Who Do You Think You Are?

Who Do You Think You Are?

a memoir

Laura Lyn Donahue

W. Brand Publishing
NASHVILLE, TENNESSEE

W. Brand Publishing is committed to publishing works of quality and integrity. In that spirit, we are proud to offer this book to our readers; however, the story, the experiences, and the words are the author's alone and portrayed to the best of their recollection. In some cases, names have been changed to protect the privacy of the people involved.

Copyright ©2025 Laura Lyn Donahue

All rights reserved. No part of this publication may be reproduced, distributed, or transmitted in any form or by any means, including photocopying, recording, or other electronic or mechanical methods, without the prior written permission of the publisher, except in the case of brief quotations embodied in critical reviews and certain other noncommercial uses permitted by copyright law. For permission requests, write to the publisher, addressed "Attention Permission Request" at the email below.

j.brand@wbrandpub.com

W. Brand Publishing

www.wbrandpub.com

Cover design by JuLee Brand / designchik

Cover photo of Laura Lyn (Baker) Donahue by Robert L. Baker

Back cover photo by Jeremy Cowart

Who Do You Think You Are? / Laura Lyn Donahue –1st ed.

Available in Paperback, Kindle, and eBook formats.

PB: 979-8-89503-010-3

eBook: 979-8-89503-011-0

Library of Congress Control Number: 2024923342

CONTENTS

Preface ix
Introduction 1
Chapter One: A Storybook Start 9
Chapter Two: It Runs in the Family 17
Chapter Three: Modern Performer 31
Chapter Four: Sing a Song for Me 41
Chapter Five: Rules Rule 45
Chapter Six: Way Out West 59
Chapter Seven: Major Codependency 69
Chapter Eight: Pretty is as Pretty Does 79
Chapter Nine: Making Music 81
Chapter Ten: Split Image 85
Chapter Eleven : Nothing But the Truth 89
Chapter Twelve: I Do 93
Chapter Thirteen: Good Counsel 99
Chapter Fourteen: Natural Instinct 105
Chapter Fifteen: Who Are You? 115
Chapter Sixteen: Milk Jugular 123
Chapter Seventeen: Houskeeping 129
Chapter Eighteen: The Pill Pact 133
Chapter Nineteen: Party of Six? 141
Chapter Twenty: As The Music Fades 145
Chapter Twenty-One: Natural Disaster 151
Chapter Twenty-Two: The Unexpected 155
Chapter Twenty-Three: Looks Like We Made It 169
Chapter Twenty-Four: Face to Face 177
Chapter Twenty-Five: Here We Grow 187
Chapter Twenty-Six: Mom, MD 197
Chapter Twenty-Seven: Trapped By Grace 213
Chapter Twenty-Eight: Pro Mom 219

Chapter Twenty-Nine: Crisis Management 223
Chapter Thirty: Naive is as Naive Does 227
Chapter Thirty-One: I Can't Fix It 241
Chapter Thirty-Two: Flying the Coop 245
Chapter Thirty-Three: Shut It Down 251
Chapter Thirty-Four: Go West 257
Chapter Thirty-Five: Kansas City, Here She Comes 271
Chapter Thirty-Six: Shifting Sand 275
Chapter Thirty-Seven: Yellow Petals 277
Chapter Thirty-Eight: We're Moving Out 279
Chapter Thirty-Nine: Waterlogged 287
Chapter Forty: Do the Hard Things 295
Chapter Forty-One: Write On 299
Chapter Forty-Two: Drowning in Disorder 301
Chapter Forty-Three: Diet Drama 307
Chapter Forty-Four: (Wo)Menopause 315
Chapter Forty-Five: Unending Love Song 319
Acknowledgments 323
My Kickstarter Team and Backers 325
End Notes 327
About the Author 329

To my husband Don, my prince: *You are the love of my life. Thank you for your unwavering support and constant encouragement. You were right. Dreams really do come true. I love you with all of my heart.*

To my children, Baker, Brennan, Cara, Eliza, and Jordany: *You are the living joys of my life. Thank you for believing in me and for cheering me on along the way. Your births and your lives are evidence that dreams do come true. I am forever blessed by each of you, and I love you with all of my heart.*

PREFACE

These are my life experiences. I share each account according to how I recall it happening, along with how I feel it has affected me, both then and through the years. Other stories recount what others have told me and how I have visualized the events in my mind's eye. I have altered some details, names, and minutia to protect identities; however, the experiences and their effect upon my life through the years are true to me. My encounters from day-to-day, year-to-year, and decade-to-decade shaped me and ultimately led me to research myself to answer the question, "Who do I think I am?" My accounts—honest, vulnerable, and significant to me—are not meant to be compared to anyone else's story. They are not a reflection of anyone else's perspective; nor are my stories told to shame or point fingers at anyone. What is written in the pages of my memoir is more than my heart on my sleeve. This writing is personal open-heart surgery, an examination, and yet only a beginning.

INTRODUCTION

How many times have you been asked: "Who do you think you are?" How many types of answers to this question do you think exist?

Have you ever turned to another person and asked *them*, "Who do you think you are?" Certainly, the context and tone of your asking, whether accusatory, rhetorical, sassy, or demeaning, matters greatly and affects the answer you receive.

However, "Who do you think you are?" could also be issued to invite self-reflection. In this scenario, instead of feeling berated, one might feel compelled to thought; maybe astonished and perplexed because they don't know the answer. They've never really thought about it.

Well, over the last few years, I've asked myself this question in both derogatory and sensitive ways. This book is a reflection on the latter. It's not a comprehensive analysis but a memoir—a remembering of space, time, and experiences—to help unearth who I was before, who I am now, or both.

We evolve, though, don't we? Upon reflection, we may now think differently about what we saw in a past moment. I'm looking for both the truths of my past and present, and I see this stage of life as a time to honor myself. I want you to honor yourself, too, because we are all worth it.

As I pose the question, "Who do you think you are?" to myself and to you, we may answer according to what we do in a present role or reality:

"I'm a child."
"I'm a student."
"I'm a woman."
"I'm a runner."
"I'm a wife."
"I'm an employee."
"I'm a mother."

If you think like me, these types of replies do not adequately answer the question. We are more than what we do; we are how we do it, whether by being authentic or by wearing a façade. *There's* an answer.

Finding the Truth Behind the Question (and Why It Matters)

At age fifty-four (at the time of writing), it's fair to say that I've lived over half my life. That's a hard pill to swallow. You would think that at my age I could easily answer the question of who I think I am. However, I have discovered that at times I view myself as an imposter. I have often wondered, to borrow a phrase from modern jargon, *Do I have imposter syndrome?*

For example, for most of my life I did not describe myself as a writer, even when asked, "What do you do?" Why would I leave out "writer" in my response? It was long the role of my most authentic self but was never part of my retort. I think that until recently, I didn't feel worthy of the descriptor, because I had very little to show for it in the way of publication.

Do you have to be published to be a writer? No.

Do you have to have work hanging in a gallery to be an artist? Of course not.

The path that I set upon a few years ago was to write a book. I've started and stopped many versions and have completed none (until now). In fact, I never called myself a writer until just a few years ago, when I took an online class in which the instructor said that if you write you're a writer. *Duh.* "Write" there in my face.

Who we are is not what we do, but how do we separate the two? I have learned that how we view ourselves can shift from year-to-year and decade-to-decade, and the dissection of those years may be the answer to unraveling the question of who we think we are.

Change is inevitable.

Growth is optional.

We evolve, and in our evolution, we can look back and see who we have been and how it has changed where we are now. The choice to see the change is one thing. The choice to grow from the change is ours to make.

Some remain static. I've seen it firsthand, and, in some instances, I've experienced the stalemate myself. Failing to embrace life's highs and lows—staying stuck, buried, or stubborn—is one way to process (or not), but it's not the only way, and it is certainly not *the* way to process.

Life is a lesson.

It is a stretch.

Living is an opportunity.

Becoming. Transforming. Transitioning. Learning. Each is part of the answer and at least an equal part of the reason why the question matters. "Who do you think you are?" is the pause button, the signal indicator, the tipping point. When we can stop and ask ourselves, *"Who do you think you are?"* and answer authentically in the moment, it is then we find the opportunity to move from stagnant to stretching, and that is why the truth behind the question matters.

While sometimes I feel that age is an advantage in my self-discovery journey, I have also uncovered some glaring truths that challenge my ability to remain true to myself. The modalities of comparison, shame, insecurity, and more still find their way into my life as if they were old friends. I ask myself, *"Why am I still listening to the negative tapes of the past despite decades of therapy, self-study, and personal research?"* Answering that question has not been easy, but I have discovered that the depth of who we are lies beneath the layers we peel back as we search for the treasure. The work is not for the faint of heart. It has been like pulling a bandage off slowly or waiting for a sneeze to come that doesn't—uncomfortable.

This book is hard-won affirmation of who I have become and the life events that have helped to shape my answers. It's my turning of the tables, peeking out from under the covers, and exploring who I think that I am and how my definition of self has changed through life experiences.

Why Write?

Having grown up in an affluent home with privilege, love, and acceptance, how did I emerge without knowing the core of who I am? My life and circumstances impeded this knowledge. I don't think this is abnormal; it happens whether one is affluent or not. Environmental factors certainly play a role in shaping us, but thankfully we also have the opportunity to become who and what we want to become.

With enough therapy and self-discovery (and a lot more therapy), I'm making progress. Weaving through a tapestry of the major events in my past and the seemingly insignificant blips on the map is part of the hard work that uncovering the self requires. That is the work of peeling back those layers.

For me, journaling has been a major method of self-discovery. Writing is cathartic, self-revelatory, and a good way to process major, complex moments as well as discover how the simple moments make a difference. In frustrating times, I've found that the act of "putting it on paper" is diffusive—a way to let off steam. Sometimes journaling is the only processing that I need. Other times, it is a way for me to start processing—a jumping off point.

My first journal was stamped with the title, *My Diary*. It was a nostalgic, pink book with a lock and key for privacy. Since *My Diary*, throughout the years there have been thousands of pages filled in various formats—spiral-bound books, Moleskine notebooks, floral-covered, lined journals, and more intricate, thought-provoking journals like *The Artist's Way*. My writings have varied from stream of conscious to poetic prose and reflections, and my middle and high school entries often held tales of teenage romance, heartache, and breakups.

At the time of this writing, I have the most beautiful journal, filled with pastel-painted pages with wonderful prompts woven into the fabric and design. *Being You* by Elena Brower has opened my self-awareness to another level. Divided into chapters, the watercolor pages are quite thought-provoking. This book holds writing that is unlike any self-reflective work that I have ever done.

Almost every morning after yoga, I sit down in the living room with Don in our matching "comfy" chairs. Inherited from my parents, the original, yellow floral aviary fabric is slipcovered with white matelassé. When I journal, I sink into my over-stuffed, white chair in the living room. If it's cold, the fireplace is burning for warmth and coziness. From my seat, there is a view of the woods. The atmosphere provides a feeling you might have if you were in a tree house. The elevation of the main living floor is on the second story. So, when you look out, you are about midway up the trunks of the trees, and your only obstruction is the forest—deep and magical. On any given day, you will see squirrels, chipmunks, deer, turkeys, and our most recent visitor, Henrietta, the red-tailed hawk.

A setting both peaceful and inspiring.

At any rate, one morning I opened my journal to the prompt, "Learning to love my struggles is my practice." This phrase resonated with me, but not in the day-to-day sense of loving my struggles as my practice. Instead, I immediately thought of yoga because it is called a "practice." I *practice* yoga daily, and the welcoming theme of "come as you are" presents an opportunity to love yourself right where you are—on the mat.

Taking the title at face value implies that there will be mistakes or struggles along the way, which has benefits. If we are to "get it" on the first try, we forgo the struggle altogether, which stunts growth. In yoga, as parallel to life, we must make room for errors and missteps. Finding ourselves off-balance is part of the routine.

However, *learning* during those struggles is where we have the chance to gain strength and confidence. We are always in the right place to learn and observe whether we are on the mat in Child's Pose, content in the moment, or curled up in the fetal position, crying our eyes out on the floor.

My life struggles and research into myself and my circumstances have become opportunities for self-revelation, the doors through which the core of who I am has been revealed. My prayer is that through my vulnerability, I might in some way connect you with your own. While digging down into the nitty-gritty, I feel that, at our center, we are much more alike than we are different. Each of us has a story.

Thank you for being here and for taking a chance, whether by persuasion (thank you, family and friends) or by choice (thank you, one and all). I desire that you find a connection, come to know that you are not alone, and, perhaps, find a sense of solace, belonging, and acceptance within the pages of my experiences.

You belong.

You matter.

You have a purpose.

Join me in exploring the question, "Who do you think you are?" While this memoir is my narrative, I invite you to apply this same question to your life and use it as a catalyst for vulnerability in your story. Your response to the question will reflect your own unique and intricate design. There are no right or wrong answers.

Our stories are different. Some are earth-shattering, devastating, and tragic. Some are publicly known; others are peppered with heartache and pain and kept private. Regardless, every story matters; no experience is too small. Our individual lives, shaped by our personal joys and sorrows, are worthy of recognition. Every bit of vulnerability is significant and unique to who we are.

Before we step into this story; I want to share one of my poems. It is written with *your* heart in mind, as an opportunity to peek behind its door, with no expectation of the door flinging open wide by revelation. Although what you glimpse inside your heart might be a little messy, know that love exists amid the clutter. This love may be hard to see but take the opportunity to know yourself. Whether you're a diamond in the rough, one right at the surface, or a discovery yet to make, you are a diamond all the same.

Hearts

*Visible hearts are
vulnerable
"hearts on sleeves."
Hidden hearts are
protected—
"hard-hearted."*

*Neither negates the other, though,
they coexist:
each,
both,
one.*

We decide who shows up.

*Hearts throb.
Hearts pump.
Hearts break.
Hearts mend.
Hearts pulse.
Hearts connect.
Hearts give.
Hearts sustain.
Hearts listen.
Hearts guide.
Hearts prompt.
Hearts caution.
Hearts return.
With every beat,
hearts love.*

Laura Lyn Donahue, 2021

CHAPTER ONE

A STORYBOOK START

My childhood home was idyllic. In my mind, I can vividly recall how it looked and felt to come down the driveway. First, we'd head down the steep blacktop hill, along the pasture where the Cooks' miniature black-and-white pony, Polly, grazed all day. We'd continue around the bend by the pond on the left, past the leg of the drive that led to the Connors' log cabin. With a sharp right, at the fork in the road wending around the curve past a big field to the right, we would come to the split rail fencing on the left. With a lurch of the car, a shift in horsepower, up the drive and around to the left, our home, built snugly in the woods, stood surrounded by four dense acres of privacy. Our driveway was discreet and marked by a three-foot log turned on its end with the words "PRIVATE DRIVE" etched in it. As you exited our winding drive, the back of the post read, "THIS IS THE DAY THAT THE LORD HAS MADE" (Psalm 118:24).

Tucked in a true storybook setting, my childhood home was a fitting comparison to how life felt as a little girl—safe, embraced, and ideal. I lacked nothing and was provided almost anything I wanted. While *idyllic* does not mean perfect, as a little girl growing up in this environment, our life certainly conveyed a fairly perfect appearance on the outside, and, to me, felt comfortable, happy, and secure.

Dad found this treasured property in the early 1970s. He purchased sixteen acres of forested bliss and subdivided it into four, four-acre lots. Just two miles from the nearest grocery store, we were close to necessities yet worlds away from the busyness of life.

This home was no ordinary home, but I didn't know that until many years later. To me it was all I knew of home, and it was where I felt most at home within myself. Both Mom and Dad put meticulous detail into designing it, from the antique leaded glass windows to the old, brass-knobbed front door to the understated chandeliers, carved mantels, and more. It was built of old brick recovered from a Mississippi church that had been torn down. There were five windows across the second floor, and symmetrically below them were four sets of mock French doors with the front door in the center.

Over the years, English ivy grew up the brick exterior, neatly kept with seasonal trims that kept it from going awry. To the left of the main portion of the house was what looked almost like an addition—a smallish, one-level breakfast room built with mixed materials of wood and brick, and its unique roofline, set on a lower plane.

Around the breakfast room, there were more French doors—some operable to the front, to the side, and to the rear. The back of the home had a deck off the breakfast room that spilled onto the brick porch spanning the length of the house. Yet again, there were more French doors. Some provided exit from the kitchen and others opened into the family and living rooms.

Aside from the front door, the most used door in our house was the one off the kitchen. Mom kept a cowbell on the interior handle—one that had at one time belonged to grandparents who passed it along to us. To get that kitchen door open from the outside, you had to give it a little nudge with your knee, which in turn jingled the cowbell that was almost impossible not to hear throughout the house.

Our kitchen was the heart and hearth of the home. Large by 1970s standards, full of thoughtful design and detail, the kitchen sinks were avocado green. There were two sinks: One was a double sink to the side by the dishwasher, and in the middle of the kitchen was the main sink with a countertop to either side. The stove was tucked into an arched, old brick inset. The cabinets were hung with antique glass doors, and an old, dark green, burnished brass lantern dangled from the ceiling over the tiny dining area.

All of our bedrooms were on the second floor. My room was pink and covered with a lovely spring green shag carpet that felt like soft, just cut grass under my toes. I had a double bed and a dresser that had been my great-grandmother's. Originally a bright turquoise, Mom and Dad had it painted in soft creams, pinks, and greens, detailing the flower garlands on the head and footboards that were secured by hand-turned bed posts. No canopy, but it still felt like a bed for a princess.

The walls of my bathroom were papered in a miniature, rose-and-vine pink floral pattern by Laura Ashley. Over the sink hung an antique gold mirror with two iron rosebud sconces flanking either side of it. What were once holes for wax candles had been retrofitted with electric light bulbs. A tall, narrow window looked over the wooded hillside and let in some natural light. Just off the bathroom, I had a wonderful walk-in closet with dark brown built-in cabinets, shelves, and a hamper. More times than not, my closet was a hideout, a doll house, and a refuge.

What I loved most about my bedroom, though, was its set of French doors. Pink-and-green, with hand-painted cloisonné handles, they opened wide to the back porch and its canopy of woods and sky. A porch swing to the right held room for daydreams, cat naps, and serenades.

From the middle of the balcony to the opposite end, there were two more sets of double doors—behind one set was my parents' bathroom, and through the other was their bedroom. Often, I stepped out onto the porch in the dark of night for comfort or solace. Oh, how I loved looking at the stars in the clear, nighttime sky, swinging on the porch swing, or staring at the moon—with no city lights to distract any view. Some evenings, I leaned forward against the railing, my arms stretched out as though I were holding a beachball and lifted high toward the heavens. It was here in this holiness where I talked to God. I felt closest to him there in the stillness of the evening, in the beauty of creation.

The children who lived in two of the nearby homes were close in age to my brothers and me. At night, at least in winter, you could see the glow of bedroom lights through the trees, but in the daytime, you couldn't see any of the homes, even through the nakedness of the woods in winter. The neighbor kids, my brothers, and I took advantage of our surroundings and cleared paths as we traipsed along the narrow trails left by deer and other woodland critters.

Of course, what is an adventure without forts in the woods? Our creations came in all shapes and sizes, most with imaginary walls outlined by fallen branches and divided into rooms with sticks and stones. If we were feeling super cozy about a fort and its longevity, we brought out toilet paper to make it feel like home.

However, I'm not sure that any of us took advantage of that amenity.

We buried secret treasure in jars in the backyard with promises to return when we were older. We played hide-and-seek in the Civil War trench carved through our side yard. We uncovered arrowheads and ran from snakes.

We owned the woods. We knew its secrets. We observed its wildlife . . . the woodpecker, the fox, and our resident hoot owl, Ollie. In the snows of winter (back when it snowed more in Nashville), we took our sleds to the top of our steep driveway and flew with abandon down the slope . . . sometimes too fast and too close to the pond at the bottom of the hill.

In the hot, sultry summers, we raced through the trees collecting lightning bugs in Mason jars with holes punctured in the lids. When we had caught our fill and had our fair share of fun, we took our blinking lamps and placed them at our bedsides as temporary glowing nightlights.

The field in the middle of our property had a flat center where we played kickball until the sun went down. Meanwhile, our unleashed dogs ran uninhibited and lived outside with their own little cedar dog houses as shelter from the elements. We had cats. We had kittens, some birthed in the back seat of a car because of a window being left open, and others delivered behind our air conditioning units. These babies that were born out of reach were wild, perhaps feral. We couldn't get our hands on them. We tried, but they hissed and swiped at us from their secret hiding place. These kitties were never domesticated. They lived life on their own, wild and free. On occasion, we caught a glimpse of one bounding through the fields. Often, they were heard and not seen—a mating call here, a crying screech there.

The woods had many heavy, grappling vines on which we swung through the "wild" like Tarzan and Jane. Not all were reliable; however, there was a tremendous one in our front yard that hung thick and gnarly from an old Oak tree. On our way into the house, on our way out, it wasn't unusual to catch one of us kids swinging across the yard bellowing out our version of Tarzan's call.

This front-yard vine was a favorite because it was low enough to easily grab but high enough to be tethered, tangled, and twined close to the top of the mammoth tree. To launch ourselves, we grabbed the end of the vine, walked it back far enough to get a lofty start, leaped on, wrapped our legs around its scaly, knotted rope, clasped our hands above us, and swung across the dip in our front yard, across the lawn and almost to the dining room French door windows at the front of the house.

I don't recall how many hundreds of times we took off on that vine, yelling, whooping, and squealing in delight as our stomachs dropped with the sensation of a roller coaster flying downhill. What I do remember most about that grapevine, though, is the last day my brother and I rode tandem. We each found a side of the vine, wrapped ourselves somewhat in our own combined knot, and swung toward the house. The thrill and stability of swinging across the front yard quickly turned to shock, as the tightly-tethered tendrils loosened their hold, and the vine rapidly unraveled through the tree and dumped us on our butts in the front yard. We said goodbye to our "Old Faithful" that day, and life deposited a lesson, a kernel of comparison, for me to later understand more thoroughly.

My home, its thoughtful detail, my parents' love, and our wooded surroundings were elements that helped provide me with a childlike sense of abandon, which I'd later learn was not what every child felt. Like the vine in our front yard, what was "faithful" to my sense of home in childhood would unravel in adulthood—only the fall would be further and far more complicated.

CHAPTER TWO

IT RUNS IN THE FAMILY

DAD'S FAMILY

Dad grew up north of downtown Nashville, only a few miles from the home he built for us. His family home was a simple colonial, white and modest. A sweeping front lawn sprawled up to an overgrown gravel drive, and behind the house was a gravel parking area that nestled up to the screened-in back porch—complete with a slamming door.

I don't recall the porch being used for anything other than storing stuff. What I do remember is that when you came through the door, on your left was a red-and-white Coca-Cola cooler, waist-high to me at the time. The cooler had the classic Coca-Cola logo on it and slid open from the top where Grandmother and Pappy kept the ice-cold bottles.

Originally, the home sat amid farmland. My dad had a boxer named Buddy and a horse named Red. Growing up, Dad took Red on expedition after expedition, always discovering something new. It wasn't uncommon for him and Red to travel a few miles over to Nashville's beloved Radnor Lake, well before it was a state park filled with joggers, walkers, and pet parents. As he tells the story, he would ride Red through the water to the grassy, treed island in the middle of the lake, where they would stop for a rest before swimming back to shore.

With his own two hands, Dad built a trampoline pit in the backyard where he practiced his flips, jumps, and tricks as often as possible. One year, he even built a barn on the property. Dad grew up with performance at the forefront of his mind and with a nothing-is-impossible attitude.

Pappy, Dad's dad, had kind, blue sparkling eyes—the spectacular ones that smile on their own—making it hard to imagine that his face could ever look angry. His hair was snow-white, and his face always danced with a smile. The only time he wasn't smiling was when he was asleep in his Barcalounger. It wasn't unusual for my brothers and me to find Pappy sawing logs in his chair, the newspaper and mail cluttered all around him, and the TV on full blast. If someone didn't know and love Pappy, I don't know who it was.

Pappy didn't cook much, but he made the best white Bunny Bread toast ever, with tender, squishy middles. Each piece had four pats of butter spaced evenly in a square. With the oven set to a 500-degree broil, Pappy slid the pan into the oven to cook the bread until it was browned to perfection, crisp on the outside, and tender with buttery yumminess in the middle.

Sometimes, Pappy made us cinnamon toast. He layered the buttered Bunny Bread with sugar, cinnamon, and more sugar. As it cooked, he was careful to watch the broiler for the sweet concoction to come to a crispy crunch. *Ahh, perfection.* Chomping into its candied, sugary deliciousness was delightful. Being less than gourmet, I kept this recipe tucked in my repertoire for years to come. Pappy died in 1995, just before the birth of his first great-grandchild—our first baby, Baker.

Grandmother, as we called her, was a lovely, slender woman. Her fingers were long and her red-painted nails as hard as rock. A Kool cigarette often hung limply from her lips while she pulled puffs of that sultry smoke one drag after another. Grandmother was sweet and loving. She was always ready for a hug and happy to see us when we came to visit. However, Grandmother could also be a terror—or that's how it seemed to my brothers, cousins, and me in our youth and naiveté. Because we were all so young, none of us knew why Grandmother had episodes of mania and others of calm. We just knew it happened sometimes. The adults offered little explanation as to her mood swings, and, perhaps, that was age-appropriate for us at the time.

Pappy was a pharmaceutical representative, and there was always medicine in the house, easily discoverable in various nooks and crannies, but I didn't know that some of the medicine actually belonged to Grandmother.

Now I know that Grandmother's manic episodes were directly related to her not taking her meds—whether on purpose or on accident—either way, missing medication for more than a day or so could lead to some scary times. As a child, it was hard to reconcile her behavior, because it seemed rather unexplainable and was sometimes pretty scary. In our adult years, we learned that Grandmother suffered from schizophrenia. Mental illness wasn't a topic of discussion. It was, in fact, taboo. For the most part, Grandmother's behavior was referred to as "crazy" or described as "one of her spells"—it's no wonder a stigma was once attached to those battling a decline in mental health. (Thankfully, times are changing. Education is available. Talk is not taboo; nor is therapy).

As children, we didn't know then what we know now. We only knew that when Grandmother seemed to turn mean, it was our cue to vanish. Unfortunately, there were some things we did as children that we had no idea were triggers for instability in Grandmother's mental health. My "twin cousin", Mimi, and I engaged in antics such as hiding Grandmother's cigarettes, which, at times, was a catalyst for her irritability. Had we known better, Mimi and I would not have hidden her cigarettes. We thought we were being helpful. Not only were we unaware of mental health, but we did not understand addiction and its relationship to smoking. Hindsight is 20/20. Sadly, smoking eventually caught up to Grandmother, and in the early 1980s she died of lung cancer.

When Grandmother was feeling healthy, she was up for adventure. On special occasions or when the mood struck, Grandmother would take Mimi and me on outings in her two-tone, light green Chevy Impala. Always parked in the back of the house in the gray gravel drive, it sported a low-slung, long front body and exaggerated, pointy sides that poked out past the trunk. All three of us would slide into the vinyl-covered, front bench seat that had no headrests, our seatbelts unbuckled, and the ashtray ajar.

Grandmother's keychain was distinct—a dark woodgrain disk that was half an inch thick and about the size of a coaster. It sported a somewhat animated, black ant poised upright on her two back legs. In her arms she carried a red pocketbook. The wood disk was lacquered to a glossy perfection, and it swung back and forth below the keys as we drove along.

Knowing my dad's parents is an important part of who I am. Mostly for the memories, but also for life lessons, examples, and for medical history. Not all of us know both sets of grandparents. Not all of us spent time with them. Some of us would rather not be with them at all because of trauma of one kind or another. For me, though, my grandmother's death from lung cancer was a significant deterrent that kept me from ever even being interested in smoking. Grandmother's mental health is an important part of my medical history and, perhaps, a foreshadowing of my struggles to come and a benchmark for understanding and empathy. I hate that Grandmother struggled in an era of "hush-hush," but I'm grateful for her life and what she had to give. Pappy's bright-eyed, shining smile, and his kindness still bring me joy today, and I'd like to think that some of that joy rubbed off on me.

MOM'S FAMILY

My mom was born in Raleigh, Tennessee, near Memphis, and moved to Columbus, Mississippi when she was five. I spent my childhood visiting the home that she grew up in. We always traveled the backroads to get there. In those days, there wasn't a highway, and my mom loved driving through the countryside. From Nashville we drove south through Franklin and then Columbia, Tennessee, two towns that would play significant parts in my adult life. We gawked at the Rattle and Snap mansion, bigger than any home we could have imagined at the time, and made our way down the two-lane highways and through all the tiny and unincorporated towns across Alabama. One of our rest stops along the way was the Wilson Lock and Dam in Florence—a history-making, hydroelectric construction that always caught our eye. Traveling to Columbus was a family tradition.

Mom's family had moved to Columbus in 1948 for her dad to open a car dealership. Nabors Ford became a hometown name and a family-owned business for decades. Having a dad who owned a car lot had its perks. Mom rode atop the rear seat of a classic 1950s Mustang convertible as homecoming queen for her high school. Later, she would drive everything from an orange Pinto to a pea-green Country Squire station wagon, complete with woodgrain side trim.

The Nabors called the dealership "the place," and if anyone was looking for Gran, more than likely he would be found at "the place" or at "the church."

Grandaddy was just over six feet tall. He was so handsome with his dark brown wavy hair, square jaw, and kind blue eyes. His voice was deep and authoritative, yet also gentle and wooing. Walking into any room, he commanded the space with strength, honor, and gentility.

Gran sold Ford cars and trucks until he retired and passed the dealership onto his eldest son. Even then, you could still find him at the dealership with my mom's oldest brother, who had taken the reins. Grandaddy loved the Bible. He was dedicated to studying the scripture, memorizing its verses, and knowing its stories by heart. When we visited, my pullout bed was in his small, windowless office. In the corner next to the closet was his desk with the Bible open to what he was studying at the time.

Mom's mom (we called her "Mema") was a beautiful woman with thick, blonde hair that she wore in a bouffant style. Mema was tender and kind. She worked as a stay-at-home mom raising my mom, mom's twin brother, and their two older siblings. Mema's days were filled with housekeeping, kid-wrangling, and cooking. Caring for four children born in stair-step order was not an easy task, and somewhere along the way she was able to have help in the home.

Meals were the heart of my mom's childhood home. My Mema could cook all of the Southern comfort food—roast beef, pork chops, fried chicken, black-eyed peas, purple hull peas, and turnip greens. She was at the ready with food for breakfast, lunch, and dinner. One of my favorites was her crispy fried chicken. I can still smell the Crisco sizzling. The smell of grease and chicken filled the kitchen as it cooked up extra crisp and crunchy. The Colonel had nothing on Mema!

In the South, lunch was often called "supper," and it was routine for the school-age kids to walk home to eat supper each day. I can imagine that the four kids walked home together. Girls in their dresses. Boys in their slacks. Maybe some poking and sibling-teasing going on as Mom, her brothers, and her sister came up the hill to the house with hot food prepared and ready on the kitchen table.

MOM

Mom was (and is) strikingly beautiful with high cheekbones, a straight nose, and soft blue eyes. As a little girl, she wore her light brown, curly hair short, just below her ears. She played hopscotch on the sidewalk, kick the can in the street, and, somewhere down the line, spin the bottle. She had a best girlfriend nearby and built-in playmates with her twin brother, and her older sister and brother.

Playing with her siblings wasn't always fun, though. When her family lived on Aunt Edna and Uncle Tom's farm, her oldest brother would coax the younger ones into laying down on the dirt path while he hopped on his bike and rolled over their tummies as if they were railroad tracks. I guess it was fun for the one on the bike (Ha-ha!).

In high school, Mom often wore a cardigan to cover her arms, which she thought were too skinny. She had a tiny nineteen-inch waist and a perfectly quaffed, frosted bouffant. One year she played the role of Beth in *Little Women*. She cheered for football and basketball, she ran track, and in her senior year she was named homecoming queen.

In the 1950s Mom wore fun, classic-era clothes, some of which she saved for me. Years later, I might be caught wearing her navy blue, corduroy cheerleading uniform, her suede, cape-style coat with a fur collar, or her off-white, cotton letterman jacket with a red-letter S sewn on the left placket. I've always wanted to be like my mom (in more ways than one), and as a little girl I couldn't wait to walk in Mom's footsteps and be a cheerleader myself.

My mom is my best friend. We've always been close to one another and continue to have a very close bond. Mom is kind, gracious, loving, and welcoming. Her heart's desire was to have a family and be a mother. Her dream came true, and she did just that. She rocked me to sleep in her arms and sang lullabies over me. She is wise. She is approachable and without judgment. Her voice is calming. She listens well. She is a gem.

The two of us are kindred spirits. While I didn't major in English, Mom's knowledge of grammar and love for poetry seeped vicariously into my own veins. Mom taught me to love nature as I saw the world through her descriptive lenses. She and I have taken hundreds of walks hand-in-hand by the ocean, while discussing a biblical philosophy, the grandeur of God and sea, or my latest boyfriend. Sometimes we've walked in reverent silence, taking in the feel of the sand between our toes, the cool waves lapping over our feet, and the salty breeze making our curly hair expand by the second. We've collected thousands of shells, treasure washed in with the tide—conch, lady slippers, tiger's paw, olives, and others housing hermit crabs—now sweet mementos of days gone by.

After high school graduation, Mom and her twin brother headed to Nashville to attend David Lipscomb College. It was there where she and my dad met and fell in love. Mom graduated with a bachelor's in English and continued her education at the George Peabody College for Teachers located in Nashville, on Vanderbilt's campus and earned her master's in education.

Degrees in tow and smart as a whip, she was quickly hired by David Lipscomb College and became known as the hardest English professor on campus—but also the prettiest! Smart and pretty ruled, and her classes were always full—and maybe a little heavy on the masculine side.

When I was born in June of 1969, Mom shifted her career from teaching to being a full-time mom. Once my brothers and I were all in school, Mom returned to David Lipscomb to teach freshman English. She had an office on campus in the basement of Elam Hall, which would later become my first dorm. When school was over for my brothers and me, we took the sidewalks that wove through our campus over to the college where we met Mom to head home.

Before I graduated from college, Lipscomb began a master's program in Biblical studies. Mom was very intrigued, astute with knowledge of the scripture and a deep love for the Bible. It was only natural that she enrolled. She finished the program with straight A's and honors and became the first woman at Lipscomb to graduate with a degree in Biblical studies. Wiser than ever, my mom's ambition led her to teach both English and Bible at Lipscomb. She was beloved and remains so to this day.

DAD

Dad and I had a special bond, and, as much as my mom and I were joined at the hip, I was also a daddy's girl. On the weekends, he and I jumped on the trampoline together, my blonde pigtails bouncing with every rebound. Dad taught me seat drops, forward rolls, flips, and cartwheels.

I never wanted him to leave for work, but, alas, he had to. After he kissed Mom and me goodbye, I would run from the front door down the short hall to my bedroom. As quickly as I could, I'd plop down on the floor, my nightgown billowing, and wave goodbye with my feet. Why? I don't know, but Dad always got a kick out of it. So much so that we continued the tradition in one way or another until neither of us could lift our feet that high!

As evening rolled around, and while my mom was getting dinner ready, I would peer through the window looking out for Dad. When I'd see him getting out of the car, I could hardly stand it. I'd run to his open arms and plunge myself into his big bear hug. Dad was generous with "I love you" and affirmations. He is, and always has been, very smart. He knows something about almost everything. He was a hard worker, he traveled often, but he rarely missed dinner when he was home, and he was never short on affection.

If we were to take a vote, it would be unanimous. Dad was super handsome with thick, brown wavy hair, deep blue eyes, and long, thick eyelashes that would melt any girl's gaze (and fill her with envy for the same).

Dad was full of adventure, always doing something fun. One of my mom's favorite memories in the early days of dating Dad was when he offered up a tempting alternative to Bible study. He suggested they skip church and go see Ray Charles, and that's exactly what they did. Sitting just an arm's length from the stage, that memory will never fade.

Dad, a member of the Hall of Fame now, was a celebrated gymnast and trampolinist at David Lipscomb. The gymnastics team was always the half-time show during the basketball games. My dad would soar on the trampoline, high enough to make you gasp (or so I've been told), all the while doing flips and twists in the air that risked a crash through the springs of the trampoline or onto the hardwood floor. Thankfully, that was not the case for Dad. He was pretty much always on point, whether it be on the trampoline, the rings, the horse, or the mat—Olympic material.

One year, he and his team put together a Batman and Robin show to wow the crowd at halftime. He and a teammate rigged a zipline of sorts from the furthest corner of the gym ceiling to a bolt in the middle of the basketball court (it was hidden in a trap door under the floor). He attached his line, taut and seemingly secure, to a carabiner and then to the zipline itself. With the Batman theme playing in the background, and the crowd antsy with anticipation, my dad leaped from the rafters and set sail for mid-court. Much to his chagrin, the line snapped on his way down. However, fall he may, he put his gymnastic skills to the test and landed on his feet—just like any cool cat would have done. *Ta-da!* The breathless audience erupted in cheers thinking the fall was all part of the show. Needless to say, that was the first and last stunt of its kind.

After receiving his bachelor's degree, my dad went on to law school at Vanderbilt University. He was later snapped up for his savviness and specialty in transportation law, when A.O. Buck entered our lives. "Buck," as he was affectionately called, took my dad under his wing. They worked hard together and eventually partnered to open their firm, Buck & Baker. From the moment Dad met Buck, he and his wife, Frances, became a dear part of our lives. Beyond a professional relationship, the Bucks became parental figures to my parents and also our adopted grandparents.

BABY MAKES 3

Long before my dad opened a law firm, my parents met one another in college. Three years older than my dad, Mom was a junior when Dad stepped on campus as a freshman. Being the gymnast he was, it made sense for Dad to use his skills not only on the trampoline but also on the sidelines as a cheerleader. Muscles flexed, he hoisted the girls, including my mom, into stunts and provided strong arms to catch anyone in a fall. While Mom vowed she would never marry a younger man, her plans changed when she met my dashingly handsome and super fun dad.

Full of love for one another and with life and adventure ahead of them, they married in the late summer of 1968. Not too many months later, their party of two became a party of three. On June 27, 1969, they welcomed their firstborn into the world and named her Laura Lyn. "Laura," as suggested by my great-grandmother, and "Lyn" after my dad.

As the story goes, Mom went into labor. Already packed for the hospital, Mom was ready to go. Dad, on the other hand, was a frantic mess of excitement—

much like you might see in a movie when the dad, so nervous, just can hardly see straight. Not only could my dad not see straight, but he also failed to notice the car keys before locking up and rushing out of the house. Classic. He managed to get back into the house through a window and got Mom to the hospital in plenty of time.

It was culturally unusual for the husband to be in the room while his wife was giving birth. At the same time, before the labor pains got unbearable, it was common for the OB to give the mother a healthy dose of the opiate pain reliever, Dilaudid. The scenario was the same for my parents. Dad nervously paced in the hall, while Mom drifted to dreamland and had a baby during her slumber.

No worse for the wear, little me emerged with healthy lungs and a head full of hair—not just any hair, as I'm often reminded, but frosted curly locks of which the nurses were in awe. My parents were in love all over again.

CHAPTER THREE

MODERN PERFORMER

Most of my life, I've sought acceptance. I'm a performer, a pleaser, a helper—you know the type. Either you experience life similarly, or you know someone else who does.

I've stepped back to a simpler time in life while researching the trajectory of my performance-oriented mindset and how it came about. My childhood, as I described earlier, was a somewhat carefree time, when I was happily unaware of the ramifications to come of being prematurely, and perhaps unintendedly, labeled by adults in my life.

What I now know, having looked back on these critical moments, is that I had *no idea* that my behavior or my mindset would become self-defeating. These outcomes are not my fault. Living in an environment and culture of perfection, it was all too easy for adults, perhaps unbeknownst to them, to take advantage of a young, coming-of-age girl and her desire to please. Whether intentional or not, those who knew better allowed a part of me to be taken away under the guise of *it being the right thing to do.*

My own experiences and my learned behavior set me up to maintain the status quo or somehow make the circumstances especially conducive to everyone but me. I did not rock the boat. Characteristically, I was not a risk taker. Challenging authority was not part of my MO. Performing, pleasing, and helping is how I thrived, and when those skills were praised, I was continually being validated for something less than myself and more about someone else.

Mema, Mom's mom, and I used to watch television together when I was young. Mema loved the classic, black-and-white movies starring Shirley Temple. I learned to love her too. Her tight, curly locks, her iconic polka-dot dress, the ability she had to break into song, tap-dance, and her all-over sunny nature, come what may, brought joy and ambition to my heart.

Not necessarily in secret, but I certainly held close my desire to be like Shirley: Singer. Dancer. Actor. Like that tiny, stage-stealing princess, I too, wanted to draw praise and adoration from the masses for my disposition, my talents, and my cuteness.

A seemingly simple dream to me, in reality it was a long stretch. My overall environment lacked the opportunity for stardom, unless, that is, if you wanted to be a "country and western" singer! Although I took ballet, tap, and jazz, I ended up quitting them all because I didn't really enjoy them, and I was also often the last to arrive and the last to be picked up. On the surface, I was a little girl embarrassed because her parent was tardy. But deep down, the child in me did not want to inconvenience the adults around me by making a fuss. Being timely would have been so much easier, or so I thought at my age. In retrospect, whether my ride was prompt wasn't the main struggle; but it was my desire to please.

If my dream was to be a star, you'd think that I would have prepared better for it. I shunned piano lessons because all my friends hated it. Boy, I wish I had taken the risk just to see what I could have done. Voice lessons were probably available, but I never took those, and as far as exposure to the stage, I had none—aside from school plays, which would ironically be what stopped my pursuit of acting. What I wanted was to be a natural. I hoped to wow my peers and the adults in my life with my amazing, innate talents.

Yes, I was naive and unaware of the difference between "having what it takes" and "learning what it takes," which was not a priority or even available to me then.

That's not to say that I didn't take some opportunities. I played Lummi Sticks in music class. (Remember, "Ta Ta Ti-Ti Ta"?) Every year of elementary school I was in a play—as was the whole class. Like I shared earlier, I tried dance on for size but not any star-worthy instruments. On top of my desire for notability and excellence in acting, singing, and dancing, being a model was also on my list. At five-foot-two in the 1970s, I was certainly not model material.

One modeling chance that I took was in the eighth grade. Mom took me to our local department store, Castner-Knott, where there was going to be an opportunity to walk the runway. I wore a wonderful peach jumpsuit with an elastic cinched waist and sandals. My thick, long, curly hair flipped into terrific wings—not just any wings, though. Mine could easily have rivaled Farrah Fawcett's own. My deep blue eyes reflected blue-shaded lids, blue eyeliner, and super long eyelashes that I coated thick with black mascara and curled high enough to get tangled in my eyebrows! If I couldn't make it as a traditional model, then I was certain I would be discovered for my eyelashes and cast in Revlon mascara commercials. No joke. I longed to be plucked from a crowd for something extraordinary. In my mind, there was a lot at stake for me in this audition.

Mom parked us in the parking lot, and we climbed the lengthy steps to the top to the entrance and walked into Castner-Knott, which was next door to Cain-Sloan—both family-run department stores in the Southeast. We made our way through cosmetics, shoes, and accessories, and stepped onto the "down" escalator. Surrounding the runway were loads of model wannabes—giggling girls ripe with excitement—and a palpable air of competition.

The stage crew had spotlights set up to shine on each girl as she walked the runway (alone). I was very, very nervous. However, my name was called, and I took the double steps up to the stage. Walking down this runway, with all eyes on me and the TV camera pointed in my direction, my only desire was to please the judges enough to be picked. Light shining in my eyes, I smiled my biggest smile and did my best to mimic models I'd seen on the "boob tube" waltzing down the catwalk. *Turning, smiling, posing, smiling. Smiling . . .* smiling so deliberately that the muscles around my mouth began to quiver. They shook so hard I could not possibly halt it. As I arrived at the end of the runway, mouth shaking uncontrollably, I posed for the Canon camera staring straight at me. Whether I ever got those photos, I don't know, but I would not have been surprised to see them blurry from all my facial movements. Alas, I did not get to join the chosen few who would be featured in the coveted newspaper inserts or the local fashion shows sporting the latest trends.

Defeated. *Heartbroken.*

I felt waves of self-pity and echoes in my head taunting, *You just don't have it.* This would happen to me time and again in many situations. My desire to be randomly "discovered" and also to be a pleaser really set me up for disappointment. For one, "being discovered" in a crowd was not common (but I'd seen it happen), but for another, I was not assertive. Drawing attention to myself made me uncomfortable. I didn't like that feeling nor did I want to be vulnerable. I kept so much of this inside, though, not knowing how to articulate my feelings—also not feeling confident enough to set myself apart. I didn't give up though—perhaps I did on modeling—but not on singing and acting.

At some point in middle school, I tried out for the school play. While I don't recall the name of the play, or its premise, the cast was comprised of several Disney princesses along with other characters from Disney's lineup of fairytales. I tried out to be a princess—any princess—and I also auditioned for a solo. To my great delight, I landed Snow White. My part included both a short speaking role and a partial solo of the song, "Someday My Prince Will Come." I was beside myself with pride and excitement. This was my time to shine.

We practiced for weeks. Singing alone was a challenge for me, and I knew that I didn't measure up to the confidence of another's voice. I sang anyway and my confidence started to rise. While play rehearsals were still ongoing, a new classmate joined our grade. Sally also loved to act and sing. Since we had already had tryouts for the lead roles, there were not any prominent parts left. I assumed Sally would be a woodland animal or flower. I was wrong. Little did I know what was brewing in Sally's mind, and in her ability to speak up for what she wanted.

Regardless of where we lived, any school community would expect the student body to be warm and welcoming to any new incoming student, especially mid-year when friendships had been established and clicks locked. Nothing less was expected from us, but something more. Living in the South, being a Christian, and attending a religious school, set us up for a welcome that included a more intricate, selfless, sugar-laced, and other-focused style of warmth. Being the good people that we were (not that there's anything wrong with being good—far from it) we took the Southern, legalistic, be-like-Jesus approach. If you're not familiar with this style, think, "Be as perfect as possible; do as you're told; do the right thing; make everyone else happy; gain approval, and *do not* be selfish, even at your own expense." No one knew what self-care was (if anything, self-care was *self-ish*).

Just what would the school decide to offer Sally that would help her find her place? I would soon discover the answer in a much more personal way than I could have imagined. The drama teacher and others approached me and asked me if I would be willing to give my princess role to the new girl. *Seriously?* Yep. No joke. The question was presented to me by one of the administrators. I was asked to offer this selfless opportunity to solve someone else's predicament and desire to please. The meat behind the ask was that if I were to make this big sacrifice, then that would mean Sally would at once feel accepted and included.

There were at least two obvious things wrong with this request. First, as far as I recall, only one princess was asked to give up her role: me. The implication of this was that I was not as good as the other princesses, and those girls were preferred over me. The second problem was that I was asked because the chance that I would say yes, and with a smile to boot, was pretty much guaranteed. And I did exactly as was expected of me. My smile remained fixed while in the presence of those issuing platitudes, but it melted into a frown and tears by the time I got home.

I was *devastated*. Shocked. Undone.

I handed over my role as Snow White because it was what everyone else wanted me to do. The back-patting and approval ratings seemed worth it at the time. My circumstances didn't afford room for my feelings or self-esteem, and I was not comfortable advocating for myself or rocking anyone's boat of expectations for me.

From the fairytale princess to the do-the-right-thing girl, it seemed to me that my sacrifice would be worth it in the end because it garnered the approval of others—which is what I viewed as successful at the time. To me, in my youthful thinking, this trade surely had an upside. I was "the pleaser," and I mistakenly took my compliance and the approval I garnered from adults as paramount to my ability to achieve. My self-denial, added to my pleasing behavior, would surely equal adult approval and my future success. I was unaware of the fault in this logic. It was what I knew. It did not occur to me that there was an alternative way of behaving by which I took care of myself.

I gave away my glittery ball gown—hopes dashed—and put on the familiar cloak of perfection. While choking back tears and sweeping my feelings under the rug, the sweet, nice, always-do-the-right-thing girl succumbed to the pressure to please others because in that moment, it seemed that a positive payoff would come in return.

I don't want to paint the wrong picture of the teachers and administration at school. They were doing the best that they could at the time, and they were kind-hearted folks who I know loved me; however, our culture then considered self-care and awareness to be selfish. Hopefully, most of us know better now.

Opportunities for growth always exist if we choose to see them, and cultural shifts over the decades are often the catalyst for positive change.

Because of the internal, negative effects this experience had on me, it took some time for me to get past it. I did not try out for another part in a play while in middle or high school. While in grade school, I did, thanks to a relative, play a small role in a college play with the theater company at Lipscomb. As far as other acting opportunities go, during my senior year in high school I appeared in a commercial for Lipscomb K-12 that aired on TV and radio, and in print. I was proud of the recognition I was given, and I was honored to have been asked. This did afford me a little local notoriety, and my name would occasionally be recognized. As far as my future as an actor, there was only one more play where I went for it—all in and for myself.

During my freshman year at Lipscomb College, the big production on campus was a variety show called *Sing Song*. Somehow, I mustered up the courage to sing for a part. I remember standing in line for the audition with many other excited students. I was quite nervous, but my turn came, and I stepped on the stage for the judges and sang. I don't remember what song I sang, and I didn't make the cut, but I did muster the courage to try. I was proud of myself for that, but I lost confidence in myself and put my dreams of being a singer to rest. Still, the desire to be "discovered" for something stayed with me for decades.

Moments that seem simple or inconsequential are not always so. My early experiences of people-pleasing set the stage for how I thought of myself and how I performed for others—neither of which represented me truthfully. It would be decades before I could begin to undo what I had not known I had done.

In the undoing, my reply to, "Who do you think you are?" has morphed and matured. I'm a recovering performer—aware of my tendencies to please but also attuned to my ability to advocate for myself. Some situations are easier than others. When fear or anxiety grip too tightly, I revert to the default of my youth. However, today I know what it feels like to take care of myself when my individuality is threatened by the pressure to choose someone else's well-being over my own.

My story may remind you of your own in one way or another. Perhaps you have also learned that pleasing others evokes a positive response, and, in turn, gives you the acceptance that you thought you needed through praise. Your childhood experiences are certainly different from mine, but part of becoming is learning about where you started and what patterns may or may not have shaped some or all of your life. Reflecting on your experiences can provide "ah-ha" moments, helping you delve deeper into who you are.

CHAPTER FOUR

SING A SONG FOR ME

The stardom of the big stage was left in the wake of a young girl's dashed dreams. As I grew, I became fully aware that for me there would be no career as a professional singer, as an actor, and certainly not as a dancer. There would be no big stage, no filled stadiums, no crazy fans, and no paparazzi.

However, melodies are part of my heritage. I had learned songs and hymns from my mother, from church, and from school, and I was never far from a song. That love of music became a dream that evolved as I did. My full focus shifted to being a mother, and I became a mom with a song in her heart and on her lips. I was given a tiny, captive audience with the births of my five little children. To them I would sing one thousand lullabies and ten thousand hymns, all on a stage unlike any I could have imagined. This stage required no perfection and no people-pleasing. It required no perfect pitch or pose. Instead, my stage was arms cradled around babies, rocking chairs tipping to the rhythm, while my adoring fans cooed, drooled, and even screamed.

I curated a catalog of music and sang memorized songs that became the backdrop of tender mama-and-baby moments and the rhythm of many surly, sleepless nights. When my first child, Baker, was born, I sang "O, Holy Night," "Jesus Loves Me," "She'll Be Coming

'Round the Mountain," "How Great Thou Art," and "The Wheels on the Bus." Hymn after hymn and lullaby after lullaby, I sang until I had subconsciously memorized the order, with one song leading right into the other and from one child to the next—Cara and Brennan, Eliza, and Jordany.

As insignificant or simple as it may have seemed to the outsider (whom I was not trying to please!), these cherished moments were privately, personally, and melodically underscored in the key of Motherhood. How much more beautiful could reality be for me? My heart's desire came true—different than I thought, but in a way more authentically suited to me.

My singing didn't stop with babies. I sang in the car, in the shower, and throughout the house. I had a song for everything! If I were cleaning the house, out popped Diana Ross's, "She Works Hard for the Money." If a Peter Cottontail hopped through the yard, "Little Bunny Foo Foo" spilled from my lips, and God knows what I would have done if not for Barney's (in)famous "Clean Up! Clean Up!" anthem. If I didn't have a song for the circumstance, then I made one up.

Song lyrics were not the only melodies I knew, though. During my youth and into adulthood, pen-to-paper, I wrote the prose of my poet's heart, and it is in this role where I find myself most comfortable. As a poet, I can claim my talent. It's often appreciated by others. I do receive praise and kudos, but my motive for writing has never been to please anyone other than myself.

No fame and no *Billboard* number ones (or any number, for that matter!) ever crossed my threshold, but poetry did. My innate ability for prose and creative writing is my personal claim to fame and where my authenticity shines.

As I've grown older and wiser, I am different than what I had hoped to be, but I am nestled into a skin more my style. I have autonomy in my creativity. I am talented. I can sing when I want to and write when I feel so inclined, and I have moved toward being myself—a natural.

I tend to believe that a lot of people have dreamed of being famous in some form or fashion—if not famous, then perhaps recognized and affirmed by those around them. With the dawn of social media, especially TikTok, the opportunities to stand out seem almost limitless. However, fame seems to rarely, if ever, be the answer to anyone's problems or the cure for low self-esteem. In fact, quite the opposite is often true. In our "Look at me!" culture, fear of missing out (FOMO), jealousy, and envy seem more likely to result from watching others. Looking inside ourselves, though, and uncovering the layers of our "wannabe" selves can also help us understand why what we thought we wanted is not what would have been good for us at all.

CHAPTER FIVE

RULES RULE

Growing up, our family attended church three times per week—Sunday morning, Sunday evening, and Wednesday night. We had no choice of whether or not to go. We went.

Our church was not far from where we lived. If we were snowed in, then we would trek through the snow and woods, climb over fences, and traipse down a narrow lane named Laurel Hill. At the end of the road, we had only one major street to cross, and we were there.

On a lovely corner lot with trees and a creek was our church. It sat in the forefront of the lot, easy to see and easy to enter. With its tall, lofty white steeple, peachy brick, and stately columns, it was rather imposing and large, but welcoming. Large white doors flanked the front with various side entrances around the building, complete with a portico in the back for when the weather was temperamental.

While oxymoron-ish, yet consistent, two or three men often stood at the side entrances smoking cigarettes and greeting the dallying members as the service got underway. The Church of Christ was our religion and our "perfect" compass for all that was deemed "right" or "wrong." *Perfection* was important—praised. Provocative for a rule-follower, potentially detrimental for a rebel.

The Church of Christ is not considered a denomination, even though in my formative years most C of Cs operated in the same legalistic way, sans a universal governing body. There was a hierarchy of sin. Cheating on your spouse was up there with murder—it was an impossible stain to erase—whereas telling a lie or coveting your neighbor's wealth was uncomplicated and easily wiped away. There were countless rules and regulations, and, of course, as a child I didn't understand the intricacies of church for anything other than what it was. We went. We obeyed. When I failed, there was plenty of guilt to swallow me up—not from my parents, but rather it was self-inflicted.

Our religion boasted that we were the only ones going to heaven because we were the ones who interpreted the scripture without flaw. Yikes. This monumental declaration would time and again present an impasse for me over the years. I could not reconcile selective salvation in my young mind. Into my teens, the idea of anyone being excluded from the grace of God continued to haunt me.

The routine of church was familiar, full of fellowship, and its body of people was like family. The sense of community in our church was deep—from Wednesday night potlucks in Fellowship Hall to church picnics at the park, and from Sunday school classes to revival meetings under huge white tents pitched in the parking lot.

My family usually sat in the same row each time we went. I recall that in my younger years we sat in the middle three or four rows from the front of the stage. As I got older, we moved from the center to stage left, about four or five rows back.

Aunt Maggie, Uncle Pete, and Aunt Lena (not blood relatives but like family) always perched on the second row, center of the stage-right end of the pew. Our song leader sat on the front row, and sometimes my friends and I would sit a few spaces down on the same row. Other times, I found myself sitting with a friend who enjoyed pinching my leg during the service, tempting me to make a peep. I held out pretty well each time. Why I allowed this infliction of pain in a house of redemption, I have no idea, other than I always rose to the challenge of perfection even to my demise.

We had hymnals full of beautiful songs that we sang completely acapella. There were no instruments; they were not allowed because they were not deemed "biblical." We were served the Lord's Supper (cracker and juice) every single Sunday morning. If you missed it, you had the opportunity to come back Sunday night and take it. You didn't want to let a Sunday pass by without having had your bread and grape juice. There was an implication that if you skipped the Lord's Supper, your salvation was in jeopardy. This type of rules-oriented religion managed to create a whole lot of necessary boxes to check if you wanted to go to heaven.

Because I spent so much time in church, studying the Bible became second nature. I memorized countless scriptures and whole chapters. Throughout my life, I have leaned on the words of wisdom and comfort found in these writings. Beautiful. Sacred.

What wasn't so affirming was the literal interpretation of the scriptures, which I didn't reconcile until my early twenties and am still recovering from today. I have friends from other denominations who, like me, consider themselves in religious recovery as well.

There were *so many rules* and failure to uphold each one put your eternity in the balance between heaven and hell, good and evil. There were no other remedies for this problem besides confessing your sins to God, asking him for forgiveness, and starting over.

As I mentioned, you didn't want to miss taking the Lord's Supper on Sundays. You also needed to be baptized, not sprinkled. It was very important to understand at a young age that Jesus was your Lord and Savior who had died to save you. It was critical that you confessed your sins, committed to following Christ, and were immersed in water in front of the congregation.

Don't get me wrong, this ceremonial tradition was (and is) beautiful. Seeing someone go from "sinner" to "saved" was transformational. But it was also requisite for your soul's immortality in the presence of God and his heavenly empire of gold, pearls, mansions, and sinlessness. Otherwise, you were infinitely condemned to the fiery furnace of Satan and everything evil.

Our religion had a lot of scare tactics. While I believe religious denominations were generally created for good, the ability for their rules and regulations to destroy you was (and is) unsurprisingly dangerous—perhaps lethal to some. How could one ever be good enough? The bar was set too high; it evoked a my-sins-are-not-as-bad-as-yours type of piety, and the exercise of grace and mercy was fairly nonexistent and did not look like the Jesus we studied and followed.

I was naive to the potential for harm that these man-made, entirely patriarchal rules and check boxes risked. The idea of perfection was forever an insurmountable, unsustainable expectation. Organized religion was designed by men, for men. There existed a toxic environment within this culture that boxed God in to suit a need for structure and to tick off tasks to keep the church body in line with man, not God.

There was nary a role for women in the church service when I attended church—nothing other than taking care of the babies in the nursery or teaching Sunday school or Wednesday night class to the youth. Women were to remain quiet and were not allowed to stand on the stage and speak, become members of the church's governing bodies, or to pass the communion or collection plates as volunteers. There was more, of course, and a ripple effect from being bullied into submission by someone else's opinion of what "gets you to heaven."

Who am I after this type of indoctrination? I am a woman who knows what legalism looks like. I am a woman who has a moral compass based on who she is and not a check box that someone else has for me. Being bound by "commandments" is hard to shake. Remnant effects of the past extremism I endured still pop up; that's what trauma does. However, I am now able identify these recurrences, and instead of suppressing them, I can acknowledge them and let them go.

Whether you've been part of a religious institution or not, are you living by an unrealistic set of legalistic check boxes? If so, why? Examine your parameters. Ask yourself if your conditions for being a "good" human being are actually contributing to your goal or pulling you away from it. A lot of times, the things that we think are good for us are getting in the way of our becoming fully known to ourselves and others.

LOSING MY RELIGION

As an outsider looking in, I can only imagine how the culture of religious institutions might look—maybe not so welcoming if you don't know the flow. For example, in every church I attended, the audience knew when to rise, when to kneel, when to bow heads, when to sing, and all of the dos and don'ts. It didn't even occur to me that the ritualistic behaviors within a church service were foreign or confusing until a friend I brought to church for the first time asked me how we all knew when to stand up and sit down. These cues were demonstrated to me from the first moment my mother held me in her arms while she sat in a pew. These movements were essentially intrinsic to the regular churchgoer and understandably odd to someone looking in.

When I started to date my now husband, he introduced me to a church community where it seemed grace did abound and there were fewer parameters—but still, there were some rules that to me seemed to oppose Jesus and His example. Unfortunately, I found there to be an underbelly—a riptide, if you will—where grace was absent and ultimate acceptance was conditional upon your ability to follow the rules. There, the foundation of love could be more like quicksand, not solid but sinking.

The skein of religion has done a big disservice to the whole concept of unconditional love with its patriarchal hierarchy. To a hurting world, the attraction has dimmed and faded and is close to being blown out. It's a shame, because if love was truly at the forefront there would be a lot less hurt and a lot less pride.

An endearing song we learned as children was a hymn by C. H. Woolston, "Jesus Loves the Little Children." What a beautiful thought, but in my experience, there was little to show for this diverse, all-inclusive acceptance of color and race as explicitly stated in its lyrics:

Jesus loves the little children,
All the children of the world;
Red and yellow, black and white,
They are precious in His sight.

In my religious community, the churches were predominately White and American. I wonder, *Did people of other races feel welcome in the church that I attended in my youth?* In hindsight, color was noticeably absent, and the modeling of overall acceptance of diversity seemed lacking. If nothing else, there was certainly an air of oppression and a law of subjectivity for those who were not both White and male.

I think if this same song were written today, perhaps the lyrics would be something like, "Jesus loves everyone," and perhaps, if this example was practiced consistently, there would be more love, grace, and harmony, or at least the opportunity for more. "Actions speak louder than words" was a consistent thread in my life, but it was not always demonstrated in church or in the everyday. My intention for sharing this observation is not to condemn or unfairly criticize those who were doing the best that they could with the skills that they had at the time, only to bring it to light as significant to me and my journey toward love and acceptance of everyone.

It would be easy for me to take a much deeper dive into the destructive ramifications of religion, but my goal is not to attack. It is to expose the detrimental effect that a rigid-rules approach had on my well-being. Legalism, as I mentioned earlier, was designed for accountability, but in hindsight, this type of conditional accountability was not a reflection of the Christ-like theme of the Bible which is, in a nutshell, *love*. Unconditional love.

Unconditional love was difficult, if not impossible, within a rules-oriented church body. Love was often under the guise of conditions, exclusivity, shame, or more. We may have followed the said requirements of the Bible, but we did not account for error, misinterpretation, or current culture—except when we wanted to. There was always a verse for what you should do and what is forbidden.

The LGBTQ+ community has long been ostracized from many denominations and non-denominations alike. I participated in many church bodies where it was a sin to be homosexual. There was room for forgiveness, but it was often conditional upon denying your personhood. Growing up in church, I was taught that being gay was wrong and acting out as a homosexual, lesbian, or trans person subjected one to an eternity in hell. In Bible class and in church services, this tenement was routinely instilled in me. I was taught scripture to use to defend my position against people who loved differently. This type of weaponization subjected precious individuals to shame, exclusion, and condemnation, and for a greater part of my life, I held onto these beliefs.

Two or more decades ago, I walked away from these teachings into acceptance and love for all who have been created—without condition on sexuality. In my opinion, the words of the Bible are for edification and encouragement, not for holding over the heads of those who do not abide by its man-interpreted commands. The God that I have come into my own with is the God of the universe, the loving and almighty God who does not impose conditions on his love for any of us. If you grew up in a religious institution, you may have experienced condemnation yourself, and I am sorry. In the Church of Christ, there was little tolerance for acts that were an affront or violation to the rules.

It was not only those who were gay who were outcast, there was also an insufferable stigma around having sex before marriage, and getting pregnant before marriage was even worse because there was evidence. I knew of unwed mothers who were kept hidden by their families to avoid the unrelenting judgment of others. More than one woman shared with me her plans for an abortion because the persecution and stigma of being pregnant and unmarried were too much for them to bear. I was traumatized by the experience of witnessing congregants come to the front of church to reveal their sins to the whole body—extra-marital affairs, financial improprieties, impure thoughts, sex out of wedlock, and more. One Sunday, a woman came forward and admitted her sins of having sex before marriage and becoming pregnant out of wedlock. To be clear, I was not traumatized by this woman's actions, but by the fact that she "had to" tell everyone what she had done so that she could receive forgiveness—not just from God, but from all of the people in the room. I recall that I heard wailing during the service.

At times, shame and pain that the "sinners" endured was palpable during worship. The scorn that some experienced was unacceptable. Once someone had confessed to carrying a baby without a husband, it seemed as though an invisible Scarlet Letter hung indelibly around their neck. Unfortunately, our church did not have or know a better way forward at the time. It is my hope that this type of shaming and condemnation has come to an end in the church at large. What I can say about the women who experienced indignity around being a single mother, or those who harbored the secret of abortion, is that they were all brave. They are beautiful, and I am grateful to have known them in one way or another.

Persecution is not acceptable. Passing judgment over someone else's choices is not right. Shaming is damaging. Only love is healing.

While my husband and I took our kids to church regularly, became involved in ministries, and joined small groups, we were naive (or in denial) over conditional religion and its effect on our family. Not to say that all was bad—it wasn't—and we enjoyed community, learning more about the Bible, and hearing inspiring lessons intended for growth.

We grew. We transformed. We evolved, and when the COVID pandemic hit in 2020, we exited "the church." We did this firstly because no one could attend in person, and secondly, because we had come to know more about the fallacies of religious culture. It was never more evident than during the COVID era. Politics took a turn, and divisiveness seemed to ravage hearts and relationships. A loud voice of many who claimed Christianity stung in my heart with echoes of heresy and exclusivity, of piety and a better-than-you mentality.

Despite all this undoing, I haven't abandoned God, the lessons from the Bible, or the example that Jesus lived. Instead, I have embraced what Jesus did—albeit, far from perfectly (perfection is not the goal and is unattainable)—but with an end goal of loving others well. *Period*.

Having evolved in womanhood and with better-defined beliefs, I am a now woman who seeks to include others, exhibit kindness, love myself, and love others. Thank God, I don't hold myself to the standards of perfection that others created. I have only one priority, which is to hold all my life and my interactions with others under the banner of love.

SCHOOL RULES

When I began grade school in 1975, I was on a small campus of a growing primary school in the heart of Green Hills, a suburb south of Nashville. David Lipscomb was a unique school in that it offered education from kindergarten through college. I attended the same school in all twelve years of elementary, middle, and high school.

School was not very different than church. It was also a Church of Christ school, so the legalism of the church married seamlessly with school. When I was in first grade, women were not allowed to wear pants anywhere on the campus. Not in grade school. Not in college. Female adult or child—no pants unless it was freezing outside. Then and only then could we girls put on a pair of pants. The caveat? Our pants had to go on underneath our dress. *Ugh. Eyeroll here.* Thankfully, this rule evaporated fairly quickly into my schooling.

Wearing shorts was forbidden. Skirts had to be knee-length. Shirts had to be tucked in for boys, and on and on—there was little margin for error. Falling short of the rules risked a trip to the principal, a call to your parents, or a paddling (for the guys), depending on the number of your infractions.

No public display of affection (PDA) was allowed. There was to be no handholding, no arms around one another, and, God-forbid, no kissing. Well, no wonder—if dancing led to sex, then what chance did you have if you were kissing? With time, the rules around PDA loosened, and holding hands was no longer taboo. Wearing shorts, though? I think it was allowed during PE class, but never while going across campus in public. This rule changed somewhere along the way during my college years.

Dancing was also frowned upon. We were told that dancing could easily lead to premarital sex, a baby, and a life ruined. We didn't have dances—no prom, no homecoming dance, and no dance themes. Instead, we had banquets, which were much like dances but with no dancing. We dressed to the nines, had dates, ate hotel ballroom buffet foods, and sat at our tables while we *watched* the band play.

My parents weren't too keen on the no-dancing rule. In fact, they were less conservative than the church or school, but at home legalism still ruled the roost. I did go to dances with boys from other schools. So, I got to experience prom, homecoming, and other dance events.

SCHOOL DAZE

Beginning with first grade, elementary and middle school classrooms were pod-like, portable buildings with windows and steel railings and steps, each connected to another like a train. Through the years, I moved from one temporary building to another until I eventually entered high school. Then most of my classes were held in the same building—Harding Hall.

Our grounds included a "Central Park" of sorts, where we had PE and free play. The space was like an island with a concrete drive around the whole parcel. There were tall oak trees, a playground with a slide, a merry-go-round, monkey bars, and more. Large greenspace allowed room for kickball fields and picnics. On one end of this greenspace was a historic bell tower and on the other was an original-to-the-property, white Victorian cottage where one or more of my Bible classes were held.

I had a love/hate relationship with the foot-worn path around the playing fields. There were two routes you could take: the Marathon, with a turn halfway around and through the middle of the fields, or the Super Marathon, which was twice as long. When participating in races, I was fast—small, but fast nonetheless—and I loved winning the girls' race. I was always nervous, with sweaty palms and revved up energy, and more than likely I was in a dress. When the starter would call, "On your mark. Get set. Go!" I'd run with my arms bent and my feet treading just as fast as possible, taking advantage of my short stature and quick feet against taller boys and girls with longer strides.

I spent a good portion of the twelve years from elementary to high school running around something, whether it was the track or the kickball field. My dream of being a cheerleader came true. I excelled in academics, I was homecoming queen my senior year, and I left for college at Lipscomb University just across campus. Lipscomb and its ways were part of me. Continuing into college at the same school felt natural at the time. Not only natural, but familiar, and close to home, and I didn't seriously consider any other school.

However, after having spent fourteen years at the same school, I became restless with what felt like monotony in my life, an endless repetition of church, school Bible class, and chapel.

I mentioned that Sunday mornings, Sunday nights, and Wednesday nights were all devoted to the church. Monday through Friday also included chapel, devotionals, and Bible class. In fact, all of my schooling had always felt the same. I was not only steeped in religion, but I was also drowning in it. I didn't know "me" apart from the rules and expectations.

Come my sophomore year of college, I had had enough of the sameness. At age twenty, I was ready for the change I wasn't ready for at eighteen. So, I met with one of my professors for advice. He gave me some things to think about like, "Why are you at Lipscomb?" and "Isn't it time you did something for yourself?" His questions struck a chord with me and prompted me to look into other schools. Little did I know this meeting would change the trajectory of my major and my schooling.

It's at this juncture that I began opening myself up for discovery. Self-discovery. Heading out on my own was a big leap of faith for me. I still recognize this young woman in myself today, but she is more reserved. That's because being willing to step out into the unknown has brought challenges—some healthy, some not—but opportunities to grow, nonetheless.

CHAPTER SIX

WAY OUT WEST

Transferring to another school and being far from home was a big deal for me. Before this, I had not considered going to school anywhere other than where I was. Because it was easy? Maybe. Although, I also believe I hadn't been ready, which is not uncommon.

Having grown up in the Church of Christ, my natural tendency was to look at other Church of Christ-affiliated schools where there would be some familiarity, and my academic scholarship would transfer with me. I considered only two options: Abilene Christian University in Abilene, Texas, and Pepperdine University in Malibu, California. The choice seemed like a no-brainer. My parents were supportive of either school but preferred for me to be closer to Tennessee. With Abilene being 850 miles away and Malibu more than twice that, neither was truly close to home.

With my mind set to explore the two colleges, I planned my trips. The first visit was to Pepperdine. Early on a Friday morning, my parents took me to the airport and I flew out to California alone to visit Pepperdine.

If you've never been to Pepperdine, let me tell you, its campus is nothing short of a showstopper. Just off of Pacific Coast Highway and Malibu Canyon Road in

Malibu, Pepperdine, in all of its glory, is nestled in the Santa Monica Mountains and commands a mesmerizing view of the Pacific Ocean. In other words, this place was *drop dead gorgeous*—a slice of paradise.

I only knew one student there, Chris, who was excited to pick me up at Los Angeles International Airport (LAX) and show me Los Angeles and Malibu. He pulled up to LAX in a convertible, I tossed my luggage in the trunk, and we took off into the California sunshine. Dreamy.

Chris had arranged for me to stay with some of his girlfriends in the dorm so I would have the full-on campus experience. After meeting the girls, Chris took me to a party in Malibu. Ironically, the venue was a church that had been converted to a nightclub. Other than having a lot of fun and waking up in the girls' dorm with a headache the next day, I don't remember a whole lot else from that evening.

The next morning, despite being slightly hung over, I pulled myself together and took the official campus tour. I vividly recall walking into the university library. I don't remember anything about the layout, where books were housed, or what amenities were available. The only thing in that building that made an impression on me was the view of the Pacific Ocean! As I stood looking out the window at the sea and the beach, I immediately said to myself, "I will *never* study here!"

My second college tour was of the Abilene Christian University campus. To get to Abilene, I flew from Nashville to the Dallas Fort Worth International Airport where I boarded a commuter flight to the tiny college town located two hours west of Dallas. This was my first trip to Texas, and I had been forewarned that it was flat, but having come from lush hills and mountains, I really had no idea what flat was or how stark it can be on first site. It brought to mind a song with the lyrics, "Abilene, Abilene, prettiest town I've ever seen." I instantly found this ode to Abilene, written by George Hamilton IV and sung by Bill Anderson and Waylon Jennings, to be a bit misleading. Abilene, dusty and flat, was not quite the prettiest town that I'd ever seen, and, granted, few places hold a candle to the beauty of the Pacific Coast and the rolling hills of Tennessee. Perhaps unfair to Abilene, I was comparing apples to oranges.

Driving around in pickup trucks were actual cowboys and ranchers, wearing everything a cowboy wears from Ropers to Wranglers. I'd never seen anything like it. In Nashville, cowboy hats and boots weren't uncommon, but the difference was that these Texas boys wore it all with the complete authenticity you would expect and quite akin to what you might see on a TV Western.

Before visiting Texas, I had only seen cartoon tumbleweeds on Saturday morning episodes of *The Road Runner Show*, but when I arrived in Abilene, I saw my very first ones that were true-to-life. In West Texas, the ground was often dirty and dusty and windstorms whipped up without a moment's notice, turning the dry ground into a frenzy by gathering and blowing everything and anything across the roads and fields. I was less than impressed.

Between Pepperdine and Abilene, the choice seemed obvious—at least from a visual standpoint, but the decision wasn't easy for me. I weighed the immediate pros and cons of both locations—beauty, distance, and beauty! After weeks of deliberation, I chose flatlands and rattlesnakes over sea salt and sand.

Looking back, it seems an irrational decision, but I know why I chose Texas over California. One of the positive factors about Abilene was that I had a very close cousin who was there and just a year ahead of me. She was excited for me to come and lovingly set me up with an apartment and roommates who became close friends. Also helpful was the fact that I had more family just a couple of hours away in Fort Worth. The underlying thought process, though, involved choosing not just what fit within my comfort zone, but what fit that of my parents. It seemed the most pleasing choice to make.

After the excitement of the new town, new friends, and my first apartment wore off, the scales fell from my eyes. I loathed Texas and its endlessly unvaried landscape. The scrub brush left the nature scene lacking in comparison to the beauty of the evergreens and the tall, billowing trees from home.

Experiencing the change in landscape from Nashville to Abilene tore at my heart and love for nature. The environmental contrast with where I had grown up was stark, and I also encountered culture shock that I could not have truly prepared myself for. I was sad, and I had a hard time adjusting to that first semester.

My confidence in myself was low. Yes, I had friends, sweet ones, but starting a new college mid-year meant that I had missed out on the *social club* scene and had half as much time to forge new relationships.

When I started at Abilene, I was in broadcasting and journalism hoping to be a news anchor or similar. Self-doubt crept in, though, and I moved behind the scenes. Even there, I couldn't find my comfort zone. Nothing felt natural and I felt alone. Once again, I shifted my focus and settled on Human Communications. Why in the world was it called that? I don't really know. It is self-explanatory but it sounds weird. Weird or not, I found myself more comfortable in my new area of focus. Human communication classes included brushes with psychology, philosophy, and the sociological side of studying the human condition—that's what I liked.

As my first semester in Abilene was ending, I had all but decided to move back to Nashville. I just couldn't reconcile my ache for greener pastures—literally—and I had yet to find solace in what Texas could offer in exchange.

Set on leaving Abilene, and as the last few weeks of the first semester were closing in on us, there was an announcement about a brand-new study abroad program in London. I recall sitting in the large gymnasium during chapel, probably uninterested in much at the time, and feeling like an answer to prayer had just emerged. I gathered all the information that I could and called my parents right away. My promise was to get a job over the winter break and make some money to go toward the cost of the program.

My parents both agreed (and probably began planning their visit right away), and in January of 1990, I joined a group of about ten schoolmates (two of whom I knew) and a chaperone couple to spend mid-winter to early spring studying at Regent's College.

The college itself was located in the beautiful Regent's Park where Queen Mary's Gardens and the London Zoo were located. Within easy walking distance to Madame Tussauds, and an easy stretch to the aptly named Tube, was Baker (my maiden name) Street.

Living in the heart of London, taking classes four days a week, and traveling almost every Friday through Sunday, I found a freedom that I had not experienced in my life. Because I had not had much time completely on my own, I almost didn't know where or how to release my inner self. However, I took cues from others, sewed all kinds of oats, uncovered my ability to confidently travel alone (much to my mom's chagrin), and tapped into more of who I was in the middle of everything unfamiliar.

It was in London that I became a vegetarian and an explorer. My eagerness to travel to as many places as possible was on fire—hardly quenchable—and was fed by one trip launching into another.

My classes were easy and enjoyable—European Geography (which came in handy to a girl with a poor sense of direction), acting, and one other class insignificant enough for me to forget.

Groups of us traversed the whole of the United Kingdom, from Ireland to Wales to Scotland and a major portion of England itself. My first taste of solo travel happened during my trip to Dublin with one other classmate. She and I had similar goals when we boarded Ryanair, but those changed quickly. After one night in a grubby hostel, I was uninterested in staying in Dublin. I like cities, but I crave the sparse countryside, and the grassy green hills of Ireland were calling my name.

This was long before the internet and cell phones. Computers were around, but Google wasn't. Nor were there any sites dedicated to the student traveler. Instead, the bible of our youth overseas was the famous *Let's Go Europe*. This book went with me everywhere I went. At more than five hundred pages, it offered loads of resources about where to stay, what to avoid, how to travel, what to bring, and so much more.

With *Let's Go Europe* as my guide, I left Dublin alone, boarded a rurally bound bus, and headed to the rolling hills and pastureland. Before leaving Dublin, I had made arrangements to stay at a bed and breakfast in the middle of a sheep farm. I was both excited and nervous, but less nervous because *Let's Go* had assured me that Ireland was the safest place for a female to travel alone.

While I did find it fairly easy to travel by myself, I did not find it easy to calculate directions and distances on my own. So, when my stop came along, and the bus pulled up alongside a row fence on a one-lane road, I stepped off in the middle of *nowhere* at dusk. Down the road, I spotted a pub and I headed straight there. They were not officially open yet, but I walked in to find the bartender setting up for the evening. I didn't have any idea where I was. I felt fairly confident that my B&B wasn't too far away, but there were no road signs, no markers, nothing.

Somewhat nervous, I stepped up to the bar to ask the bartender if he could point me in the direction of my lodging. He was happy to oblige and began, in a lovely Irish lilt, to talk and gesture the directions for my route. While I listened and watched the sun set lower in the sky, it dawned on me that there was hardly any way I would make it to the B&B before the sun set behind the hills. Talk about dark—Irish countryside, no streetlights, no cars to speak of—just a dusty gravel road heading through pasture after pasture.

Lucky for me, I was in Ireland, which made the coming luck all the more appropriate. The bartender called out to a younger guy who was helping set up the pub for the dinner crowd. With that, Keiran walked over to greet me, and he became my four-leaf clover.

Keiran drove me to the sweet, ranch-style home where I would stay, along with another guest. Nothing fancy. Perfect, though. Two bedrooms at the end of the hall and a lovely host, Molly, who greeted us as we pulled up the drive.

Again, as luck would have it (I can't help it), the next day was St. Patrick's Day, and before I got out of the car, Keiran told me he would come back in the morning, drive me through the countryside, and take me to a Gaelic football game in Dublin. This proposition sounded good to me—perhaps a little risky. I waved goodbye and before I even stepped into the house, Molly, who had heard Kieran's offer, had started a chain of telephone calls around town to figure out who this young man was and if it was safe for me to travel with him. The overwhelming consensus was yes. Keiran's family was well-known in the village. His parents were famous folk singers who were currently touring the country while Keiran and his two sisters held down the fort at home. So, Keiran was approved, and the next day dawned.

After I ate a steaming hot bowl of oatmeal while gazing at the grazing sheep, Keiran picked me up and we drove through the most beautiful hill country, stopping at castles and monastery ruins along the way. The day could not have been more ideal. The cherry on the top was that we ended it in Dublin watching a soccer match and eating fish and chips. I could have made this up, but I didn't.

Opinions aside as to whether my twenty-one-year-old self was making smart decisions, this trip was a victory for me. I felt myself come alive. The young adventurer in me, the one who used to build forts in the woods and sled monstrous hills in the snow, showed up like I had never seen myself in the past. If there was anything that I now knew about myself—aside from anyone else's version or expectation of me—it was that I could do something on my own, in my time. I discovered a newfound sense of freedom and reaped the benefits of traveling alone and figuring things out for myself.

There were many adventures that semester, many stories to tell—not all as shiny as a penny and some a little scary—nonetheless, looking back on myself, I flourished in this setting, and the ache to discover new worlds has always remained. Whether I've been true to it all of my life is part of my story too, though.

There is a time and season for everything.

Seasons change; everything changes.

Looking back now, I can answer the question "Who do you think you are?" I was a brave, adventurous, spontaneous, and confident young woman. I have to remind myself that I still am.

"WHO DO YOU THINK YOU ARE?"

he yelled at his sitting audience and he looked down at me then, as I reddened. "That Paul, he was a hot-shot until his part of us came in. I thought there was more and gave us less of life now, we're fools if anything changes."

Looked over to me. "I can answer the question, why we're here. Every I one's a name. That's us, a what's-that one: a million, a sign, a meteor, a tree, means Independent of us all."

CHAPTER SEVEN

MAJOR CODEPENDENCY

The study abroad program and new friendships gave me a fresh perspective and a desire to return to Abilene to finish my undergraduate degree.

If you've ever lived in Texas or even visited, it's almost impossible not to see that it is truly like its own country. Everything is bigger in Texas, and Texas has a culture of its own, from rattlesnake round-ups to Tex-Mex to margaritas to two-stepping, and I hadn't missed any of it.

Of course, all these things are much more fun with friends. Throw a cute boyfriend in the mix, and the whole package works—until it doesn't.

Margaritas caught up with me. Drunk decisions are never good decisions, and alcohol impaired my judgment when it came to relationships with the opposite sex. When I partied, I loosened up. When I loosened up, there was sex—not random sex, but sex nonetheless—which was a way for me to escape. Naive to this underlying motivation at the time, I now realize that what I sought was another level of intimacy and dependence; I tried to gain approval by using my body in the arms of someone who "cared" for me. My body served me well in that I had worked to make it attractive, but my body, sex, and alcohol were only vices to fill a void—one that I could not name nor that I wanted to recognize. The numbing felt better because it was what I knew. Not too much time passed, though, before I decided to dig deeper into what my need truly was.

It may not be a shocker to some that I was having age-appropriate sex, sewing my oats, and behaving like a college student, but none of these natural areas of exploration were allowed in my religious culture. Sex outside of marriage was a big sin, not as big as adultery, but not far from it. Drinking alcohol was also a big no-no. The difference, though, is that having premarital sex was done at the risk of hell, or so I believed because of my church doctrine. Further, in my religious community we did *not* talk about sex or drinking—to anyone, ever. *Don't talk about your struggles (not the nitty-gritty details, anyway), and deal with that yourself.* These were universal understandings. Meanwhile, I secretly walked around filled with guilt and shame. All the acting out, though, finally came to a head.

During my last year of college, a mutual friend introduced me to a charming Texan named Chad. Chad drove a dated, sporty car and worked as a lifeguard at the Abilene Country Club. Originally from a Dallas suburb, Chad had come to Abilene for college but had taken a break for a semester to reevaluate what he wanted to do. He wasn't feeling the college vibes, but this was an era when *everyone* got a college degree—so it was still on the table for him, even if just for appearances sake.

Chad was adorable and handsome. He made me laugh and was a lot of fun to be with. I loved the way he said my name, "Laaaw-ruh Liin," stringing out the syllables in his West Texas twang. He was a really good kisser, and on top of all of that he needed me. *Hallelujah.* I could be his savior, the one who could steer him back to college, right where his family wanted him. Bonus:

The parents loved me, and who better to step up to the plate than the perfectly poised pleaser and performer? If anyone was up to the task, it was me.

Not only did I have a handsome boyfriend, but I also now had a purpose—at least that's what it felt like to me. Chad and I liked each other so much that he flew to Nashville during my Christmas break. This, for me, was like saying, "You're the one," or at minimum, "Let's date." His charming, wily ways, though, got the best of me.

Despite having fun and enjoying each other's company, on a winter day after school had resumed, Chad pulled a classic. We were sitting in his sporty car talking, when out of the blue he said, "It's not you. It's me. You're too good for me. I will just drag you down," and with that, he broke up with me. Crying, I was stunned and begged for him to change his mind (he didn't), and he drove me home.

Like other breakups had in the past, this led me to starve myself—eating little more than a serving of frozen yogurt at lunch in the cafeteria. I took step aerobics, I ran six miles a day six days a week, and I eventually cut my hair. (You know, ladies!) From this moment, I spiraled into a depression like I had never known in my life. The kicker, though, was that I really didn't even know how to name what I was feeling.

I had a terrible time finding my identity after the breakup. After all, I had a purpose in that relationship and people to please. How could I fail? With a desire for perfection and intimacy, I could not stay away from this boy. I returned again and again to his doorstep—often drunk, usually crying. My physical self needed some type of validation. I didn't know this feeling. I didn't know how to deal with it other than trying my best to feed it.

We never officially got back together, and, of my own doing, we had months of a toxic and tumultuous relationship. It was toxic for me. Probably not so much for him at the time. I also used his plan of returning to school as fodder for us to date again. It's what his mom and dad wanted. It's what I thought I wanted. It was not at all what I needed; nor did it come close to being what was good for me.

I kept the pressure on. I showed up again and again, only to be taken advantage of and shot down again and again. The catalyst for the crumble, though, came after a phone call I had had with his mom during which she pleaded with me to help and suggested that I mention the idea of counseling to him. Counseling? *Yes*, I thought. *This is a good idea.*

One day, I stormed into his apartment dead set on a reversal of our terms. We argued. I said that it was in his best interest, but he wasn't having any of it. Maybe he saw that none of this behavior was in *my* best interest. As our voices got louder, and the yelling started, I blurted out, "Your mom and I think you need to go to counseling!" Yikes.

I had planned for a negative reaction and hoped for a positive one. However, I had not planned, prepared for, or anticipated what would happen next. After I declared to him what he should do, he threw it back in my face and said, "*You* should go to counseling!"

Self-defeated and exhausted, I turned and said, "I think I will."

This was a "Wake up, Laura Lyn!" moment for me, and without overthinking it I walked out of his door and headed straight to our campus counseling center. I kid you not. That's just what I did. I was scared. Feeling hopeless and very lost.

I had no idea what I was doing, but I had to do something. I walked into the counseling office, a crying mess, and asked if I could talk to someone. Without much time for the reality of where I was and what I was doing to sink in, a counselor appeared from behind a door. (Keep in mind, in 1991, counseling was still taboo and pretty much reserved for the "crazy" people. If you went, you didn't talk about it. You kept it private. Personal. "Vulnerability" was a bad word.) I don't know who or what I was expecting to emerge from the closed office door, but it was not who greeted me with an outstretched handshake. He introduced himself as Major. I was thinking, *Major what?* There was no last name—like Prince or Madonna—he was Major.

At six-foot-five, Major towered over my barely five-foot, three-inch frame. I had never considered that the counselor I would meet would be a handsome, authoritative Black man named Major. Honestly, I'm sure I would have thought it would be a White woman with coiffed hair and glasses hanging around her neck! However, I believe that because Major was the opposite of who I expected, he was the perfect match for me. Maybe he was the only one. I don't know, but there was something about him that was compelling. While intimidating on first impression, he offered me a sense of safety and an opportunity to be more forthcoming than I thought I ever could be. Or maybe the circumstances simply gave me the permission that I needed to feel and do these things.

As I sat down in the chair across from his desk, the shocking reality of what I'd done came in a rushing wave of blood to my brain. I felt dizzy, awkward, and stuck—very stuck. Major took his seat behind his desk, while I looked up at him wondering what in the hell I was going to say to this guy. I didn't know what I was doing. However, I did have a couple of images in mind of what therapy looked like. One, the patient lounging on a couch, eyes closed, telling the counselor everything. Major had a couch, but I didn't lie on it! The second and scarier image was that of the patient talking to an inanimate object as if it were a person.

The second scenario came true in our very first session. Major moved from behind his desk and around to where I was seated. As he walked over, he pulled up a couple of chairs—one for him and one for "Chad." My thoughts racing, I watched as Major pulled a pillow from the couch and plopped it into the chair. "Talk to the pillow like it was Chad," he said to me.

Good grief. This was *not* what I wanted to do—so cliché and embarrassing. I gritted my teeth and began to talk to Chad, to yell at Chad, and to punch Chad, as Major guided me through the exercise of play-acting, only it wasn't a play and it wasn't acting. I got a little more comfortable with it the longer I was subjected to it, and I was able to express feelings of hurt and anger that I may have otherwise never said aloud. Thank God, though, this was the first and last time I would ever talk to a pillow—but it was not the last time I would punch one.

Because I had grown up in an environment with a man-made list of right and wrong with eternity hanging in the balance, giving up my self—my true self, and all of it—didn't seem reasonable. It was too scary to admit that against school rules I had drunken alcohol or that against the Bible I had had sex before marriage. On top of all that, admitting these indiscretions would mean admitting that I had failed. I had not lived up to expectations; I was not perfect. I would be an utter disappointment to the powers that be.

As Major and I got to know each other in those first few minutes in his office, I let my guard down a bit. I felt like I could trust this new person in my life in the same way that you might trust a stranger with no context of "you," or, of who you should or should not be. He didn't know me in any other context than a young woman asking for help.

However, I was still cautious about what I told him, making sure not to implicate myself in crime against the church. Because of this, the most pertinent information never came to light. At least I was in control of that. I knew how to gauge my talk, what to avoid, and what to reveal—all within the confines of the legalistic checklist seared into my brain. The sad truth was that I never brought up my acting out. At this stage in my life, I did not know that what I was leaving out—the drinking and the sex (mostly the sex)—were key elements to uncovering myself and why my actions were motivated by more than backlash to authority or issuing, "Fuck you!" to the rules. I'm sure that I was not pulling any wool over Major's eyes. After all, part of the training of a counselor is to be able to see deeper, even with a patient who is evasive. He was a highly intelligent man.

Before I left his office that first day, Major handed me a copy of the now famous, *Codependent No More: How to Stop Controlling Others and Start Caring for Yourself* by Melody Beattie. Beattie was a game changer on the front lines of codependency. Her first edition of *Codependent No More* was published in 1986, just five years prior to it being given to me. I don't know whether the book had even caught on yet, but it did, and it continues to be revised and reprinted today. If the subtitle alone doesn't suggest what this book covers, I don't know what does. For the first time in my life, I had an inkling of an answer to the "why" behind my actions and choices.

In the book, Beattie says, "We [codependents] rescue people from their responsibilities. We take care of people's responsibilities for them. Later we get mad at them for what we've done. Then we feel used and sorry for ourselves. That is the pattern, the triangle."[1] Bingo. I was looking for control in relationships. I was looking for affirmation in sex. I was looking for kudos, a pat on the back, a "well-done." I felt deserving of praise for changing others. I didn't know that all the while I was neglecting the one who needed me most—me. My determination to control outcomes by saying yes, to control of relationships by being the helper, and to control of my body by making it smaller—by none of these was I truly in control. Each was a denial of myself in the service of others.

All was not lost, though. My time with Major helped set me on a new course that, in my opinion, helped shape the rest of my life. In a world that didn't think too highly of therapy or recognize the importance of mental health or self-discovery, little did I know that I was on the cutting edge of change. This change would still take decades—but it saved my life and restored some sanity.

My time in the Great State of Texas was more than just a coming of age for me. It was an undoing, and a re-do, a glass half empty and a glass half full. I took these self-revelations for better or worse and did the best that I could to make my life better, not worse. This fresh, thin, buildable layer of knowing myself set me on a course to healthier relationships, to self-actualization, and to revelation—not quickly—but through years of difficult and challenging self-work and, well, *life*. Because life happens.

Every year brings with it a stronger foundation, but, equally so, it offers more layers of the onion to peel away and examine. What I learned about myself and codependence helped me to understand why I sought others' approval so much. Codependent behavior, in and of itself, is not bad. We are born codependent. In order to survive, we need the care of another individual. The challenge is knowing how to navigate life as a codependent. I have emerged as a self-aware codependent. On my best days, taking care of myself is my focal point, and on my not-so-great days, I may find myself leaning into codependency as a way to control my environment. Love of self is what we all need. Control is not.

CHAPTER EIGHT

PRETTY IS AS PRETTY DOES

Despite the struggles that I had in Texas, I walked away with a true love for the state and the people. I'll never forget the exhilarating feeling of two-stepping with a cowboy who could whisk me across the dance floor, despite the fact that I hardly knew how to dance.

Abilene ended up being a lot more beautiful to me than I first thought. I fell in love with the vast Texas sunset spread across the plains. Radiant with color, it seemed to linger for hours on the horizon. I found solace in sunsets and in watching the sun rise during morning bike rides. Beauty is indeed in the eye of the beholder. I had to look harder to see it, but it was there all along.

In the summer of 1991, I graduated as valedictorian of my small college class. There was no hoopla. No dramatic pomp and circumstance. No speech from me. But I had finished; I was proud of my accomplishment and so was my family.

After college, I left Texas and my friends and moved home to Nashville. My plan was to get a job, take a year off of schooling, study for the Law School Admission Test (LSAT), and go to law school. Plans change, and so did mine. At the end of the day, I got a far better deal.

CHAPTER NINE

MAKING MUSIC

I grew up knowing Nashville was the home of country music, but I didn't know anything about the music business—the details behind the glamor and the people behind the scenes who made it happen—or the fact that a majority of Christian music was also recorded in Nashville. During the lulls and breaks of my college career, and prior to my trip to Europe, in the summer of 1990, I worked in the music industry as a receptionist for a music management company. After I graduated from college, I continued to work at the same company and eventually became an administrative assistant to the vice president. This job changed my life forever for the better because it's how I met my soulmate.

Don was intriguing to me. He was handsome, with gorgeous blue eyes, and he was quick-witted and very funny. We worked in the same office building, a two-story, duplex-like, orangey brick building that stood alone in a parking lot just off of Nashville's West End, several miles away from well-known Music Row. Although we were in the same building, we worked for different companies. My side was artist management and his side was a record label—both companies mutually owned by the other. I got to know Don because he would frequent our side of the building to visit his best friend, my boss.

After a summer's worth of seeing him come and go, I decided that I'd really like to go on a date with him. When I couldn't get a co-worker to get a move on and drop a hint to Don, I took matters into my own hands. One day, I worked up the courage to go to Don's office and ask him on a date.

What I didn't know was that Don had a girlfriend. What I also didn't know until I invited him out was that he was flying to Kansas City to break up with said girlfriend—all very convenient, except for the fact that he couldn't say yes to my offer. I was pretty bummed, and maybe even a little embarrassed, but not for long.

The following week, while I was packing up to leave for the day, Don emerged from one of the executive offices about ten paces from my desk. I was still sitting down, finishing up for the day, when Don walked out of the meeting he was in and over to my desk. He sidled up to my chair and then crouched down to my level and said something to the effect of, "I'd really like to go out with you if you're still interested." I said, "Of course, I am," with a big grin on my face. After I said yes, we talked for a minute, and Don stood up to go back into his meeting. As he turned around to walk the short distance to the office door, he ran right into the credenza behind him—it was funny. Awkward, but also a bit of an ice breaker.

Our first date was a double date with a friend of Don's and his girlfriend. The couple had not been together too long, but they were already in counseling, and they chose to share about that over dinner at the Italian restaurant where we were eating. While we slurped spaghetti and dipped our focaccia into olive oil, we listened to the other two argue and discuss their counseling session. We survived the meal, though, and capped the evening off with the premiere of *The Addams Family* at a nearby movie theater. And, as they say, the rest is history, but there's much more to the story. Having come from a tumultuous relationship in Abilene, and while still preparing for the LSAT and looking at law schools, my mind was not on a serious relationship. But that changed, too. Everything changed.

Don was different, very different than any other man (or boy) I had dated. One noticeable difference with Don was how he dressed. Keep in mind, we were fairly fresh out of the 1980s, and even then, his style was a far cry from that of the preppy boys I had dated. He had an ear piercing and he wore round, tortoise shell glasses. On our first date, he picked me up at my parents' house wearing a gold stud in his ear, a silver cross around his neck, and a dark blue, plaid blazer. A boy wearing an earring was edgy (for me). Wearing a cross necklace was weird. Throw in the sports jacket, and his look was a bit confusing—we would change that later.

Three years older than me, Don was certainly more mature than anyone I had gone out with, and unlike past codependent partners, Don didn't need to be fixed. This was foreign to me, and I didn't know exactly how to do a relationship in which it wasn't *my job* to be the savior or the pleaser.

Don was forthcoming with his feelings, blunt (thank you, Midwest), and to the point. He was ahead of his time in that he was not afraid to show emotion as a sensitive man, a caring man, and a wise man. He and I talked about my past and my natural tendency to stuff my feelings, sweep them under the rug, and ignore them altogether. I had to be self-protective. I had to guard my heart. Years later, I'd realize that this coping mechanism was a learned behavior, unconsciously modeled to me at home.

Thank God, Don was patient with me. I was timid, skeptical, and reluctant to go deep, but Don earned my trust, and I began to feel comfortable sharing with him. As we opened up to one another, his vulnerability opened the door for my own. My high walls began to diminish in the safe space he afforded me. The bricks came down one-by-one, and our love began to grow and blossom into something extraordinary for the two of us.

CHAPTER TEN

SPLIT IMAGE

By 1992, Don and I were full-blown in love and talking about marriage, and at the same time, my parent's marriage was falling apart. We didn't know the extent of their struggle then and wouldn't understand it until we later saw it in hindsight.

One random day at work, my mom called me. She didn't ask me, but rather she told me to come home for a family meeting. We had had family meetings growing up but never emergency ones. So, I left work and headed home down the familiar streets of town, the ones I had grown up driving to wherever I wanted to go. On this day, though, I drove my practical, blue Honda Accord in dread. As I headed down the main road to our cul-de-sac, I passed the three mailboxes lined neatly together on railroad ties. I took a hard right down the steep private drive, around the bend, and up to our home in the woods.

When I arrived, my brothers were there sitting with our mom and dad in the living room. Timidly, I walked into the room. There was awkward silence—not the kind of awkwardness you feel when your mom wants to sing devotional songs together, but it was eerie, telling, frightening even.

While the tension hung in the air, our conversation began, how exactly I don't know, but probably with a casual comment from my dad in an effort to diffuse some of the brewing hostility. What came next was one of the worst moments in my life. My parents told me during their twenty-five years of marriage there had been some major breaches in their marriage vows. Shaking with anger and disillusionment, Mom and Dad told us everything. Everything we didn't want to know but had to. While the details of their story are theirs to tell, the ramifications of their story on me are mine. It felt like a tragic discovery in a hostile culture, an unforgiving one, and occurring a full generation before people would even risk taking the opportunity to look inward, to self-examine, or, God-forbid, go to counseling. It felt hopeless.

Sitting on the couch in the "family" room, suddenly family didn't feel so much like family. The whole atmosphere was unfamiliar, heavy, suffocating. There was no script for what to do next. While each of us sat frozen in our places, my brothers and I asked questions, asked for details, and longed for an answer to explain everything away and wrap up the disaster with a neat little bow. Our questions were answered to the best of Mom and Dad's ability. There were apologies and acts of contrition. The room was like a sauna. The heat of anger was palpable and the ability to breathe was nearly impossible. The steaming pot boiled over. Our family room erupted like a volcano—emotions like hot, molten lava circling our feet. As if through smoke and flames, I watched my parents split into two—literally.

One stayed; one left.

I felt my heart break into a million pieces. *Where am I? This isn't real. My parents promised me they would never divorce. How can all of this be the new reality?* I thought to myself. I did not want this burden, and that's what it was.

While the confessors' loads had been lifted, mine had become heavy ladened.

I tried to reconcile who I knew my parents to be and what was now happening. I loved my dad. He was my daddy; the one who tossed me in the air on the trampoline; the one who built my dollhouse from scratch; the one who designed our home for our family; and the one who made my dreams come true.

I also loved my mom. She was my mom, my confidant, the one who calmed my fears and created home inside of a house. My mentor. My best friend. These idyllic ruminations echoed in my head. I was dumbfounded. Confused.

Sitting in that dizzying haze, one parent tried to be somewhat reassuring to assuage our disbelief. Yet, there was no balm for the wounded, no soft landing. Bags were packed, goodbyes were said, and the open door closed. When the front door closed, I watched with tears streaming down my face as one parent started up the car and drove away. Where was there to go?

I couldn't take the hell any longer. What felt like a fever swept from my head and through my veins, and I ran up the stairs to my bedroom and straight into my closet. There in my safe space, I lay prone screaming, wailing, gripping the green shag carpet in my hands, pounding the floor, and crying my eyes out for hours. I could not process what had happened.

The picture-perfect family had shattered. The picturesque dream of family had crashed. An unsuspected bomb had been deployed, destroying a family dream.

I stayed home that night. Don was out of town, but as was his routine, he called me, and I told him everything. By this point, Don and I had dated long enough for me to know he was a safe place to land.

When he got back to town, I didn't just land. I crashed into his arms. He held me. Listened. Did not shame me. Offered grace and love and stayed by my side through every last bit, and in these tender moments, we were able to better understand what had happened before the fallout.

CHAPTER ELEVEN

NOTHING BUT THE TRUTH

Months before all hell broke loose in my parent's marriage, I had told them that Don was the one. He was the man of my dreams. My soulmate. As if my reasoning had fallen on deaf ears, Mom dropped to her knees and, in tears, told me that Don was not the one. Dad pulled up a chair for the defendant, me, and drilled me with questions like, "Has Don ever been married; does he have any children?"

In my mind I was thinking, *What the fuck is going on here?*

Dad continued, "How is he going to support you? What if he loses his job? He doesn't have a degree." Don hadn't been married and didn't have any children; his only *fault* in this paradigm of conditions was that he hadn't graduated from college. But, come on, that was far from a reason for me not to marry him.

Their reactions to my announcement were so uncharacteristically dramatic and emotional of my parents. There was so much anger and a lot more fear. Why were my parents so afraid? Why did they subject me to such harsh interrogation? I had no clue. It made me speechless and suddenly very unsure of what I had been so sure of when I walked in. I knew I wanted to marry Don, and then I didn't know—or so I thought.

Then Mom and Dad asked me to stop dating Don. Talk about confusing. I had no context or clarity, but I respected my parents and was also a pleaser. It's certainly not abnormal for parents to be questioning or to want to protect their children, but I was afraid they knew something that I didn't—not about Don specifically—but about life and choosing your mate. Maybe I had done it all wrong. So, I broke up with Don.

BREAKING UP IS HARD TO DO

Breaking up with Don was terrible. It was so confusing for him, and I did know how to explain it because I didn't know what was happening. I didn't really understand why, but I knew that the only way to get the madness to stop was for me to perform well, to be a pleaser, and to steady the boat. Our time apart lasted a couple of agonizing weeks, but as devastating as it was, the forced break made it glaringly obvious to me that I did know how to choose a soulmate. I could trust my gut, and I could make a choice for myself that didn't have to measure up to whatever expectations of me were hovering in my atmosphere.

Then hindsight became 20/20: I realized that my parents wanted me to break up with Don because they were falling apart. Everything in their relationship hung in the balance. It made sense—if after twenty-five years together you uncover what feels irreparable, and if you can't control your own circumstances, then what do you do? You protect and control the ones you can. The questions, the absurdity of most of it, hadn't been about me. It had been about them.

My parents remained separated over the next two years. It would be an understatement to say that they worked hard on their marriage because that hardly scratches the surface. They spent myriad hours in individual counseling and couples' therapy. They found support groups, attended therapeutic retreat centers, and worked hard on themselves. Each of them uncovered their own shit and how one can enable another. There was much to learn.

All of the unrest, intensive therapy, and self-focus going on made it an inconvenient time for their only daughter to get married, but Don and I could not be on my parent's timeline. Marriage was our dream, and in early 1993, Don asked my dad for my hand. Their time together could have been better; it could have even been exciting, but not in that season of crisis. Nonetheless, my dad gave his blessing to Don.

THE SUN WILL RISE AGAIN

On Easter Sunday in March of 1993, just as the sun was coming up over the hills, Don snuck into my childhood home of more than twenty years and into my cotton candy pink bedroom where time stood still. Behind my bedroom door still hung a full-length mirror and a poster of Christy Brinkley in all her 1980s glamour—think *Sports Illustrated: Swimsuit Edition*. She wore a bright red, one-piece swimsuit and looked as though she had just come from a plunge in the pool, soaking wet with her famous winged hair slicked back from the water, the length of it pulled over one shoulder. She was tan and beautiful. Glistening. For so long, I had wanted to be her or at least look like her. Teenage dreams.

Back to Don, who had put together a secret plan with my mom the night before. Only, when Don walked into my preppy pink room that Easter morning and knelt beside the bed, he was surprised to discover that I was not in bed! Just as that was dawning on him, he heard the toilet flush. Yup. That's the moment, the very one, that I had chosen to go to the bathroom. I was so embarrassed. Even so, as flustered as I was, it didn't take me two shakes to jump back in bed. Once I was settled under the covers, Don leaned over and held out a porcelain easter egg. As he moved it toward me, he lifted its lid to reveal a diamond engagement ring, and he asked me to marry him.

"Yes! Yes! Yes!"

Reflecting back on those difficult two years, I can see where the growth happened. I was a woman who took a stand and stood up for herself, bucked the pleasing pony act, and conquered some fears of rejection. I was also a woman who worked to make her dreams come true. Little by little, our life circumstances inch us into our being if we let them. We take the good and make it better, take the rough and let them be lessons for positive change.

CHAPTER TWELVE

I DO

Wedding planning, it turns out, wasn't exactly how I had imagined it to be. Don't get me wrong, the excitement was there, but it was somewhat dampened by the condition of my parents' marriage issues and their attention being divided.

Still, Mom and I had a lot of fun searching for a dress, looking for a venue for the wedding and reception, and planning the decor for the ceremony. At the time, Nashville did not have many vendors for bridal gowns, so we took a fun mother-daughter shopping trip to Atlanta. I picked out lingerie, shoes, honeymoon outfits, and more. However, we didn't find my dress in Atlanta.

We ended up finding it in a small, beautiful boutique in Nashville. My gown was simple and pearl white, with a scalloped, off-the-shoulder neckline. Rosettes covered the cap sleeves, and flowing down the back of the dress was a beautiful cascade of what seemed like a hundred tiny buttons. The bodice of my dress was fitted, and the skirt was full, with layers of tulle underneath that gave it the perfect bell shape. It suited me well.

The financial side of my wedding plans was between my dad and me. Planning with my dad was all about practicality and responsible spending. He had me keep a spreadsheet of expenses and "justifiables." Along with the spreadsheet, I organized receipts, contracts, and anything pertinent to the cost of putting together a wedding. I put all these papers in a wedding notebook as proof of purchase, so to speak, for my dad. In and of itself, none of this was bad. In fact, it was a good opportunity for budgeting, keeping track of costs, and collecting relative information to support the costs. There was a shadow of perfection cast over every bit of planning. I strove to present all the information and any additional requests in a format that was both impressive and convincing. My performer rose to the challenge.

Don and I were not in a hurry to marry, but we were also not interested in dragging out the timeline. Our first choice of venue was not available on the October date that we had circled; however, it was available in September. Lucky us.

On September 18, 1993, Don and I were married in the beautiful, traditional West End Church of Christ in Nashville. The church had a newly remodeled auditorium (we didn't call them sanctuaries for some reason). The carpet was lovely and neutral, the interior walls were painted a soft blue, and the trim of the windows and woodwork was a fresh white, a perfect backdrop to my wedding's color theme—*hot pink!*

Come on! It was the early '90s. Pink was big and so was hair; although, much tamer than it had been in the '80s. My bridesmaids included childhood and college friends and a friend whose husband was Don's best man. The couple's eldest of two daughters was our precious flower girl. My cousin Mimi was my maid of honor. Both of my brothers were in the wedding party, along with some of Don's childhood friends and men instrumental in his career and in our courtship.

On the morning of our wedding, I woke up in my bedroom at home, peered outside, and grinned with excitement. My parents were both eager and full of joy. Mom and Dad could hardly wait to show me what had happened overnight. It had been a cool evening, and there was dew on the grass as the sun rose. There were also a hundred or so lovingly spun spiderwebs on the bushes, in corners, hanging between trees. Dew droplets caught on the webs and created an ambiance of wedding lace draped around the house. It was truly a stunning sight. Dad was able to get photos to capture the lovely beginning of my new life.

Midday, my Aunt June hosted a bridesmaid's luncheon for the women in the wedding party, and for moms and cousins. After lunch, I had appointments for hair and makeup. For some reason, I went to both of these alone. Near my home in Green Hills, there was a lovely skin care and makeup boutique called Private Edition where I had my makeup lovingly applied. From there, I went to my hair salon, and my stylist loaded my thick, blonde hair with curls and secured my bridal veil on my head.

Dressed in casual clothes and tennis shoes, with my makeup perfectly applied, my hair coiffed, and lace covering the back of my head, I certainly looked a bit odd. Nonetheless, it didn't bother me, and I figured folks were smart enough to figure out what was going on with my attire. Because I had been dropped off at the salon, my bridesmaid, Kay, and her fiancé were planning to pick me up. I finished with an hour or so to spare before we needed to be at the church. So, the three of us met at a next-door restaurant for a glass of wine. That was such a sweet, unexpected moment. The room was dimly lit. The wine was tasty and offered a nice bit of relaxation before the big to-do. From there, my stomach filled with butterflies as we headed to the church for pre-ceremony pictures and to prepare for the service.

The auditorium was full. About three hundred friends and family attended. The room was covered with roses donated by my fourth-grade teacher who had a prize rose garden. Our fee for these stunners was a donation to the American Rose Society. Pink, white, and red roses flanked the ends of each pew, and enormous urns stood on the stage filled to the brim with a floral paradise. The bridesmaids and I carried tightly gathered bouquets; mine was knitted together with white roses and my beautiful friends carried multicolored clusters of roses. There was a rose arbor center stage. Honestly, it looked like the Garden of Eden. The whole scene reflected what I loved most, community and nature.

After a rather lengthy but lovely service, we said our "I dos" and ran through falling rose petals thrown and scattered by our guests. (We didn't have rice because of the risk of harm to birds and for falls, but someone made sure that we got our fair share of rice and filled one of our suitcases with plenty.) Don helped me into the black limo parked out front, the photographer snapped memory after memory, and we drove away to the reception, which was held in lovely Longview Mansion, a historic home owned by our dear friends.

Because I was Church of Christ and my mom was still a professor at David Lipscomb, our reception was alcohol-free, much to the disappointment of many groomsmen. However, they knew this ahead of time, and many years later, we discovered that they had hidden a keg in the woods behind the house where our "partying" guests (and my brothers) were able to toast and toss back a couple of brewski's in the "normal" tradition. Honestly, I wouldn't have been surprised if many of our guests tramped into the woods for their own mug, but within the bounds of my religion, alcohol was pretty much a no-no.

However, Don and I did manage to slip in a champagne toast for the two of us while folks cheered. Don't get me wrong, our reception was beautiful. Our wedding cake was lovingly prepared by a friend. She recreated a Martha Stewart basketweave tiered cake I had seen in a book. Covering the creamy white cake were more sprays of fresh roses from top to bottom.

Dancing was another wedding tradition that was often skipped because of my religious parameters. So, instead of a band and a dance floor, Don's best man and a fabulous vocalist who was a dear friend performed for us. Wayne played the piano while Chris sang our favorite song, "Get Here" by Oleta Adams, and to that beautiful music, Don and I had our first (rated G) dance as husband and wife. This was followed by a mother-son and dad-daughter swing around the polished wood floors. My dad is an excellent dancer, by the way, and he twirled me around like the princess that I felt like that day.

Don and I spent our wedding night at the new Loews Vanderbilt Hotel across from the campus of the university for which it was named. First things first, though, Don and I had both been on the Nutrisystem diet to get wedding ready. We were so self-deprived of decadent food, including one of our all-time favorite date night appetizers, Outback Steakhouse's cheese fries!

Cheese fries had become a staple of our weekly outings with our dear friends, Wayne and Fran. They both knew that by our wedding we were drooling to sink our teeth into this succulent, fried substance, and so, Wayne arranged for Outback's cheese fries to be delivered to us by one of Don's groomsmen. Keep in mind, this was way before Uber Eats or any kind of delivery service other than pizza.

Mark knocked on the door of our honeymoon suite. Don answered and returned with a paper sack bleeding with grease from the French fries sizzling inside. Don tore open the bag for the two of us, and I plopped on the couch, wedding dress billowing around me, and dove into that dreamy goodness. Those fries never tasted better—plus, we hadn't eaten anything at the reception, preoccupied with greeting guests, shoving cake in each other's mouths (that doesn't count as eating), and walking around in a delightful daze. We were *starving*.

French fries devoured, the rest, as they say, is history.

CHAPTER THIRTEEN

GOOD COUNSEL

The two years between my parents' separation and my wedding offered a lot of opportunity for learning. Since I had started counseling in 1991, it was familiar to me, but it was new to my mom and dad. With that newness, though, came loads of education and offerings of wisdom throughout the process.

Both Don and I soaked in what my parents were learning, and, in turn, applied it to our own relationship. The importance of communication in a marriage could not have been better stressed. We took that seriously and committed to communicating well with one another, and when we felt we needed a boost we sought counsel ourselves.

Not only did I better learn to discuss feelings, struggles, money issues, and more during this period of time, but I gained a major glimpse into my life growing up. I discovered that where I had learned to stuff my feelings was in our family home, which lacked a deep sense of vulnerability. Personally, I preferred to look perfect for the sake of affirmation and avoided confrontation like the plague. I don't know if any of us knew what we were doing. We weren't stuffing on purpose. We were putting our feelings aside because that's what we had seen modeled to us.

Growing up with a longing desire to please others in hopes of being accepted, I missed opportunities to find or be myself. Often, I found that I liked things because others liked them. I purchased items because friends had them or wanted them. I imitated the people that I liked with a longing to be brought into the fold. From the outside looking in, it may not have seemed that way to others, or maybe it did. Either way, I worked to impress friends and strangers alike at the expense of knowing me.

Until counseling, I don't think we could have identified vulnerability or a lack thereof. Remaining calm, keeping feelings of discontent to ourselves, and suppressing disappointment (suppressing everything, for that matter) looked more like we knew how to maintain self-control. Moderation, poise, and keeping the boat afloat were all part of my parents' culture, and what they had learned influenced my way of being.

Because of the struggles of my parents, an opportunity for growth like never before emerged and changed my life forever. Little did I know, I would put my learning to use in more ways than I thought possible as I became a wife and especially a mother.

This time and space opened a door for us to stop generational patterns, to learn how by past behaviors we sabotaged ourselves, and to recognize all of this as dysfunction. "Dysfunction"—what a taboo word at the time. Combine it with "family," and you have a "dysfunctional family," which was really not something that you wanted to make public. What I uncovered, though, is that every family has dysfunction. Every. Single. One. Some recognize it and seize the opportunity for growth, and some ignore it in an effort to maintain the status quo, maintaining good appearance on the outside while the inside crumbles.

Mom and Dad continued their self-work, admirably so. I don't know that there was anything that they did not do to try to save their marriage. However, they eventually came to an impasse, and it looked like divorce was going to be the healthiest option (sometimes it's the only option).

Because Mom and I were so close, I knew that this was coming. I had come to terms with it as much as possible. Having watched my mom grow by leaps and bounds—learning to stand up for herself, identifying her ability to enable, and acknowledging the critical nature of communicating her needs—I was very proud of her. My feelings for my dad were similar. He had grown so much. By allowing himself to be vulnerable he had become a more compassionate, sympathetic person. These two had put in the work; I was sure that if anybody could survive their struggle it was them.

However, one day at work I got a call from my mom asking me to come home for a family meeting. All too traumatically familiar, as I dropped down the steep drive and turning hard through the curves of the road, I felt a queasiness in my stomach, unwelcomed moths flitting about inside. I was with Don, though, and his support helped carry me. Walking into the house, and smelling the familiar scent of home, my mind flashed through childhood memories, and my stomach cramped with the pain of what would no longer be.

Mom, Dad, my brothers, Don, and I gathered in the breakfast room just off of the kitchen. Awkward silence filled the room, and we each took a seat and ended up in somewhat of a circle around the room, each facing the other. With that, my parents began to share their divorce plans.

They had their assets divided, expenses sorted, and an amicable agreement that they were headed in the healthiest direction possible. Yet, neither truly wanted a divorce. There were hurdles that they just could not get over, though, and after two years of intense therapy and hard work, it seemed insurmountable.

As our family talked and asked questions of my parents, the younger of my two brothers spoke up to add his two cents. He was sixteen at the time and was wise beyond his years, yet simple in his approach. Basically, he asked Mom and Dad why they were not committing to commit. He told them that when he wanted to reach a goal, he wrote it on a Post-it note and stuck it to the bathroom mirror for him to see and be reminded of every day. Essentially, their goal should be to choose family.

Being seven years older, I appreciated the simplicity of what my brother had suggested, but I did not take it seriously to heart. I guess, because, well, it was just too simple of a solution. Mom and Dad had dug deep, and if the tough work wasn't panning out for the better, how could something so minor as committing to commit actually work? My parents, though, felt the deeper wisdom in my brother's words. They understood that sometimes what looks like the easiest solution is often the hardest and the most productive.

So, Mom and Dad committed to apply their hard work to the simple, yet difficult application: They committed to commit. Instead of getting a divorce, they decided to try living together again.

Not without its intense struggles, my parents' marriage began to strengthen. Because of their hard work, they had the tools they needed to forge ahead. However, those tools needed to be exercised and implemented. That's what they did. Miraculously, they found restoration through the brokenness.

They climbed out of the valley and onto the mountain top, unsteady, but there, nonetheless. They led authentic, vulnerable classes for couples at their church. My dad hosted men's groups and provided a safe space for sharing and healing. In everything that my parents did for others, the overarching theme was love and the foundational principle for sharing in a group was that these were private conversations not to be shared with others. Mom and Dad went on to help hundreds of others in crises, always with grace and understanding, while only expecting others to try.

With reconciliation and restoration came devastating fallout with extended family, something that I had not considered. As a consequence of the disapproval of my parents' recommitment, some family deserted us. Just when family was needed the most, they were no longer there. To be fair, they were also hurt. To abandon us was about them and not about us, but it stung and created a divide. For me, nothing was ever the same. Personally, I felt betrayed.

The estrangement, for me, has, for the most part, continued. I mourned them for a long time and missed having them in my life, but I have learned that not everyone can stick with you through thick and thin. That's not my fault. It's someone else's inability to cope, for whatever reason, and that is their prerogative, which I've learned to give back to them. The codependent in me had no fix for this, nor was this my responsibility to repair.

Despite all the trauma, my parents have been married for fifty-six years. Both would say that returning to commitment was worth the hell-ravaged valley they took to get there. They are whole. Not perfect but restored. Always learning; always growing.

Exposing wounds, experiencing healing, and learning more about myself, gave way to understanding. It opened the door to the significance of vulnerability and showed me my value. I was merging into a recovering codependent. I became a woman with tools to help me find my way through the next stages of my life. To this day, I benefit from my parents' vulnerability and willingness to do the work. I have circled around to claim that for myself again and again.

One of the most impactful and unexpected gifts for me was that of being vulnerable. Sharing with others became different for me. I felt more relatable and maybe more accepted. I think there's a feeling or intuition that lies within us that says, *"He/she/they would never understand me. I can't possibly share my story and still be accepted."* For me, what I found was the opposite—almost like sifting sand in search of the jewel. The jewels are the ones who have experienced trauma, every degree counts. While there is certainly a delineation between insufferable tragedy and what is less so, there is no delineation among those who suffer and grow. In fact, when you don't compare, and instead sympathize or empathize, you open a door to your heart.

Those doors need to be protected though. Safe spaces need to exist and there is no place for a betrayal of trust. What is sensitive to one may not be sensitive to another. Nonetheless, both deserve honor. To this day, my goal is to offer a safe space for others to share whatever they want, and no matter what that is, I never want to be judgmental. I want to be relatable because of the human condition. We are all subject to the negativity of life, but open arms and recognition of this is how we create community, whether for an hour or for a lifetime.

CHAPTER FOURTEEN

NATURAL INSTINCT

For as long as I can remember, I wanted to be a mother. As a little girl, I had baby dolls that I took care of, rocked, and sang to. I had a Baby Wet & Care who could, you guessed it, pee in her diaper so that little girls could learn how to change those diapers. I had a sweet, life-size Madame Alexander baby that I rocked to sleep in her crib. She had a pacifier that poked into the little hole in her mouth, her eyes closed when you laid her down, and she slept without a peep.

When the Cabbage Patch dolls rolled around, I got one of those, too. Part of the thrill of the Cabbage Patch doll was that you were able to adopt her. These dolls looked so different from past dolls; they had a soft body and were very cuddly, but they were not cute—at least not at first. Their look grew on you until you couldn't help but see their beauty (kind of).

My hands-down favorite doll was my Madame Alexander Sweet Tears. Yes, she could cry. She also had a pacifier and blinking eyelids lined with stubby, dark lashes. My baby had golden hair with sweet blue eyes. Her limbs were thick plastic, and her arms, legs, and neck could rotate. I carried Sweet Tears everywhere, dressed her in tiny clothes, rocked her, burped her, and gave her a haircut—that didn't turn out so well.

The mothering instinct stayed with me, and my desire to have children grew through the years. There's codependency in caretaking, but it's different than trying to fix someone or some circumstance because it's vital to the survival of your child. Always learning, always growing—at least I was trying to do that.

Taking care of baby dolls doesn't prepare you for having children, though. I don't think anything can prepare you. It's a leap of faith, a free-for-all. It's a lifetime of learning, of getting it right, of getting it wrong, of not getting it at all. Still, the pain points, the difficult transitions and awkward moments, make room for growth if you're willing.

FIRST BORN

Some dreams do come true, and I was blessed by the ability to get pregnant easily. That gift is not something that I take lightly. So many suffer infertility and miscarriages. Some are able to bring a miracle into the world through in vitro fertilization (IVF) and other fertility treatments, while others are never able to carry a baby. I have friends and family in every category and more. I do not take the ease of getting pregnant for granted, but I cannot pretend to empathize with those who struggle to conceive. I wouldn't want to, so as not to dishonor the pain or diminish the agony.

All of our stories are different. This is mine.

At just under two short years of marriage, Don and I decided to stop birth control. I remember being on a trip together. We were in a hotel, and I tossed out my empty packet of birth control pills. We were under the impression that pregnancy would take a few months, and that it was healthier not to get pregnant right off the pill. Well, you know what they say about the best laid plans? Expect them to change. Ours did, and within the next six weeks I was peeing on a stick in the half-bathroom of our newly finished first home when the pink plus sign appeared. Don and I were thrilled, as were all of our parents, siblings, and friends.

During our first pregnancy, we decided to find out the sex of our baby early. In the 1990s, ultrasounds were administered at twenty weeks, when you could find out if you were having a boy or a girl. We were having a boy! We knew right away that we wanted his first name to be Baker, which was my maiden name.

I continued to work while I was pregnant. I had morning sickness that eased up with a glass of orange juice first thing. I had aversions to food, especially salad (Imagine that—my body was so sick of salad!), and I definitely had cravings. I never wanted pickles and ice cream, but I did salivate for fried pickles! When a pregnant woman has a craving, it's best to help her satisfy it as quickly as possible.

On one such occasion, Don got me to the closest pickle-frying pub in town as soon as possible. This was back when pubs were pubs; there were No Smoking sections. You had to request a table away from where the most smoke was at the moment, with fingers crossed that your section wouldn't eventually harbor that hazy cloud.

The Bunganut Pig was in a court of mixed-use offerings, mostly business that had bellied-up. Walking through the court, Don and I wound our way around to the entrance, climbing down the steps that led to the basement level of the building and to the entrance of the restaurant. We stepped across the threshold and the hostess led us to a booth. Strolling over to our table, you couldn't help but be accosted or enveloped in a shroud of smoke, some from currently lit cigarettes. Old, dingy smoke creeped into the mix from the tattered carpet that covered the floor. Even the walls reeked of old smells. In spite of the dizzying scents, there was also a layer of air that wafted with the smell of fried pickles. Dipped in buttermilk, rolled in cornmeal, and fried up in the hot, bubbling grease, these crispy delicacies were just what the doctor ordered. Mama was happy.

Another craving that tugged at my tastebuds was a long-forgotten, tiny sandwich combination. In the south, we used to have luncheons where no forks were needed, and everything could be modestly picked up by the fingers. My aunt used to make these yummy little cucumber and cream cheese tea sandwiches, which were two circles of white bread punched out with a biscuit cutter, spread with cream cheese, topped with a cucumber slice, and sandwiched in with the top sphere of bread. Easy enough to make at home, I ate those until I could no longer stomach them.

My pregnancy was fairly textbook, until it wasn't. My body wanted to go into early labor, and it attempted several times to the point that I took medication to keep contractions at bay. However, later in the journey, more than one set of Braxton Hicks contractions sent us to the hospital in false labor. We were sure that our son would be born on Thanksgiving Day 1993. We had invited our dear friends Wayne and Fran to join us for the holiday at my parent's home, but now we weren't going to be able to make it. However, on our way to the hospital, we stopped by the house and dropped off my corn pudding! Don and I both felt awful about unexpectedly ditching our friends and leaving them to fend for themselves during our family traditions. Those included waiting around the table while my dad took snapshots of each section of the circle. This was long before panorama photos, and later, when the photos were printed, he would tape them all together. The family also always took turns around the table sharing what we were thankful for. We would conclude with a prayer. That year, Wayne and Fran were fine; they knew my family well enough not to feel too terribly uncomfortable.

Meanwhile, as Mom's yummy yeast rolls were being passed around the table, Don and I were at the hospital waiting for Baker to be born—or so we thought. We spent the *whole* day there, and I couldn't eat anything. While I lay in the bed, I got a waft here and there of food that had been brought for the nurses to share. Everything smelled insanely delicious, but I wanted to have my baby more than I wanted to eat any food. Alas, by the end of the day, this trip was just another bout of false labor, and I would get Thanksgiving leftovers instead of a tiny baby. *Ugh.*

Had Baker been born that week, he would have been four weeks early, his due date not being until December 29, 1993. Anticipating his arrival kept us on our toes, but here's the thing about expectations: Expectations habitually turn into the unexpected. I suppose the only consistent outcome of expectations is that they change. That's exactly what happened to me.

Over the course of the days following Thanksgiving, my body began retaining fluids. First, I noticed my ankles swelling, which isn't unusual for a pregnant woman. I didn't think a whole lot about it and on the Sunday following Thanksgiving, we had a baby shower, and I continued some work from home. I was helping to plan a big event, and my goal was to get it finished before I had the baby.

My symptoms didn't dissipate, though. Looking back on pictures from those few days, it was obvious that something was not right. My face continued to get puffier and redder. I felt as though I had the flu or a virus. As a precaution, we went to see the obstetrician. The on-call doctor checked me and seemed to think things were okay. The day after my checkup, though, things were not okay. The nausea, sweats, water retention, and more, had gotten worse. I called my OB's office, and the nurse relayed my symptoms to our doctor. Dr. Jeffery told us to come to the office so that he could observe my symptoms himself. After Dr. Jeffery examined me, he turned to Don and me and said, "How'd you like to have a baby today?" I'm sure there was shock on our faces, but the excitement took over and we replied with a resounding, "Yes!" Donald Baker Donahue would be born on November 29, 1995, however, not without fanfare and drama.

Dr. Jeffery told us to head to the emergency room at Baptist Hospital, which was in downtown Nashville and only a couple of miles from the office. Baptist was also the hospital where I was registered to deliver, and most of my information was already in their system. Obviously, I had been there a few times already. A lot of the details are blurry because I felt so poorly, but I was checked in, my vitals were taken, and I was hooked up to an IV.

If you've ever been in the ER, you can attest to the busyness of it as well as how long the wait might be just to get checked in. Luckily, Dr. Jeffrey had called ahead, and I was taken from the ER to a labor and delivery room almost immediately.

Like I mentioned earlier, looking back, it's all a bit of a haze. I was diagnosed with toxemia, preeclampsia, and HELLP syndrome, all of which, until modern medicine, had often been deadly for women in childbirth. My white blood cell count was low, and my blood pressure was high. I was retaining so much fluid that my body was as plump as the Pillsbury Dough Boy, except when you pushed my belly button, it stayed in, and there was no happy giggle!

The doctor explained the need to lower my blood pressure and swelling, and the only way to recover was to deliver the baby. Upon my arrival to a room, the prep work for birth began. I was given an epidural (Thank you very much!) and put on a Pitocin drip to fire up contractions. While my contractions did begin, after a few hours, labor was not progressing as swiftly as it needed to for our baby. We watched Baker's heart rate on the fetal monitor, and that familiar beating began to slow. Baker was in distress, the contractions were too much for him, delivery wasn't progressing, and his heart rate was dropping. My doctor, always calm and collected, walked in and said, "Let's go ahead and have the baby."

In my mind, that's what I thought we were already doing, but the doc continued, "We're going to head to the operating room for an emergency C-section." *What!* Now in distress of my own, with eyes as wide as saucers, I stared up at Dr. Jeffrey and said, "I didn't read the chapter on C-sections!"

At the time of our pregnancy, two books were all the rage. The first and more clinical of the two was, *What to Expect When You're Expecting* (the pregnancy bible). This book was full of practicality, myth-busting, and downright honesty. The author, Heidi Murkoff, walked the reader (both the pregnant one and the not pregnant one) through preconception, each week of the baby's growth, and more. The second book, *The Girlfriend's Guide to Pregnancy*, wasn't any less practical, but it was also hilarious. I laughed so much reading the words of the author, Vicki Ovine, who talks to the reader as though you're her best friend. She reveals the skinny on what really happens to your body, the type of insensitive comments that may be coming your way, and lots of embarrassing stuff that others might never tell you.

Being the high performer that I am, I read both of those books cover-to-cover—well, not quite all of *What to Expect When You're Expecting*, having skimmed the part about having a C-section. Why would I have read that part? I wasn't scheduled for or interested in a cesarean birth.

What I didn't prepare for was an emergency, and that's where I found myself that afternoon. I'm sure that *What to Expect When You're Expecting* addressed this, but, again, I hadn't thought it would apply to me. Maybe it was better that I didn't know what to expect in my case.

From Labor, Delivery, and Recovery (LDR), I was moved from my stationary bed to a gurney which would get me down the hall in a flash. I was basically prepared for surgery. I was wearing a lovely hospital gown (wink, wink) and was covered with a bedsheet and a blanket. The anesthesiologist took care to make sure my epidural was primed and pumping. I already had an IV line sprouting from the inner bend of my elbow. It was taped down to keep it in place, but I could still feel that tiny pin prick inside my vein. *Ugh.* IV lines always gave me the creeps.

Once I was settled on my rolling bed, I was whisked into an already prepped operating room just around the corner from where I had been. The sense of rush was a little unsettling. Don had called my parents. So, they were already nearby and anxious with anticipation over the birth of their first grandchild.

Unbeknownst to me at the time, a few more family members and friends-like-family showed up, too. The word about our delivery and my illness had reached them, and they wanted to be there for support.

From the gurney, I was moved to the operating table. Laying prone, knees bent, and a sheet draped over me from the waist down, I was as ready as I could be, which didn't really feel ready at all. The bedsheet acted as a curtain so that I could not see my tummy—not that I would have wanted to see it!

Before I knew it, the doctor was making an incision in my lower abdomen. Don was right by my side. I didn't feel any pain, only a bit of a tug in my abdomen, and *voila*; the doc pulled Baker up out of my tummy feet first and dangled him above the sheet so that I could see him. Don cut the umbilical cord, and the nurse gave me a quick moment to hold Baker. Then he was quickly taken for a check of his vitals and lung development and an Apgar assessment. Baker had been born early at thirty-seven weeks. Thankfully, his lungs were in good shape, as were his vitals, and he was six pounds and seven ounces of pure joy.

While Baker was small but thriving, I was neither. Attention quickly turned to me. With the baby out of my belly, I needed immediate care. The nurse put me on an IV of magnesium sulfate, which helps draw out the toxic buildup inside but also causes major swelling—remember I was already quite swollen. My liver was not in good shape, and my white blood cell count was still low. Because of these side effects, I was taken to a small, private room in the ICU, where I was watched for the next five days until my symptoms returned to normal.

While isolated, I did breathing exercises with a plastic apparatus to help increase my lung capacity and oxygen intake. The nurses brought Baker to me for feedings but kept him in the nursery at night so that

I could rest. I don't remember much about those days, but, obviously, nothing we expected had happened.

My nausea and dizziness began to subside, and the medicine I was given helped my liver function return to normal, lowered my blood pressure, and relieved the painful swelling. Once all of my labs showed the necessary improvements, I was finally healthy enough to go home. The nurse wheeled Baker and me down to the curb where Don was waiting with the car. I eased into the back seat to sit with Baker while Don awkwardly strapped our fresh little bundle of joy into his car seat. Grateful to be heading home, I gazed at my son, who, despite looking like a little old man nestled in a La-Z-Boy, was beautiful all the same.

As joyful as it is to bring home your firstborn, it's also very hard. As a new mom, you really have no idea what is going to happen next. There's no comparison to it, and even if you've heard story after story of "bringing home baby," you haven't heard your story because you've got to live it.

Because Baker was born early, he got hungry a lot. Night after night, day after day was spent breastfeeding every two-to-three hours, changing dirty diapers almost as often, and rhythmically swaying Baker in my arms, in a rocking chair, or while standing up. I rocked him until my arms were numb.

Baker had a bad case of reflux and projectile vomiting, and I often walked around with a big squirt of spit-up streaming down the back of my arm from burping him over my shoulder. The routine went round and round, over and over again. I had help, thank God. My mom stayed with us for a week, and Don was as helpful as he could be, but with this seismic change in our lives, nothing would ever be the same again.

CHAPTER FIFTEEN

WHO ARE YOU?

When I brought my first baby into the world, as happy as I was, I did not know how becoming a mother would almost instantly change the person I had been before having a baby. As I've worked on this book, a shocking truth has been brought to my attention by my publisher, who challenged me to answer the question, "Who are you—not as a mom but as a human being?"

Perhaps this quest was the most difficult of all. I mean, who am I really? I'm a partner. I'm a mom. I'm a stay-at-home mom. Yet those are descriptors not of who I am but of what I do. Where did the "me" inside the labels exist and did I even know her? Where did I go during the mothering?

Once I got the hang of things, and when there was finally a more predictable rhythm, I tuned back into myself in the best way that I knew how. I took step aerobics three times a week at our neighborhood clubhouse where childcare was available. I took Baker in the stroller for walks, became an expert at hoisting him from the stroller into his rear-facing car seat (the detachable car seat/stroller combos had yet to hit the market), and I could even manage a lunch or two with my mom or friends. I was always exhausted, though.

Never did I think, *Why did we have a baby?* Never. I often wondered, *Will I ever fit back into my favorite pair of jeans?* I considered what I could do in addition to being a mom. My soul's desire was to stay at home with my kids, but there was a part of me that felt like the role of "mom" just wasn't enough. Being asked, "Do you work outside the home?" was something I loathed. I didn't, not at the time, and I felt guilty when I answered no, as if a 24/7 job didn't cut it in the "real" workspace. There seemed to often exist a hint of placation, like when someone remarked, "Oh, I'm sure you have your hands full." That was true, but the folks who gave those replies usually weren't moms who stayed home with their kids.

All throughout motherhood I worried that I wasn't doing enough, that being home wasn't a real job, and that I needed to do more, more, and more. I had something to prove, but to whom? I wanted to impress. I wanted accolades. There it was—even in realizing my dream of a lifetime, I still found myself eager to please, perform, and be as perfect as possible to get the praise. Outwardly, I shied from the pats on the back, while inwardly I craved them like a drink of water in the desert.

While I was continually searching for myself in all the mothering, I was also living out my heart's desire. I never wanted to be a mom in order to please anyone other than myself, and after about eighteen months, I was ready to do it all over again.

WOMB-MATES

Don was "on board," and not long after deciding to try for another baby, we were pregnant again. It was thrilling. Both Don and I thought that having a family of two-to-three kids would be perfect, and we were on our way to that goal with a second pregnancy. When Baker was just over two years old, our family grew.

The pregnancy was "textbook," as my doctor often said. Things went smoothly. I monitored my food intake more than I had in my previous pregnancy. I didn't want to get "too big" and perhaps risk toxemia again, although I think it's an illness that can happen no matter your size. While I carried our second child, I decided to go back to my natural hair color, and I dyed my hair brown. I wasn't too afraid to try new things with my hair. I also wasn't averse to doing them myself, and it took me decades to learn that this was not a good idea.

My attempt at turning my blonde hair to brown landed me with a dingy purple, dusty brown color—horrifying! This was bad. If I had colored my hair myself to save money, that hadn't worked. I had to spend many hours and many dollars at the salon having color run through my hair until it was finally acceptable.

I think part of my willingness and desire to style my own hair at times came out of a need for control of something. It may seem counterintuitive given that I often ended up with an unwelcome outcome, but, at the same time, it was something that I could do for myself. After all, I was pregnant again. There wasn't a whole lot that I could do with my body. It was growing. I had only a tiny bit of control. Messing with my hair seemed attainable, and I wanted something different—I accomplished that!

During my second pregnancy, as a precaution given my history, my OBGYN immediately put me on medication to regulate early labor. As the weeks and months passed by, my belly swelled and grew just as it should. There were no indicators or markers of anything concerning or unusual, but something was nagging at me. I don't really know what peaked the notion, aside from a mother's instinct, but I began to wonder if I could be carrying twins.

Twins were in my family. Mom had a twin brother and fraternal twins are hereditary. So, my intuition wasn't out of left field. It was plausible. Four months into my pregnancy, I was at a routine check-up and decided to ask my OB if he thought there was an indication that I could be carrying two babies in my belly. He did not patronize me or make me feel uncomfortable for asking. He thoughtfully looked over my chart. He listened for a second heartbeat. According to my measurements and blood work, all signs pointed to a singleton. Given this information, Dr. Jeffery answered me and said, "No, I don't see any reason to think that you could be carrying two babies." So, I put the thought to rest as best I could.

In the years of my pregnancies, unless there was a medical need, pregnant women were routinely given one ultrasound at the five-month mark. So, at our next OB visit, we started with an ultrasound before seeing the doctor. This go-around, we had decided to delay the surprise of finding out the sex of our baby and wait until he or she was born. So, we were sure to express our wishes from the get-go.

I settled in on the exam table, crunchy paper at my back, ultrasound tech by my side, and Don just down from her. As I reclined on the table, the tech pulled up my shirt and bathed my stomach with clear jelly so that the wand could slide easily from one side to another. There was both excitement and a bit of nervousness as she got started. We were looking forward to seeing our new little one cuddled up in my tummy and were anxious to know that there were ten fingers and ten toes, a strong heartbeat, and a healthy outlook. As the telescopic wand picked up the baby's heartbeat, and its little black and white image appeared on the monitor, Don and I began to settle our gaze to take in this new miracle. Before either of us could focus, the tech exclaimed, "Oh, look! There're two!" Don and I were both breathless, and before we could make any sounds, she said, "Let me see if there are any more!"

I said, "Wait. Wait. Wait. You just said there are *two!*"

She looked at me and said, "Oh, you didn't know you were having multiples? I assumed you were on fertility treatment."

No, by God, we were not on fertility treatment, but now we needed some kind of treatment—cue the oxygen. I looked over at Don who had gone white as a ghost. I began to cry and laugh. We were in shock and disbelief.

We had told the tech that we didn't want to know the sex. Well, *now* we did. So, she started with the first baby she saw. "It's a BOY," she said. She then began to count his fingers and toes and take his measurements. He was perfect. So, on to the next little bundle, she moved the wand through the gel on my belly until she arrived at baby number two. As she settled in on the little babe, she said, "It's a GIRL!" Oh, the joy in that room. I had hoped for twins but had almost dismissed the idea after Baker was born, until that crazy-awesome Mom intuition kicked in—with accuracy, might I add.

The unveiling of our little womb-mates was historic, a story we never tire of telling. After the ultrasound, as I was cleaning off my tummy, a nurse came in and asked if Don needed a wheelchair. The shock was still hanging thick over us. He said, "No," but I think that he could have used one!

From the exam room, we walked over to the lobby to call our parents. Cell phones weren't a thing yet. So, we used the office phone. My parents picked up the phones—one in the kitchen, the other in the bedroom (these were landlines). Both piped up and said, "Well, is it a boy or a girl?" and we said, "Yes!" It took a nanosecond, but they got it and then shared lots of warm congratulations and love. Don's mom and dad in Missouri were equally excited, and I think that's when they began to consider a move South!

After the twenty-week mark, my pregnancy continued to go well. I may have had a false labor alarm once, but all in all things were good. My belly grew and grew and grew, and I knew that I was big when I could no longer slide into a booth at a restaurant. With my stomach bulging with two beautiful babies, things were getting big and heavy.

On January 13, 1998, I began to have mild contractions. The babies were thirty-six weeks along, which is considered full-term for twins. Because we were having twins, the doctor wanted us to get to the hospital right away. Don drove me to St. Thomas Hospital in Nashville for delivery. St. Thomas had lovely birthing suites and an excellent reputation for labor and delivery. This was their last year to offer maternity services, and we were glad to be there.

We had a delivery plan that our OB had discussed with us. I did not want to have another cesarean, and at the time it wasn't uncommon for doctors to perform VBACs (vaginal birth after cesarean). So, that was our plan. There was, however, a caveat. Our son was positioned head down toward the birth canal, ready to go. Our daughter, though, was transverse and reclined side-to-side across the upper part of my stomach. Because of this, I wasn't guaranteed a VBAC for both kiddos.

The babies were to be born in the operating room. The vaginal team was at-the-ready for the first birth, while the C-section team was standing by for the second birth, just in case. I'd had my epidural and was prepared for both scenarios.

The VBAC team helped me with a fairly painless and swift delivery of our sweet son. After his birth the doctor and nurse worked to turn baby number two around and get her head down. Over the course of the next twenty minutes or so, Dr. Jeffery manipulated the baby internally and his nurse worked on her externally. Their teamwork was successful, and they were able to turn, prod, and push the baby in position for delivery. Once that happened, she slid right out, sunny side up!

John Brennan weighed five pounds eleven ounces, and his sister, Carolyn Clare, came in at five pounds seven ounces—small but healthy, their lungs were developed and working well.

We named John Brennan after Don's great-grandfather, John, and my great-grandfather of the same name. We chose "Brennan" as his middle name after the writer, Brennan Manning, who had been a significant mentor in Don's life. Carolyn Clare was named after my mom, Carolyn (both being twins, it seemed fitting). "Clare," her middle name, was a nod to County Clare and the Irish heritage on both sides of our family.

Earlier I mentioned that I had always hoped for twins—be careful what you wish for! Don't get me wrong, I was in love with Brennan and Cara, but I had *no idea* what it took to take care of two babies and a two-year-old at one time!

Prior to the twins being born, Don, Baker, and I had moved in with my parents. We had sold our first home and were building a second with a bit more room for our growing family.

Thankfully, when we left the hospital with two babies in tow, we went home to a supportive and helpful environment. For our first week home, on the advice of friends who had twins, we hired a night nurse to give us some help, relief, and direction. Mary was a miracle worker. When the babies woke up hungry in the night, she brought them to my bedside so that they could nurse. I had breastfed Baker for exactly twelve months and was planning to do the same with Brennan and Cara—much easier said than done.

CHAPTER SIXTEEN

MILK JUGULAR

It seemed every time I nursed the twins, it was different. I tried various setups, positions, and holds. They were hungry every two hours (which is normal, but remember, there were *two*). While my mom, Don, and Mary were helpful and brought the babies to me, because I was the sole source of food no one could help with the feeding process itself.

During some rotations, I nursed Brennan overlapping Cara and used the cross-cradle hold. Imagine cradling one baby on one breast and then cradling the other on top and positioned under the other breast. My other popular option was the football hold. In case you're not familiar, picture holding a football under each arm. Now consider that each football is a baby, but they are not just tucked in like you would carry a football. Instead, they are each latched onto a nipple!

Talk about awkward and uncomfortable situations. Breastfeeding two was extremely difficult and tiring. Not only was I nursing, but I was also fixed to one spot on the couch. Sometimes Baker, the babies, and I were the only ones at home. Baker took full advantage of this opportunity to wreak havoc in the room while I was held captive. He opened drawers and dumped out its contents or ran around the antiques and vases still precariously positioned on table corners. Baker was smart, though, and he knew he could get away with most anything while the babies were attached to me.

As the days went on, Brennan became less satisfied with nursing on only one side. After all, he was growing and hungry. So was Cara. We switched the feeding schedule to try to accommodate both appetites. Instead of waking both babies up at the same time to eat, we waited for them to wake up. At this point, I was then feeding each baby on both breasts, one at a time.

Feeding them both at once meant they nursed routinely about every two hours, but when I started doing "private sessions," I surrendered my breasts to feedings almost every hour. On top of that, Brennan needed a bottle after breastfeeding.

Physically, I was utterly exhausted. While bottle-feeding Brennan gave others a chance to help, I still was overloaded and was hardly getting any rest in between feedings. Finally, an intuitive voice inside me said, *"Laura Lyn, you need help. Ask for it."* I took my words of self-care to heart, and after about two-to-three weeks, I retired my little milk jugs and we took up buying formula, bottles, and more bottles. Alas, though, I now had help.

Unfortunately, our night nurse had been temporary. While we were grateful for all of her help, we had no idea just how grateful we should be until all of the caretaking had shifted to us. After Mary left, a sleep-deprived stupor had set in for both Don and me and an utter tiredness like none I had ever experienced.

With the chaos and difficulty of having three children so close in age, I began to lose more of myself. I don't know that I was conscious of it, but if being tired was any indicator, then at some level I knew. I vividly recall standing in the kitchen with my mom and Don.

My hands grasped the edge of the avocado green sink, and I thought to myself, *I don't think I can do this anymore.* As I stood there feeling utterly overwhelmed, tears began to stream down my face. I could feel my knees shaking, threatening to buckle. Quite frankly, I wanted to collapse. As the physical and mental toll visibly took over my body, my chest heaved, my heart raced, my breathing became shallow, and eventually, I sank to the floor.

I didn't faint but felt collapsed through and through—physically spent and emotionally undone. I honestly did not know if I could do it anymore. There's tiredness, and then there's debilitating tiredness, the type where you feel like you can hardly get up or can't even get up at all. Having children was not depressing, but the demand on me with three small children was more than I could handle. My ragged body, spiraling hormones, and sheer overtiredness eventually led to a diagnosis of postpartum depression.

All told, we lived with my parents for six months, three of which I carried the twins and the other three after they were born. I know having the extra help and support did me a world of good, but we were anxious to get into our new home and settle in as a family. Having more bedrooms and more room in general was great, but it wasn't a cure-all. I continued to feel depressed and spent. I was moody, and my energy was so low. I had no sense of self and no energy to look for her.

Lying down on the couch one day, those same tears from my mom's kitchen came back in spades. I was in a stupor and didn't know what to do. I got up from the couch and wandered across the room to the kitchen. There on the bar was a book that Don had brought home. It was common for him to be given books, CDs, and other gifts at random. For the most part, gifting was common in the entertainment industry.

This wasn't the first time that I had seen this book sitting there conspicuously on the counter. In fact, I had been passing by it for weeks. Peering at it. Uninterested and even too tired to pick it up. If someone had said, "Here. Read this. You'll enjoy it," I probably wouldn't have taken their advice. That day, however, at that moment, the book looked different when I walked by. If inanimate objects can cry out, this one did, and it said, "Pick me up. Read me." Taking the book in my hands, I held it and read the title, as I had done so many times a day over the last month or so.

Do You Think I'm Beautiful? That was the title. If you're wondering why I hadn't picked it up sooner, it's because nothing about me felt beautiful, not physically, but more importantly, not mentally either. So, when I had repeatedly spied the title of the book, my eyes had glazed over. I knew the answer. Why should I read a book about it? The answer to the question was an obvious "no," despite the fact that I did not know who was even asking the question.

So, for whatever reason, perhaps divine intervention, I snatched the book from the counter, lay back down on the couch, and read it cover-to-cover. I have no idea what the children were doing—napping? Climbing all over me? I don't know. Whether they were sleeping or playing, I somehow managed to read while whatever was going on because I was captivated. The someone in this book knew me or was like me or had experienced many of my same feelings—all of it and more. The author, Angela Thomas, had words for what I felt and what I didn't know other people experienced, too. A bit of my loneliness subsided while I took in the fact that I was not alone. While the book wasn't a self-help book or a guide through postpartum depression, it was an expression of feelings that I could relate to on so many levels. I just had not "heard" it in real life scenarios, or if I had, I had forgotten.

As I read through these pages, I felt loved and covered. I saw God's faithfulness to me. I claimed his love for me and submitted to the fact that I needed his help. Divine intervention is what I didn't know that I was waiting for. I needed love to fill my cup, not people. People fail us, but love does not. You may have heard it said before, "God doesn't make mistakes. He is perfect." I believe that to my core. The mistakes, the lack, and the disappointment all come from people because, well, that's what we do. We make our own choices with what we're given. If the choice turns out to be the wrong one, all is not over. God didn't fail. His universe of love and light did not disappear. Instead, all of the good is still there. For me, it was just hard to find because I was utterly exhausted.

CHAPTER SEVENTEEN

HOUSEKEEPING

Before being diagnosed with postpartum depression, I saw the psychiatrist that I had seen multiple times throughout my parent's undoing. She, along with others, encouraged me to ask for help and hire help. Asking for help didn't come naturally to me, but out of desperation, I did. I also hired someone to clean the house for me while I watched, cared for, and fed the children and changed dirty diapers one after the other. This extra help gave me a good amount of relief. Having postpartum depression, or any kind of depression, puts you in such a vulnerable position. Help is what you need. While I did get help, I also got gossip. I mean, come on.

I was so grateful to be able to hire a housekeeper at the time. She checked so many things off of my to-do list and eased my burden. Unfortunately, the housekeeper had an opinion about me and had no qualms gossiping about me. She eventually quit or I couldn't manage her fee anymore. A few years later is when I found out that she had been talking badly about me.

The housekeeper felt inclined to talk about how messy my house was (umm, three kids and two under two), how gross my Diaper Genie was (umm, three kids in diapers, and wasn't this gadget made to hold your baby's mess until you could get it to the trash can?), and that I was lazy and spoiled (umm, being clinically depressed and chasing three kids were both exhausting, mentally and physically). Why would the person that I hired to help me through this season criticize me and talk behind my back?

She also talked about how I didn't tip or give a Christmas bonus. Well, for fuck's sake, I didn't know that was a thing. I'd never had someone clean my house. I didn't know the rules or the courtesies. I suppose I'm glad that I was inexperienced because I don't think she merited the extra. However, because of this lesson in etiquette, going forward I knew what to do.

For a co-dependent, people pleasing, broken mom of three, I was so embarrassed. I felt isolated, alone in my failure to be someone else's definition of a "good" employer. My young mom's heart wanted nothing but approval and support. Even in this moment, as I write, I can feel the anxiety, the weight on me during that time of my life.

While I wouldn't wish it on anyone, mental trauma and anguish of other kinds led me to seek and get counseling. I had experience talking to someone about my life and vulnerabilities, and I was both willing to do it and had reaped benefits from it in the past. Maybe it sounds weird to be thankful for trauma, but without it, I would have been so far behind and unfamiliar with how to go about getting help and healing.

ALL KINDS OF CRAZY

Desperation set in at this time in my life. I identified my need for help, and I answered my body's cry for relief. I was able to set myself apart from the chaos of life then. I was able to separate enough to ask for what I needed. It started with tears, was met with loving kindness by my family, and not too much later, I began seeing my psychiatrist on a more regular basis.

While I had experienced counseling and therapy in other settings and for other needs, I had not seen my psychiatrist for medical treatment. Dr. Alice was very well respected in her field with especially keen insight on medications. She had also seen my parents over the years and had a deep knowledge of my parents' story. The two combined, gave her a foundation for treating me both for past trauma and for my present circumstances. Dr. Alice gave me sympathy and empathy. She gave me tools to deal with my codependency, and she prescribed Prozac for my depression, all of which changed my life for the better.

I don't know if the medication worked as fast as I recall, but it worked, and the transformation was miraculous. I don't think that I will ever forget that feeling, and I don't know that I will ever have it again.

One morning, after having been on my new medication for just a few days, I remember waking up, coming down the stairs of our new house, walking into the kitchen, and feeling a type of euphoria I had not felt in I don't know how long. What I felt was joy. Honestly, I couldn't believe it, but I was experiencing it. Prozac wasn't a cure-all, but it did help put me on a road toward rediscovering happiness, feeling motivated, and reviving hope in me.

By the time the twins were eighteen months old, we had a routine. All of the kids were sleeping through the night and I was back to feeling more like myself. Not that it was easy. On beautiful, warm days I took everyone outside to play, and almost as soon as we set foot on the sidewalk, they headed in three different directions.

When we went swimming in the summer, I kept all of them in life jackets because I had no other way of ensuring their safety. It was all too likely that one might dash out of my reach. Inevitably, one or more would start to run across the pavement surrounding the pool. All I could think about was a fall, skinned knees, tears, and a need to go home. Much to my chagrin, we had our fair share of "catch-me-if-you-can." Thankfully, though, we never had a water accident.

CHAPTER EIGHTEEN

THE PILL PACT

Having self-proclaimed that I never wanted to have another baby, my mind began to wander. There's a phenomenon called "pregnancy brain." I think it has different meanings for different people or in different circumstances, but, at this time, for me, it meant that I had forgotten (or blocked) any pregnancy difficulties or the tedious care of newborns and the exasperations that piled on so quickly. Somehow, though, the idea of never getting pregnant again seemed absurd, and the euphoria of having another baby set in.

God bless him. Don had *no idea* what kind of crazy I was thinking. It was easy for me to explain, though: I had always wanted three children (which we now had), and while we now had three, beautiful and healthy children, I had not been *pregnant* three times! That's the kicker, the mom-brain thought process that Don couldn't quite grasp. I understood, but I was still determined.

To help my case, I went off the Pill. I was sick of taking it and tired of how it made me feel, and, quite frankly, I was tired of being the one in charge of birth control. So, I transferred that responsibility over to Don, who understood clearly what his job was if he absolutely did not want us to get pregnant again.

And then there were four.

RIGHT ON TIME

I was twenty-nine when the twins were born. When we got pregnant with our fourth child, I was thirty. Baker was four, and Brennan and Cara were two. By the time I delivered baby number four, we became parents of four children aged five and under. Yikes.

While both of my earlier pregnancies turned out not to be "textbook," it turns out, the *third* pregnancy is the charm. Shortly before going to Super Bowl XXXIV to watch our Tennessee Titans play the St. Louis Rams, Don and I found out we were going to have our fourth child, and we could not have been more excited.

Any prior thoughts of being unsure about another baby were put to rest immediately. This was the first time that I had been pregnant over the summer months, and July and August of 2000 were brutal. Humid days and steamy summer nights left little room for relief for a pregnant mom. Spending time at our community pool was my best chance to feel somewhat cool and a lot more weightless. I towed the three toddlers in the minivan to the pool. I chased them (more like waddled after them) from baby pool to big pool, from bathroom to concession stand, and around and around again. Thank God for the life jackets and the person who suggested I buy them. They were literally lifesavers!

The little kids were excited to be having a new brother or a sister. Cara was rooting for a girl since she was already outnumbered. Don and I felt confident during this pregnancy; however, in the early days before our ultrasound, we considered the fact that we could possibly have twins again. It's true. With fraternal twins being hereditary and because we already had them, our odds rose. On top of those odds, the older the mom is, the higher the chances are for multiples. Percentages, though, were in our favor for a singleton, and our five-month ultrasound didn't have any surprises. We were right on track. Only the pregnancy seemed to last forever.

With Baker, I delivered at thirty-seven weeks. I carried Brennan and Cara to thirty-six weeks. A typical pregnancy is forty weeks. In my mind, and by my own calculations, I was certain that I would deliver in July even though the baby was due August 6, 2000. Come July, I was exhausted and praying for an early delivery if the baby was healthy. The baby, though, was supremely content.

The Fourth of July came and went. The sultry, Southern heat showed its true colors, and combined with humidity levels 80 percent and above, there was enough reason to avoid being outside altogether. I was truly spent in new ways and experiencing new challenges, and yet I was eager for the new baby. As the end of July rolled around, I had carried this baby almost a month longer than the others. I was healthy but drained and ready to deliver.

We waited. Nothing. I researched homeopathic ways to induce labor. From swallowing castor oil to chewing parsley (which still makes me gag) to eating spicy Mexican food, I tried one safe recommendation after another. The second to last suggestion I tried was mowing the lawn with our push mower in the sweltering heat. Our yard was flat and not too big. I had mowed it before, but I had never done it while pregnant. I was sure that having the sun beat down on me combined with over-zealous exertion would kick-start a labor pang or two. Nothing.

The baby was healthy, and theoretically it was safe to deliver, but still, my cocoon was its preferred place of residence. I was not content, and I longed for the baby to be out of my tummy and in my arms. As August fifth approached and still no baby, I decided to go for the final natural induction method that I had avoided for obvious reasons. There are a lot of awkward scenarios to find yourself in, and this was not only cumbersome, but it was also almost impossible. Nonetheless, I was determined to go through with it, and Don was game. So, I gave myself over to this last-ditch position, if you know what I mean. If you don't, I'll relieve you from the suspense—we had sex.

It worked! The morning of August 6, 2010, contractions started up in my belly. They became consistent enough that the doctor told us to go on over to the hospital, get checked in, and settled into triage to wait. This go around, we delivered at Centennial Women's Hospital in downtown Nashville, a wonderful facility with nice birthing suites and large hospital rooms with a sitting area for families.

Once all of the pre-work was done, I was given a curtained-off room and the nurse measured my dilation. At my most recent OB checkup, I had been at three centimeters. My expectation was that I would be at least four centimeters. That wasn't the case. There had been no change, I was stagnant at three centimeters—about the circumference of a banana slice—not nearly ready. I was having contractions but not making any progress.

There was the suggestion this may have been a false alarm, but I wasn't having any of that. The nurse completely understood and suggested that Don and I walk up and down the stairwells at either end of the hospital. That's exactly what we did—we climbed the stairs, descended the stairs, traveled the hallways, and did it all again and again. We took this circular path for an hour or so, and I began to feel the contractions coming more consistently and a bit closer together.

I was still a little nervous that I might not be moving along, but when I was measured the second time, I was at four centimeters which meant we got to stay! Even though a show of movement had begun, my cervix needed to dilate to ten centimeters. (That's the size of a cantaloupe—of the miracles of the female body in growing a human, there's got to be enough room for it to leave!)

The hospital moved me to a beautiful labor and delivery room. I'd never given birth in one of these before, given that my previous deliveries were both in operating rooms. It was exciting to be in the "LDR"—not to mention *normal*—textbook, even!

Yes, I got an epidural. I'm a proud woman who has a high tolerance for pain. I'm also a pleaser and performer, as I've told you, but I was never interested in proving anything to myself or anyone else when it came to being numbed waist down for delivery. I won't compare the pain of getting an epidural to the pain of delivering a child without anesthesia, but I will say that it hurts! In order for the epidural to be administered, the anesthesiologist instructs you to bend your body in the cruelest of ways. At forty weeks pregnant with a significantly protruding belly, my task was to curl my body up into a ball. Ha—it's nearly impossible, but once I had myself contorted into my best version of the fetal position, I was told to remain absolutely still. *What the heck?* With hardly any control of my body—contractions, rapid breathing, and pain—I had to maintain some sense of stillness while the anesthesiologist inserted a needle into my lumbar spine in the epidural space. The needle was retracted, but a small catheter remained so that the analgesic could continue to be administered.

So, with my epidural in place, contractions on cue, and family gathered around for the excitement, the waiting began. My brother Christian was there. He was visiting from New York and had celebrated his birthday the day before. My parents were there. Don's parents who were celebrating their anniversary that very day were there, and my brother Rob and his wife joined us.

As the time passed and the contractions strengthened, I forgot to ask for another push of pain meds through the epidural and my belly began to seer with pain. Very unlike me, but very appropriate for my circumstances, I screamed, "Fuck!" With that, the room cleared out as the nurse took care of my pain.

Dr. Jeffrey, who had delivered all of our kids, was not on call that night; however, he had asked us to tell the nurse to call him in case he could make it. Unfortunately, he was leading his son's Cub Scout meeting and couldn't get away yet. Dr. Jeffrey was a family man and always kept his commitments to his kids as best as he could. Dr. Jeffrey asked the nurse to let us know that he would come over to the hospital after the scout meeting. We were disappointed but glad that we could at least get to see him.

Just as we were coming to terms with the fact that our OB wouldn't make it, the stars aligned (everything was right on time), and Dr. Jeffrey joined us in time for the delivery. You may have guessed it already, but we did not know the sex of the fourth baby until the moment it exited my womb and entered the room. Dr. Jeffery exclaimed, "It's a GIRL!" We erupted in cheers.

She was eight pounds nine ounces and perfectly healthy. We named her Laura Elizabeth ("Laura" after me, and "Elizabeth" after my grandmother) and called her "Eliza" for short.

Eliza was right on time, born on her due date. Because of her healthy weight, she slept well at night, affording me more rest than I had been able to get after my previous births. She hardly fussed, was go-with-the-flow (she had to be) kind of girl, and a delight for all of us.

Quiver full—two boys and two girls—each healthy and growing. Each is unique and beautiful.

CHAPTER NINETEEN

PARTY OF SIX?

We were quite the sight in public. We streamed into restaurants. We felt all eyes on us as our collective tinkling of forks on plates sounded in the background. I don't know how many times I was asked, "Are all of these children yours?" It was a question I enjoyed because I was so happy to be able to say "yes." Inside, I was pleased to impress, to receive approval, and to be noticed.

When grocery pickup and delivery became options, I lunged at the opportunity because I have never really liked to shop for groceries. However, this was the year 2000 and those little luxuries weren't around yet. Why don't I like to go grocery shopping? Well, I think it dates back to when I had to rapidly pull needed items from shelves while babies dumped shelves of other items into my buggy!

Trips to the grocery were hilariously exhausting. I carried Eliza in a Baby Bjorn that was strapped to my front and filled up one cart with Baker, Brennan, and Cara. Meanwhile, I pulled along an empty cart to fill with formula, snacks, and food, along with whatever someone else pulled from the shelves and into the cart (sight unseen by me) as we paraded down aisle after aisle.

At this stage of life, we felt complete. Our family of six was more than we could have ever asked for, and we were beyond grateful for the privilege of being parents.

By the time Eliza was born, I had the older three in a Mother's Day Out program around the corner from our house. It was nice to have a few hours as a break from a house full of kids. With just one at home, I enjoyed two days a week that were less hectic than the other five. When Eliza was eighteen months old, I went to teach at the Mother's Day Out program where the three elders were enrolled, and Eliza was able to attend as well. I taught Monday, Tuesday, and Thursday. The kids were there on those days plus Wednesday.

Working at the Mother's Day Out program gave me an opportunity to make a little money. I had some time off to get things done, and I also had the opportunity to connect with other women of varying ages. They were blessings to me. Each one treated me with such kindness and brought me adult interaction and joy, all of which are important at any age. I felt like I belonged. Quite honestly, I had forgotten what that felt like, and I had no idea how much I needed it.

Women helping women is so important. Not only did I have wonderful co-workers at Mother's Day Out, but I was also included in a prayer group with a special handful of other young moms. A few of these women were just a little further ahead in the game of parenting. They understood the need for support, and the fact that they extended an invitation for me to join made a huge difference for the better in my life. We were made for community, and I don't want to think about what it would have been like had these moms not welcomed me.

However, my days were full. "Tired" was not a good descriptor of how I felt, and "exhausted" was hardly adequate. I was depleted; but looking back what I recognize about myself when in the throes of motherhood is that I did it. I did what was needed and then some. I learned the importance of having other women in my life. While it's hardly easy to be on the clock twenty-four seven, I have no doubt that the job of motherhood and the calling to be a mom is also the most rewarding job I will ever do. I see my strengths and my weaknesses, and I am proud of that young mother. She did her very best.

CHAPTER TWENTY

AS THE MUSIC FADES

For as long as I had known Don and for as long as we had been married, he had always worked in the music industry. It was his passion. An entrepreneur by heart, he sought a larger role and more opportunity for fulfillment. Don exited the record label where we had met to start up his own, independent record label. His potential partner in the new company was dubious at first, but the thrill of the startup and the successful foundation that was already laid gave way to the planning, budgeting, forecasting, and more. Once the important details were in place, the company began its inception with new artists and a fresh philosophy toward running a record company.

Rocketown Records launched in 1996 to a wave of support and unimagined success. The artists, musicians, staff, and our families all became entwined. In fact, we often described the atmosphere as, "feels like family," because, well, Rocketown did feel like family. We not only watched the label grow, but we also experienced pregnancies together and new additions to our growing group. Baby showers, Christmas parties, and sometimes traveling together for events were some of the joys we shared. Our bond was real and very special.

As Rocketown continued to succeed, we experienced a high from its quick rise to the top in its category as a unique, small, and independent label that felt like family.

Little did we know that change—*big* change—was headed our way.

In 2001, Apple launched its first edition iPod. Music has not been the same since. CD sales plummeted. Why buy a twenty-dollar album of songs when you can get one song for free, with Napster and other illegal forms of streaming? Even with the dawn of paid music services, people were still paying less than one dollar for a song. It was the beginning of curated playlists, shareable music, and cloud storage that afforded people the opportunity to have thousands of songs at their disposal and in their pocket. It was the end of the CD, liner notes, and collections of work.

Change is good, but it can also be hard, very hard, especially when it sneaks up and you're not prepared. Musicians and artists were hurting. Record labels were going under. The rug was pulled right out from under our feet. As a small label, Rocketown had the disadvantage of losing money but also the advantage of being able to pivot—unfortunately, not fast enough to keep up with the quickly changing tide of music in general.

For us, that meant eventually closing shop. There were great efforts made to keep the company afloat. A huge deal with a major record label looked like it would be the saving grace, but, instead, at the eleventh hour, the contract lacked one signature—that of the big label. Without the deal being fully executed, there was no deal. Simultaneously, the "mother ship" of record companies was absorbed by another, and everything that had been in place no longer existed. Poof. Gone. All of it!

Worthy attempt after attempt was made to try to save the business, but none were successful enough. Although he fought to the bitter end, Don eventually had to shut the doors of Rocketown and close this chapter of our life. Our dreams of forging ahead in a once burgeoning entertainment industry were left unrealized for the foreseeable future.

As Gen-Xers, we had become accustomed to the American dream of climbing the ladder. Rung after rung up the ladder meant better money, healthy year-end bonuses, bigger titles, and perk after perk. But in the entertainment industry, the ladder climbing slowed down, as did the "wealth and health" that had once come with it. We found ourselves on what felt like the bottom rung.

Our future was unknown, with four kids, no job, no income, no insurance. Mortgage, car payments, bills and more bills—all of it—our financial picture dimmed.

Don had new opportunities that eventually came together, but the road to that end was anything but easy. Thankfully, we had some savings to help us, but the savings-to-income ratio was off balance. This was a time of life that I had, ignorantly, not really expected. The perks of working in entertainment were exciting, sometimes glamorous, and seemed extremely lucrative to the outside world. While that was the case for some, it was not the case for most.

Don and I had to figure out how to navigate this new chapter in the best way possible. Our commitment to each other and to our children never wavered, but that's not to say any of it was easy; it wasn't. However, the lessons we learned were invaluable.

While I helped pull in some income, I was also taking care of the children full-time. It was hardly financially feasible for us to put four kids in daycare so I could work outside the home. I would have basically been paying tuition that would outweigh my earning potential.

This wouldn't be the only time when we didn't have a job, income, or clarity on the future. It would happen again and again, through no fault of Don's, but as a result of seismic changes in the industry. Disruptions that used to signal a head's up that change was coming were no longer obvious. With the rate of the advancement of technology and its ability to effect change almost on a dime, pivoting to accommodate each new direction was challenging at best. With a somewhat bleak outlook on our finances, we were able to manage the crisis as best we could. We became more aware of needs versus wants, essential versus nonessential. In hindsight, the lack of funds made us resilient, creative, and much more in tune with life's reality.

In the not-too-distant future, we experienced being bled dry of our money on a new level. This was after Don and I had invested our money in the success of a financial planner who promised excellent returns on our investment. We had trusted friends who had benefited, and we felt the advisor had been well-vetted. For a few years, our returns were good. If we needed money, we had access to it. There were never any qualms about getting us what we asked for. What we didn't know was that our investor was scheming. Our money was in gold, a seemingly solid investment. However, that's only true if your money is truly in the market, which, unbeknownst to us, it was not.

One day, out of the blue, Don received a call from a friend telling us that our investor was not as upright and honest as we had all thought. In fact, it seemed he was a mini-Bernie Madoff. The news reported that the office of our investor had been raided by the FBI, papers and documents seized, computers and more taken as evidence. From the office raid, the FBI had moved on to the home of the perpetrator and uncovered the (seemingly) unimaginable. In the basement, there was a vault—one that no family member knew about because of how well it was hidden—when the door was opened, there was our gold! Bars and bars and bars of gold lining the walls and shelves that were tattered with "I Owe You's" scrawled across yellow Post-it notes.

Everything of ours was gone—*poof*—nil, *nada*, none. We were dumbfounded by the reality that we were victims of a Ponzi scheme; albeit on a much smaller scale than the ones you've heard about in the news; nonetheless, money is money, and ours was gone. Some of our friends, much further along in their years of saving, lost huge sums of money.

Job shifting and uncertainty, coupled with these ass-whipping financial losses, made for a bitter cocktail to sip and a hard pill to swallow. We had no choice, though. We had to sip and swallow. We prayed. We asked our friends and family to pray, and we prayed some more, but our lost money was never recovered, which is a whole other story.

Nonetheless, the bond that Don and I had grew stronger. Finances are a rough topic, and when the money goes, it's not unusual for the marriage to go with it. In spite of the struggle, we emerged.

Walking this valley was significant. Not only did it help me learn to better differentiate between needs and wants (or pay attention to what I had not been mindful of), but my past desire for more and more shifted. The amount of success and the amount of loss that we experienced actually made us more responsible, less greedy, and more transparent about spending.

Losing never feels good. My "keeping up with the Joneses" mentality was never fully alleviated. There were moments and seasons of envy, especially living in an affluent area. There were also welcome cries of relief when we traversed a difficult road and made it out on the other side. We were humbled. We were incredibly grateful, and our appreciation for all that we did grew in immense ways.

As I wrote earlier in the book, change happens. We have no control over that, and we cannot predict when we'll be faced with it. It's what we do with the change that matters. We move through discomfort in order to grow. As I've heard said in more ways than one, "You have to get comfortable with being uncomfortable." Such is life. I'm better because of the discomfort, but that doesn't mean that I have to like it.

CHAPTER TWENTY-ONE

NATURAL DISASTER

Plans? The only thing consistent about plans is that they change. Guaranteed. Life has proven it time and again. A lot of life happened over the course of the next ten years, and more life than we could have imagined came to pass.

On Tuesday, January 12, 2010, about sixteen miles west of its capital, the country of Haiti experienced a severely devastating earthquake decimating the presidential palace, countless government businesses, and an endless number of homes, shacks, and shanties housing its people. The news reports were shocking. From images of people being pulled out alive from under the rubble to mass graves being filled with dead bodies to complete villages devastated and people crying in pain, I watched the TV in horror as the poorest country in the world took on more losses than ever. Hearts broke all around the world as the scenes played out on television, with news of fundraising, aid, and support flying into motion.

We had friends directly affected by this horrific natural disaster, and we focused on what we could to help them. Friends for a decade, Matt and Mandy had not only been to Haiti as missionaries, but they were also currently in the process of adopting two daughters who lived in a creche (what Americans would consider an orphanage) in Port-au-Prince. There were extraordinary efforts to help this family. After the earthquake, Matt was in Haiti as fast as humanly possible, arriving with the first media on the scene. He immediately located his two girls, who, along with the rest of the children in their creche, were safe—scared, but safe. While the creche itself had sustained damage, the children and adults were ok and were moved to a secure location after vacating the volatile building.

Because of the immense destruction of buildings, much was lost, including all of the adoption paperwork that Matt and Mandy had prepared over the years during the process of their adoption. The paperwork wasn't just missing, it was under the rubble of the building where it had been housed. Because of archaic record keeping methods and no digital records to back anything up, any hope of recovering a sliver of paperwork was in vain.

As a family, we prayed and did what we could to help and support our friends, and through a lot of coordinated efforts and miracles, Matt was able to bring one of the girls home. Their second daughter had to wait a few extra days, but, again, forces rallied, God acted, and their second daughter came home as well.

As a mom, I couldn't fathom what our friends had felt about their daughters' safety and well-being amid all of the destruction and chaos. I don't know what I would have done had I been in their shoes. Would I have felt helpless? Maybe. Would I have sprung into action? You betcha! I might not have been able to jump on a plane headed straight to Port-au-Prince, but I do know that Don and I would have figured out a way to get there. What I know about who I am, especially as a mother, is that I fight for my children. I have a maternal instinct that kicks in if the safety of any of my kids is in jeopardy.

ATTENTION, PLEASE

Like children do, they pay attention to what's going on around them even if they don't say much. It was no different for our kids. We were forthcoming about the details of the earthquake during age-appropriate conversations, and we answered questions as we could.

Eliza, about nine-and-a-half at the time, was very watchful of this entire situation. Being our extra-sensitive child, her heart for the broken, the small, and the hurting, whether child or animal, was wired to attach to circumstances and to help however she could.

One day while I was standing at the kitchen sink, Eliza came up to me and asked me if I could get her savings for her. Each of the kids had a Mason jar filled with bills and change that I kept tucked away for them on a shelf in my closet behind my hanging clothes. When Eliza asked me for her money, I went and got her jar right away and gave it to her. She carried the jar by its mouth, took it to another room, and spilled it out on the floor to count.

Not too long after she had left to tally up her savings, she was back. However, instead of handing me her jar, she handed me a baggie filled with what was once in her savings jar. On the outside of the baggie, she had taken a Sharpie and written "$162.74." I took her life savings in my hand, looked at it, and turned to her. She said, "I want to give this to Matt and Mandy to help bring their girls home from Haiti."

A soft smile crept across my face as I looked into my little girl's big blue eyes, and I asked her, "Do you want to give it all?"

She replied, "Of course I do. What am I going to do with it?" My eyes filled with tears as I witnessed the tenderness of her beautiful heart.

We arranged for her wish to be granted, and she was able to present her tiny treasure to our sweet friends, who received it in a big way. So began a new journey for our family. Little did I know that from this point our lives were about to change forever (again). If we are not changing, we are not living, and if we are living, we are experiencing change of some kind almost every day. Knowing that fact in my heart, some changes have been small and somewhat expected. Others were huge and seismic, and we were never the same.

CHAPTER TWENTY-TWO

THE UNEXPECTED

While Eliza wanted to help our friends, which she did, she also wanted to go to Haiti to serve at the creche and care for the children. At the time, *everyone* wanted to go to Haiti to help. Eliza continued to watch folks head south to minister to the hurting, and she begged to do the same. As parents, Don and I felt like this request came of a phase, an inspiration of the moment, which was understandable. Eliza was too young to go to Haiti, especially given the circumstances, but Eliza didn't give up. She continued to ask to go day after day, week after week. Seven months passed, she turned ten, and she was adamant. She pleaded to go to Haiti.

At this point, Don and I were taking her a lot more seriously, and as summer turned to fall, Thanksgiving rolled around, and with Christmas just around the corner, we decided to give her the gift of our permission to go. On Christmas Day, 2010, Eliza unwrapped a certificate announcing the opportunity for her to go to Haiti.

The conditions around going, though, included raising money through acts of service and donations that would pay for her trip expenses. She was ecstatic, and within days she had designed her own flier to pass out in the neighborhood. On the flier, she used Crayons to draw a red heart with a blue-sky background. Across the heart in black she wrote, "Heart for Haiti." Inside the flier, she wrote a note asking neighbors for odd jobs and donations toward her trip. With her tenacity and determination, she managed to raise what she needed, and in July 2011 (a month prior to her eleventh birthday), she and I joined Matt and Mandy on our first trip to Haiti.

Let me pause and be honest. Haiti was never a destination to which I had any interest in going. Quite frankly, I was scared to go. Haiti is a *fifth* world country, one of the poorest in the world, and that was *before* the earthquake in January 2010. I was afraid and couldn't fathom what we'd witness after our flight into Port-au-Prince, the capital of Haiti.

The water was not safe to drink. Most of the conditions were deplorable, with trash on the streets and unmasked poverty. I had traveled to both Ecuador and Central Mexico and had seen the dilapidated circumstances of the very poor, such as one-room homes built from a hodgepodge of available items. Dirt floors, grass growing in the corner housing guinea pigs, one bed shared by several family members—these were not uncommon sights. Having seen this, I thought that I'd seen a great deal of the impoverished. I was wrong. I had only gotten a taste of what poverty looked like. Multiply these conditions by 100, and you might grasp an image, but without seeing the country of Haiti with your own eyes you will never have any idea.

Eliza had a heart for Haiti, and that was her campaign for fundraising. I did not have a heart for Haiti, and I was soon reminded of the nature of life. There are turns at every corner; it's like a merry-go-round, a seesaw, or a roller coaster spinning faster and faster. There is dizziness and confusion. We're plopped up to the sky and down again with a bang, stirring the dust and muddling the eyes. Climbing toward the sky, flying down the mountain, life can put our stomach in our chest and our heart on the ground.

Through myriad life situations, each begged the question: "Who do you think you are?" Sometimes I didn't have a clue. My best way forward was to step out in faith and allow my boundaries of comfort to be tested. How else was it possible to know myself? How else was it possible to claim my individuality? I was constantly being tested in every stage of life—likely, who I was changed too.

With uncertainty in the air but determination in our spirits—Eliza's for Haiti, mine for Eliza—we flew from Nashville to Miami and then from Miami to Port-au-Prince. When we arrived at the airport, it was chaotic to say the least. We were warned in advance. So, it wasn't completely unexpected. However, the number of men who were clamoring to carry our luggage was pretty frightening. Eliza and I stuck with Matt and Mandy (the pros) and made our way outside.

Immediately, a wall of heat hit us. Remember—it was July. Everywhere, there were tent cities within sight of the airport parking lot. The dust of the ground swirled around us, getting in our hair and lungs. The stench in the air was unfamiliar, and people continued to vie for our luggage with lots of shouting—too many, too close, hands out for anything.

The protective side of me rose with a passion I had never experienced. All I could concentrate on was the safety of my little girl. Hand-in-hand, eyes locked on one another, to say we were overwhelmed would be an understatement. I remember looking at my towheaded angel and thinking, *Why in the world did I bring her to Haiti?* I knew it was for her and not for me. My intention was to walk alongside Eliza and support her in her passion.

So, with one foot in front of the other, we walked into the dusty parking lot and boarded the ten-passenger van waiting for us. Once we were all loaded, the driver wound his way through the maze of cars, and we headed into the streets of Port-au-Prince, where there were no rules of the road. There were no stop signs, few traffic lights—certainly none at major intersections—narrow lanes, unexpected one-way streets, and utter chaos on any and every type of wheels imaginable.

On the outskirts of the airport were miles and miles of tent cities; people had to live this way after the earthquake because they could not afford to rebuild, and no public housing existed.

As we drove down the pothole-ridden, half-dirt road, we bumped and bumped along. The driver came to a screeching halt without warning, no gradual tap on the brake. It was no wonder, as other vehicles had veered onto the sidewalk to get ahead of the standstill traffic, and there were people darting unexpectedly out into traffic. I learned that driving in Haiti was not for the faint of heart, and emergency braking was part of the game. Mopeds and motorcycles whizzed by weaving in and out of the cars, barely missing the blue gingham-uniformed school children crossing the street. People drove on the opposite side of the road if they thought it would get them further along more quickly. Horns beeped and blared, the smell of rubber burned in the air, while meat smoked on makeshift grills under red and white umbrellas.

Vendor after vendor lined the road. There were tall rotating displays filled with sample sizes of pain relievers, antacids, and other medications, each hung precariously on little steel hooks that overwhelmed the frame of the rounders. One person after another, peddled kebab-like meat sticks, slices of mango, or slabs of some kind of roasted animal. There were carts of papayas, mangos, pineapples, bananas, and avocados. Goats were tied to the sellers' chairs, while the business owners hawked their wares. Chickens ran around in a frenzy, trying to avoid the emaciated, undomesticated, rabid dogs looking for morsels here and there.

The scene turned my stomach at the time, a feeling in stark contrast to how I found the beautiful people there. Lovely women of every shape and size displayed unbelievable balance as they walked along the road with huge baskets on their heads. It amazed me that they managed this, especially with everything around them in constant, chaotic motion. Street sweepers—not machines, but men and women in straw hats with straw brooms—vigorously tried to push the trash from the road to the littered gutters, all in vain. Yet, they persisted. We witnessed sad begging faces, but also big smiles and shining eyes.

While some buildings were in shambles, there were also brightly painted ones—peach, red, and green in pastel and primary shades—all of it. Alongside them and all around were tap taps that sputtered and stuttered. Tap taps were either open bed trucks or, more often, miniature buses equipped with roofs, tiny windows, two sets of benches inside, and rear exits/entrances, where passengers climbed in or jumped off depending on the speed of the tap tap. An unofficial mode of public transportation, free rides could be taken in these colorful, unmuffled mysteries.

We learned why they were called "tap taps." Unlike traditional buses that have a bell to be pulled for stops, tap tap passengers *tap-tap* on the side of the bus when they want to get off. People jumped on and off everywhere.

As our van moved along the curvy road up the mountain, we realized that our fifteen-mile ride was going to take several hours given the landscape of all that had to be traversed. The van chugged and stuttered as it ascended the mountain. Tightly dotted up, down, and across the sides of the mountain were colorful houses, some just cinder blocks, others dilapidated, others intact. Loads and loads of laundry lined the steep incline around the homes. Shirts, pants, underwear blew dry in the dirty breeze. Below the homes were rivers, ravines, and ditches, each filled less with water than trash—not just bottles and cans, but broken bikes, fallen wheels, and rusted appliances mired in thick, sticky mud and feces. These areas served as public toilets. Flies buzzed everywhere, and the smell of hot, fecal trash rose up from the ground.

At once breathtakingly beautiful and breathtakingly horrific, the dichotomy of what we witnessed on our drive up the winding mountain roads continued, not just on the climb but during the whole visit.

The beautiful in the broken. This was the theme of our trip. Our van delivered us to a pink compound secured with an iron gate, a concrete perimeter wall, and security guards. This building held who we had come to serve, the little children. Both a creche and a guesthouse, the two buildings stood in the shape of an L, with a courtyard and a swimming pool in the center.

The property had a generator for frequent power outages, a freshwater filter for clean drinking water, a covered basketball court for many types of games, and an observation deck that offered a stunning view of the mountains and tropical foliage. While it was clear we were still in Haiti, our home base offered dorm-style rooms with beds and showers, fresh cooked Haitian meals, places for the travelers to gather with one another, and an opportunity to be with the children, either in their accommodations, on the playground, or in the common areas.

Over the course of the next week, Eliza and I played with the precious kiddos with soft chocolate skin and dark chocolate eyes. The girls had tightly braided hair, and the boys wore buzz cuts for sanitary and practical reasons. It was common to see the girls sitting at the nannies' feet having their black, tightly coiled hair vigorously brushed and securely braided, a process that could easily last hours.

The kids wore clothing donated mostly from the United States and France. Outfits bore logos from American sports leagues and universities to French and English graphics of superheroes and beyond. During the weekdays, the school-aged children wore light blue-and-white gingham shirts, skirts, or shorts, and the little girls donned pigtails with blue and white checked ribbon, made to match their uniforms.

Aside from a few of the older kids, the people spoke mainly French Creole. Our French Creole was limited. My limited French vocabulary from seventh grade came in handy, but not all French words were also French Creole. We quickly nailed the basics, *oui* for "yes," *bonjour* for "hello," and the easiest, *no* for "no."

CRECHE SWEET CRECHE

The playground was the place to be if you were looking for the fun stuff, and that's where we often were. Eliza and I hoisted one baby, toddler, or kid after another into the baby swing, while some hopped up onto the slab seated swings and either sat on their bottoms or stood on their feet. Just like most children, they couldn't get enough of being pushed on the swing, and they could easily go for hours if we agreed. Every day our arms were worn out from pushing them higher and higher, while our backs ached from all of the bending over.

The kid's noses oozed endlessly. Clear nasal drip or snotty green goo were permanent fixtures on their faces. Remnants of congestion caked onto the skin above their lips, while little tongues tried to bat away the impending waterfall from their noses. We moved as fast as we could with tissues and wet wipes and tried our best to keep them clean.

At the creche, books were coveted. Just like swinging, some of the kids could not get enough of hearing us read to them. Most of the books were in English, and the kids knew them by heart from all of the repetition. By books, songs, and English-speaking visitors, they had been exposed to the English language. The school would begin to teach English a year or two later.

We rocked the fussy or crying babies who needed some undivided time and attention. While there were wonderful nannies there to help, there were not enough for all of the children. Mealtime was pretty amazing to witness. All of the kids who could walk picked up their porridge for breakfast or beans and rice for lunch from the counter and carried it to their child-sized lunchroom table. They seated themselves in tiny chairs lining each side of the tables—boys at one table, girls at the other.

Once all of the kids were settled, they bowed their heads and recited a prayer of thanks. If you peeked during prayer time, you could see many antsy faces and squirming bodies hardly able to wait for the "amen." Once grace was said, the kids gobbled up every last bit. Wary eyes kept watch on seatmates who might make a move to steal a bite. When the meal was over, the kids scraped off any tiny remnant of food into the trash and carried their plates to the sink. There was definitely a rhythm to eating and to the day itself. Having a routine was good for the children. It provided structure and predictability in an environment filled with children who needed consistency.

Off to the side of the dining area were the sleeping rooms, each divided by age. There were pieces of paper taped on the bedroom doors announcing both the names of the children in the room, as well as the family names of those who were being adopted. The babies slept in wrought-iron cribs, each painted white, and stacked one on top of the other three high, each with a door for the nannies to access the littles. While it felt sterile, unfamiliar, and somewhat barbaric, the children were safe and not at risk of falling or climbing out. Some rooms had bunk beds and twin beds, others had more traditional cribs.

The first day that we had walked over to meet the children, almost every one of them had run out to meet us, each trying to outdo the other for attention. They truly loved having visitors who were there almost solely for them. Some of the group included medical professionals who gave each child a physical and made recommendations for his or her health. Those of us who were not in the medical or nutritional field were there to love on the kids at the creche and host a soccer camp in one of the nearby villages.

EMOTIONAL OVERLOADS

In the evening of the first day that we arrived, a devotional had been planned for the group. A couple of hours before we gathered, I was having a really hard time not breaking down into tears. In less than eight hours, Eliza and I had witnessed poverty and devastation like nothing we could have ever imagined. The visual impact was overwhelming to say the least. The emotional toll was almost too much to handle.

During the devotional and reflection over our first few hours in Haiti, my emotional walls began to weaken. I managed to hold my tears back to be strong for Eliza, but when I turned to look at her, I saw that she was sobbing. As she cried almost uncontrollably, I slipped her out of the room and headed down the stairs to the director's living area. Eliza needed a break and reassurance that her feelings were normal. The director and his wife spied us in the dark, sitting on the couch, and the two of them joined us for some very sweet and tender time together. In those few moments, Eliza made an instant bond with them, and they with her.

Eliza and I both got back on our feet emotionally, at least we felt a bit steadier and understood. Plus, several others had experienced or were experiencing similar feelings. The whole scope of what we were taking in was far more than culture shock.

Later in the week, we hosted a soccer camp in a barren field in a nearby town. We set up games and courses for practicing and playing. While we put out cones, soccer balls, ropes, and other objects to assist us in camp, there was tension rising in the community that no one had expected. Some of the teenagers in town wanted to join the games but had not signed up.

They were somewhat bent on causing trouble, but the security guards that were with us were able to sort things out so that those who had signed up could enjoy their time.

As the ball literally got rolling, we did a lot of running up and down the dusty field all throughout the day. I was wearing tennis shoes; they weren't new, but my left sock kept slipping down below the ankle line. It was impossible for me to keep it in place, and a blister started to form. It got worse with every turn and run that I took. It didn't just hurt. My shoe rubbed the area raw, and it bled and stung so much that I limped from the pain (you've been there). There was no clean water to wash it off with or bandages to protect it. Germs and bacteria lurked around every object from the dirt trodden ground to the soccer balls, and pretty much whatever came into contact with an open sore.

It kind of freaked me out not to be able to clean and bandage this wound. The back of my sock was blood stained and filthy from all of the dust. I limped over to the van that had brought us to the village. I climbed in and showed my blister to one of our security guards hanging near the bus. With limited English but talented facial expressions and hand signals, he picked up a big bottle of hand sanitizer.

My eyes bulged. I knew that this was my one and only option, and it was not going to feel good at all. I had no other choice. I stripped off my bloody sock which, by this point, was stuck to my skin, and Henri poured hand sanitizer all over the open blister. My God, it stung like the devil. I held my ground though and didn't shed a tear. Do you know how something can "hurt so good" (not what you're thinking, but you get the idea)? I felt cleansed and relieved as the back of my heel bubbled and burned. There weren't any bandages though, and with our day almost over, I called it quits.

On another day, we had the option to spend our time at the creche with the children or at an orphanage for children with disabilities. The fact that such a facility existed was, in and of itself, a miracle. We were forewarned that it would be a difficult experience, but Eliza and I decided to go.

Historically, Haitian culture has viewed children who suffer physically or mentally as evil. We were told that these dear ones were often kept out of sight in the home, perhaps in a closet, or, worse, not kept at all, and discarded by the wayside in a ditch. Thank God, the children in this home had been rescued, and although the conditions themselves were lacking, they were being taken care of by locals who cared for their disabilities as best they could. I think this visit to the special need's orphanage was one of the hardest parts of my trip to Haiti and certainly the most heartbreaking to witness. Haiti could not take care of its people, including those with disabilities.

As we approached the building, there were chickens clucking in the dust, laundry pinned to the clotheslines strung across the courtyard, and little eyes peering from the balcony above. When we stepped inside, it was dark and dirty, and it took a few minutes for our eyes to adjust to the scene. Makeshift ramps made of leftover carpenter's boards were stacked on cinder blocks as pseudo-ramps for children who used walking aids and wheelchairs. Unanchored floorboards creaked and rattled as we walked from room to room and up the stairs. On the second floor, there were babies in crib-like crates covered with dingy blankets. To my horror, there was a tiny, emaciated baby that heartbreakingly died while we were there. Children lurked in every corner, some eager to touch us, some anxious about our white skin, and others who didn't know what to make of us.

I looked around and tried to take in the impossible, excruciating circumstances. It felt as though I was having an out-of-body experience. My self-identity was confusing to me. I didn't know myself at this moment. There was a feeling of being selfless and giving because I was there, but there was also a selfish, self-preservationist that wanted to get Eliza and me the hell out of there.

This was more than I could take. I wanted to leave. I needed to get out of this nightmare. Guilt rushed through my body. *How could I leave them? How could I not?* Despite my motherly fortitude, I was spent in every way. Eliza was just as shocked, and we could hardly wait for our bus to return. This setting was just too much to handle. We were there for a few hours. We did the best that we could, but it felt like we were there for days. I was in flight mode. That's the sum of it. That's the ugly of it. I felt ashamed for wanting to leave. Looking back, my feelings were valid. My feelings were natural.

CHAPTER TWENTY-THREE

LOOKS LIKE WE MADE IT

While a lot of Haiti was hard, a lot of it was joyful and beautiful. We made bonds with the staff and guards at the compound. We experienced unity of heart and mind over the care of children and the love for people. We enjoyed Haitian culture, getting to see hills and mountains, the crafts of its people, and the resiliency of an impoverished nation—nothing short of inspiring.

As our days in Haiti slipped away, Eliza's tender heart for the hurting was exploding. She turned to me time and again and told me how much she wanted us to adopt a child. I have to admit, being there didn't just tug on your heartstrings, it exposed a dire need for children to have family. Ideally, that would mean birth parents who had the means to keep their children and raise them or other Haitian families who had the ability to adopt the parentless children and raise them in the Haitian culture. Unfortunately, at the time, neither of these options were easily afforded or offered. (In just a few short years, though, our friends Matt and Mandy would make the seemingly impossible, possible. They helped build a community where Haitian children, both typical and atypical, are raised in loving environments with family, foster-family, education, access to food, daycare, medical care, and more).

At any rate, a day or two before we left, Eliza and I were on the phone with Don giving him an update on our trip and experiences. Eliza could hardly contain herself, certainly couldn't wait until we returned to the States, and before I knew it, she begged Don to let us adopt a child from Haiti soon. I knew this was going to make Don nervous. That's a whole lot to consider over an international call and right out of the blue. Don answered her wisely, and said, "Let's get you home first before we talk anything about adoption."

PRAY ON IT

Once we were finally home again in Franklin, Eliza's determination for the Donahues to adopt a child from Haiti shifted into high gear. She was so adamant that, after being home only a week or so, we had a family meeting to talk about it. One Sunday afternoon, the six of us gathered in our home library, the room with the bookshelves, books, leather couch, and picture window looking west toward the sunset. We talked about what adoption might look like and asked everyone to spend the next thirty days praying about it, discussing it and envisioning what that might look like to our family.

On a Sunday afternoon in the Fall of 2010, we gathered again in the library for our thirty-day check-in. We went around the room and talked about where each one of us was in our thought process. When Eliza and I left Haiti, I was already about 80 percent on-board with the idea of adopting. So, the needle didn't have to move far for me over our month of contemplation. Of course, Eliza was full steam ahead from the beginning, and both Brennan and Cara were game. Baker voiced his agreement. However, he admittedly felt a bit indifferent because he thought that he wouldn't get too involved. Given the length of the adoption process and his departure for college just a few years away, he didn't see much of a role for him other than a supportive one. Don, on the other hand, had just not warmed to the idea of adoption and I understood.

We already had a lot of kids, but we had made it through the baby and toddler years. We had traversed elementary school and were entering middle school and high school. Don and I spied the empty nest on the horizon, and to be honest, we were looking forward to what our next chapter held. In just a few short years, all of the kids would either be in college or on their own. I would be remiss if I didn't say that we were tired. We had lived a lot of life as a family of six, and we had spent a lot of energy–emotional, physical, and mental–making precious memories over the years. The empty nest was in sight, and it was provocative. Understandably, Don was hesitant and cautious.

We sat in the room together, and after everyone had spoken, it came down to Don who, up until that morning, was still leaning toward "no." We had attended church earlier, and the message centered around helping others, which really struck home for Don. During our time together as a family, Don told us that as he listened to the pastor speak, he thought to himself, *I can help one.* That Sunday message and Don's shift in mindset changed the course of our family history forever, and we are more blessed than ever to be a family of seven.

I was forty-one when our family said "yes" to adoption. Why did I agree to begin parenting all over again when the end of my children's dependency was almost touchable? My heart was pulled in two directions. Either choice would have been okay. There were two perspectives from my point of view—selfless and selfish. I was still learning what self-care was. Regardless, the woman who chose adoption made the right choice for her time of life. I was strong. I was learning. I was growing and stretching, and I had no idea how much more of each would come about over the next few years.

CASEBOOK

As you may be aware, adoption is not an easy process. Nothing about it is quick. Everything takes extra effort, and not one bit of the journey is simple.

Things were no different for us aside from the fact that each step was even more complicated than we could have imagined, including the paperwork, home visits, education requirements, fingerprinting, background checks—not to mention the difficulty of resurrecting documents from verified birth certificates for all of us to our marriage license to the vet-verified health of our dogs.

Recalling everything that had to happen for the adoption to come to fruition is exhausting. Adoption is not a fantasy. It is not dreamy. It is not about you. Instead, it is all about the vulnerable human being you want to bring into your family.

The United States side of the adoption process *was* fairly efficient, whereas the opposite was true on the Haitian side. There was no hint of urgency whatsoever, and no concern for the time of those waiting for one document completion before we could get to the next. The paperwork itself was a mountain to climb. I took on the lion's share of the work and was immediately crushed with what looked like tasks that I could never finish.

We needed original copies of all of our birth certificates, the ones with the raised stamp on them, which made them authentic. Don was born in 1966. His mom had saved his birth certificate, but we couldn't send the original. He made calls to the "keeper of records" in St. Louis where he was born, and finally, after paying a fee for its generation, he landed an official copy that was mailed to us. Born in 1969 myself, my mom had my birth certificate as well—but I repeated a similar process to Don's and for all four of the kiddos. Again, I couldn't give up the originals. I had to get government certified copies instead.

These types of tasks went on and on, dragging out the process. I gathered documents from the vet for each one of our dogs. We needed recommendation letters from friends and members of the community vouching for our character. Current physicals for all of us were documented. Don and I had our fingerprints taken by the FBI. We had six passports to get and/or renew. Taking on these responsibilities was a full-time job, but as you may recall, part of my nature was to please which also included being thorough and outstanding. I could recount each step ad-nauseam, but in the end, this growing mound of paperwork stacked up until it was filled with *every single* requirement. This representation of our life, this proof of identity, constructed the necessary evidence to build our dossier, our casebook.

We took one day at a time and tried our best to practice patience. Some days the waiting was crushing and depressing. Other days, there was excitement when something came through like a document being acknowledged as received on the Haitian end. Often, I walked with my headphones on, tuned to an encouraging playlist or podcast, and I cried. Until we were in the throes of adoption, I had no idea what waiting truly looked like.

Eighteen months had passed since we started the adoption application process. We were far along on the completion of our dossier, but we still had not been matched with a child. Until there was a child to adopt, nothing could proceed.

ONE MORE

We knew that our child would be from the creche where Eliza and I had visited. The director, Dr. Bay, had made a heart connection with Eliza when we were there and he was moved to match us with a girl, a little sister for Eliza. Our application was not gender specific, but we trusted the instincts of the director and waited for one little girl between the ages of four to six. In all of the months that passed, there were only sibling sets or single boys. There were no single girls ready for adoption. So, we continued to wait and wait and wait.

Finally, Don and I talked to Eliza and the other kids and asked them if their hearts were set on a girl. None were, and they all wholeheartedly agreed that a girl or a boy would be wonderful. So, Don and I called the director, Dr. Bay, and explained that we were not adamant about gender, and we no longer wanted the focus to be on just a girl.

On our call, Dr. Bay told us that there were two sisters waiting to be adopted and also one little boy. We told the director that we did not feel equipped to adopt more than one child, and, by no means wanted to separate a sibling set. As we wrapped up our conversation, Dr. Bay offered to send us photos of the sisters and the little boy in an email. I still don't know why he sent both photos when he knew our wishes, but that's what happened.

I had taken the call from home, and Don had joined me from work. After we hung up from our call, we waited for our inbox to chime. Simultaneously, from home and work, we opened the email from the creche.

The first picture was of the two precious little girls holding hands. It was excruciating to scroll past them, but we didn't have another option. As we scrolled down to the second photo, there appeared a little boy dressed in a light brown shirt and dark brown shorts. His face was beautiful, but there was a sadness in his eyes, a longing.

We knew then, this was our child.

He was the one, Jordany Jean-Baptiste, our son.

There was a caveat though, he was only two years old, and our paperwork requested a child between the ages of four and six, which meant we had to make an amendment to our application. This meant more tedium, more room for error, and another slowing of the process, but we gladly made the change.

While Don and I looked at our future child on the screen of our computers, the kids were at school oblivious to what was happening. When they came home, we had, you guessed it, another family meeting in the library! Don was home by that time, and prior to the kids arriving, he had queued up the photo of this little boy so that we could broadcast him on our TV.

The room was quiet aside from Eliza and Cara shifting on the leather couch. They didn't know what was going on. I asked them if they were ready to meet their new sibling. The energy in the room rose. You could feel the anticipation and hear the squeals of excitement. With that, we told everyone to close their eyes and keep them that way until we said, "Open."

"OPEN!" Twelve eyeballs stared at the projection of this little boy on our TV screen. There were screams of delight and tears of joy. Brennan stretched out his arm and pointed straight at the TV and announced, "Now, *that's* what I'm talking about." Brennan wanted to be a big brother, and he could not have been more thrilled. Baker, too, was excited but a bit more reserved. There was a lot of contemplating going on in his head, which I noted.

After we reveled in the excitement of being matched with Jordany and the sheer relief from the waiting to see him, I turned to Baker and said, "Baker, I know that you won't be living at home for the majority of your new brother's life, but I want you to be sure that you will know him and have a relationship with him in the perfect way for the two of you. You will be his big brother, a mentor, a hero. When you come home from college, this little brother of yours will run to you, leap into your arms, and wrap his arms around your neck—never happier than to have you home." Baker imagined this visual with some degree of plausibility. Not only was the image plausible, but this very scenario also came true over and again. To this day, these two greet each other with laughter and hugs every time—as do all of the kids.

At this stage of life, I was in labor again, not the labor of a typical pregnancy, but the labor of adoption. There was no promise of a timeline, no promise of a delivery date, no promise of a delivery, no option for an epidural, no prenatal care, no mercy (or perhaps only mercy)—just waiting, praying, hoping, exercising patience, and falling apart when I could no longer bear the pains of this type of labor. Whether I realized it at the time or not, I was such a strong woman to follow this process from beginning to end. Every step was worth it.

CHAPTER TWENTY-FOUR

FACE TO FACE

Over the course of the next eighteen months, the adoption process picked up speed a bit. In June of 2013, Don and I went to Haiti to meet our son for the first time. When we arrived at the airport in Port-au-Prince, the scene was very similar to that of which Eliza and I had experienced in July of 2010—craziness. Bodies, faces, hands clamoring to help with our luggage—all with promises of some kind or the other.

However, Don and I knew what to do and kept our luggage to ourselves as we searched for our driver. Expecting him to be in the airport or just outside holding a sign with "Donahue" on it, we were distraught when, after looking for over a half hour, we could not find him—all the while, people continued to grope toward us until one man in particular advanced and announced that he knew where our driver was.

He answered a few questions that gave us some hope, albeit with trepidation, and we reluctantly let him pull our bags across the dusty, gravel parking lot toward "our driver." Was it luck that we arrived at the right person? Perhaps. But I'd venture to bet on divine intervention. In a sea of strangers and no picture of the man we were looking for, we were ushered to a lone driver who assured us he was the right person. Our bags were tossed in the trunk, Don and I loaded ourselves into the sticky back seat, and we headed out into the barrage of city traffic.

The driver spoke little English but enough that we felt somewhat sure that we were with the right person. Phone calls to confirm had been to no avail. So, we were going out on a limb.

The car bumped and bottomed out along the pothole-filled road, people in the streets yelled, cars raced around one another and used sidewalks as passing lanes. We were under the impression that we were driving up the mountain to the creche, but instead we pulled up to a building in downtown Port-au-Prince, our auspicious Whiteness on display while our hearts thumped loudly with anxiety. *Where the hell were we?* The driver told us to get out, gave us our luggage, and took us upstairs into an office space where no one spoke English. We were then led to an empty room to wait.

Honestly, we thought we might have been kidnapped. Neither of us could find the clue that we needed to reassure ourselves that we had made the right decision. We were at the mercy of our circumstances.

Finally, Dr. Bay showed up at the office to ride with us up the mountain to the creche. We spent an enjoyable time with most of his attention on us, aside from a phone call here and there. We were able to ask lots of questions, and he told us what we should expect while we were in Haiti. Not only were we meeting Jordany for the first time, but we were also there to file paperwork, attend court, and verify our adoption process.

Eventually, we pulled down the tiny, one-lane road that led to the compound. Men arrived at the entrance, unlocked the bulky, iron gates, and pulled them apart for us to enter. The car rolled over the cobblestone driveway up to the front entrance, and we tumbled out, relieved to be safe and sound at our destination.

We got settled in our room, and soon after, we met our son. A nanny brought him to the room where we were staying in the guest house. It had a queen bed and a twin bed for Jordany, so he could spend time with us while we were there. He was three now. He had chubby cheeks and eyes of pure milk chocolate. His skin was soft as silk. The nanny handed Jordany over to me, and as I took him into my arms, he screamed and bellowed, big crocodile tears running down his face, and, *poof*, the nanny was gone.

Don and I were simultaneously freaked out and overjoyed, but the overriding emotion was definitely the freaking out. We were not able to get him to stop crying. We had brought gifts from home, so we started to pull these out as bribes for smiles. First, the coloring book, but it was of no interest, and he pushed it off of the bed. Books were no help, but songs caught his attention. After an hour or so of crying, I sang him the lullabies and hymns that I had sung to his siblings at his age. He began to quiet as I lay down on his bed, and he lay next to me with his head on my chest. I sang until he fell asleep. Don and I were not far from dreamland ourselves.

Our first night was all about the unknown. The three of us piled up in the queen bed in our room. Don and I on either side and our baby boy in the middle, cuddled up to me, leery and unsure of Don—men in general were strangers to him. Jordany was still in diapers at night, but well on his way to being potty-trained, he woke after midnight and attempted the toilet with some success once everything was pointed in the right direction! (I had forgotten about this part and many other toddler-era experiences.)

MAKE IT LEGAL

The morning of our first day, we had to leave the creche to go back to Port-au-Prince to take care of paperwork and other adoption related business. Between the hours of 6:00 a.m. and 1:00 p.m., we would attend three different court proceedings. Just before we pulled out of the compound, a Haitian woman and a two-year-old boy got in the car. At first glance, I thought it was Jordany, and I was confused. Even though it wasn't Jordany, I was still confused, but Dr. Bay explained that the little boy would be coming with us for a little while to be connected with someone along the way. I didn't completely understand, but I went with the flow.

Our first stop was the United States Embassy, a stark white, contemporary building on the outskirts of town. Upon our arrival, we were met by JP, our translator, guide, and overall walking book of knowledge who helped us every step of the way. As we climbed out of the car, the little boy, Jean, got out as well. What I didn't realize was that he was going with us. I went with the flow and carried Jean in my arms.

There were throngs of Haitians lined up for blocks outside the embassy. Anticipating we would soon be queued up as well, I was already tired. Thankfully, being Americans at the U.S. Embassy, we did not have to wait in that line. We did, however, have to wait in a large sterile room filled with chairs and a handful of people. It felt somewhat like we were in the lobby of a bank—not so much the waiting room, but there was a row of thirty teller-like windows lining one side of the room. Despite the number of stalls, I don't know if there were even three people working.

We waited over two hours. Jean was partial to me, and I had snacks. He stayed in my lap and clung to my side. The people in the room looked at us warily but also with compassion, perhaps assuming that he was my son despite our ethnic differences. The length of time that we had to wait combined with the care of a toddler compounded the whole event, but we did our best.

In between entertaining Jean, we filled out paperwork, sat through the employee lunch break (and other breaks), and through a shift change until, finally, it was our turn. Jean wouldn't let me go without him. So, I carried Jean and walked with Don up to the window. Jean melted into a fit of tears when JP took him before the proceedings began. That was the last we saw of him. Whoever was meeting him had arrived. That was weird and a bit unsettling, but we were in Haiti.

With the wails of Jean in the distance, the "teller" swore us in, and we promised all of the information on our paperwork was truthful, and from there, the forms were taken to be filed.

TWO MOMS

From the strange scenes at the embassy, we traveled to a familiar building in downtown Port-au-Prince. When we pulled up, both Don and I realized that this was the same building that we had been brought to the day before when we thought, for a brief moment, that we might have been kidnapped. As we got out of the car and walked toward the office, JP told us that we were meeting Jordany's mom here. Unfortunately, though, JP had to leave before she arrived, which meant we would not have a translator available to help us communicate with her.

One of the office workers knocked on the door and escorted Marie into the dingy, hot room where Don and I were waiting. The look on Marie's face was nondescript—

no smile, no tears, no emotion. I was so nervous. I felt very small, inadequate even. We exchanged awkward hugs and nervous glances, all of us with tears glistening in our eyes. What do you say to the mother who is giving her child to you? Even if we had known what to say, how would she understand? The only available response was, "*Merci*," completely unsatisfactory, but "thank you" was the best we had to offer in her native tongue.

We knew that it was important to document this moment. So, we asked one of the employees in the office to take a photo of the three of us. Marie stood between Don and me. Don and I smiled, but Marie had a sullen look on her face—she looked anxious to get out of the room and away from the people who were taking her son. Self-preservation—who could blame her? Even though our time together was brief, the exchange and overall experience will always remain significant. Barely five minutes after arriving Marie was gone.

SHOES, PLEASE

Before we left the office, JP returned to escort us to our next two stops. First, we had to go to lower court followed by upper court. In Haiti there is an unspoken dress code that is important to honor. As a woman in Haiti, I wore either a dress or a skirt and made sure that my shirt covered my shoulders, no tank tops or sleeveless dresses. The day that we were going to court, I had on a pink sundress with a t-shirt layered underneath. I was wearing flip flops because it was so hot. What I did not realize was that the flip flops were a poor choice, not just because my feet were filthy from all of the dust, but also because open-toed shoes were inappropriate in Haitian court. What? No one had told me this.

I thought maybe I could manage anyway, but the looks on the faces of the office staff said differently, each conveying the message that we would be turned away. So, I did the unthinkable and asked one of the women if I could borrow her shoes. This was uncomfortable in many ways, but it was most disturbing to the woman I asked. JP immediately jumped in, though, and he told me that I was asking a great deal of her. He said that I needed to give her my shoes in exchange. This was likely the only pair of shoes this woman owned, and here was a White American asking if she could "borrow" them. Who was to say that I wasn't going to leave with them?

The exchange was awkward, but I was as grateful and as humble as I knew how to be, all the while terribly aware of my Whiteness and privilege. I graciously took the woman's shoes and slipped on her size 8 black flats over my dusty, size 7 feet and shuffled to the car, promising her that I would be back with the shoes.

We left the office and went to the Haitian lower court which looked nothing like any "court" I had ever seen or imagined. Lower court was located on a side street in a trailer. I kid you not. No building, just a cramped, uncomfortable space divided into tinier spaces that served as offices. Here we signed our names on a blank piece of yellow legal pad paper, shook hands with the person across the desk, said, *"Merci,"* and left. I have no idea what we did, but it was part of the process and everyone seemed satisfied.

The contrast between lower court and upper court was drastic, to say the least. Upper court was in a beautiful government building, a treed courtyard at the entrance, and a feeling of pride within the walls of the building. Closed-toed shoes began to make more sense, and, despite the faux pas and sheer awkwardness of having asked a stranger in a strange land to borrow her shoes, I was glad that I had.

We walked through the stately lobby and found the room number to the office where we were headed. We stepped into a hot, carpeted waiting room that looked much like a doctor's office. There were upholstered couches and cushioned chairs dotted around the walls. The room was chock full of people waiting. Yet again, we were the white elephant in the room—out of place. Dozens of sets of brown eyes watched us as we searched for a spot to squeeze in amongst the others. No smiles, just looks of curiosity, maybe some of disapproval, others of indifference.

Once we sat down, we watched people come and go—singles, couples, men, women, children, and all combinations (everyone wore closed toed shoes). Some folks went into the private offices of judges while others had paperwork collected from them by a clerk that was, in turn, taken to the judges for them. We fell into the latter category.

Having waited some length of time, a woman eventually stepped over to us, asked us for our passports, and disappeared behind one of the many doors. *Well*, we thought, *We just handed over any hope of getting out of here if we were detained for any reason*. While it felt like we had put our freedom in jeopardy, we maintained a modicum of hope. We knew others who had come before us and had returned home. So, we waited. Thankfully, not too much time passed, and the woman who had taken our passports reappeared. She approached us again, handed us back our passports, and we were free to go. It's amazing how little was spoken in both of the courts, and at the same time, how much was accomplished. We left upper court, climbed into the back seat of the car, and headed back to the office; dare I forget to return the shoes to my unwitting angel. She had saved my day. Humbly, I walked back up the stairs, greeted this sweet woman. I returned her closed-toed shoes (with a very discreet, appropriate amount of "thank you" cash), and with a smile, she returned my flip-flops to me.

From the office, we left Port-au-Prince anxious to get back to the creche and spend time with our little boy. Over the next couple of days, we played with Jordany at the creche and went on a special outing. We swam in the pool together and helped him ride a bike with training wheels. We bounced basketballs and soccer balls over the covered court and ate meals together inside the guest house at the family table.

One day, before we headed off the property to go sightseeing, I dressed our sweet boy in a cute outfit that I had brought with me. He wore a navy-blue t-shirt, tan shorts, and an adorable khaki hat with a navy and white checked band around the middle. The driver took us up the mountain to a compound run by the Baptist church. We went to the attached lunch counter, ordered French fries, and sat in bright yellow booths lining the walls of the dining area. We ate ice cream and admired the view out the glass windows. Jordany didn't speak English. So, we exchanged smiles, hand gestures, hugs, and a word or two in French Creole. Outside of the compound, there were loads of Haitian artisans selling their treasures. We admired booth after booth of tchotchkes, wooden boxes with "Haiti" carved in the top, brightly colored paintings of tap taps like we had seen in Port-au-Prince, riveted flutes bound with red, blue, yellow, and green string, and all kinds of items—each good souvenir options. Every seller had just about the same collection of wares. So, we spent time bartering to get the best deal.

We left the Baptist property, and our driver took us further up the rugged mountain. After ten minutes or so, we reached a peak in the road. The driver pulled off to the side and parked. Don, Jordany, and I climbed out and walked around to a sweet, little outdoor coffee shop perched high above the Caribbean. From the mosaic-tiled deck, and over the stacked rock wall, lay the majestic, crystal blue ocean water, white, sandy beaches, swaying palm trees, and a glimpse of the Dominican Republic in the distance. It was as if we had entered paradise—a stark contrast from what was behind our backs. The dichotomy of it all was overwhelming.

Our time with Jordany could not have been more special, but having to leave him there could not have been more painful. On our last day, we packed up our suitcases with our clothes and souvenirs for the kids. I gathered Jordany up into my arms, and the three of us headed downstairs to the lobby of the guest house. At the bottom of the stairs, just to the right, there was a sofa perched against the wall. We all sat down and took some last-minute photos, all the while holding back tears aware of the inevitable to come. Come it did. Jordany's nanny rounded the corner ready to take him. Reluctantly, and with tears stinging my eyes, I handed over our sweet son. Don and I walked to the car, climbed into the now familiar back seat, and cried. Our saving grace, though, was that we would return in not too long to get him and bring him home forever . . . the sacrifice for us paled in comparison to what Jordany's mother Marie had endured—giving up her baby boy forever.

This young woman, me, exerted a lot of patience. I was resilient through the act of practicing patience. The weight of the wait rested heavily on my shoulders, but, again, I now see a strong woman, capable of more than I could have ever imagined.

CHAPTER TWENTY-FIVE

HERE WE GROW

The winter of 2014 passed, and it began to feel like spring in more ways than one. In March, we got the call that had been three years in the making. Dr. Bay and our social worker told us that it was time to come get our baby boy! When we received the exciting news, the six of us were in Rosemary Beach, Florida on the kid's spring break, but we needed to get our flights booked and everything in order to go get Jordany. Coincidentally, it was a very rainy day at the beach, with no temptation to go outside, not that I could have focused on anything else, and we were able to make all of the arrangements. I could hardly comprehend that this day had arrived. It seemed so fleeting, so distant, so unimaginable—but here it was!

Throughout the whole process of our adoption, friends, family, and strangers alike gave us unconditional support. Donations were made. Prayers were lifted, and gifts were given. We were never alone on this journey. God's favor shined on the process, and he brought so many people alongside us to help in so many ways. Without the generosity of these individuals, we would not have been able to cover the expenses of the adoption. Our gratitude to each and every one will continue for the rest of our lives. You've heard the saying, "It takes a village to raise a child." Well, it also takes a village to bring a child home. Our village will forever be part of Jordany's life, and none of us will ever be the same—all for the better.

Throughout the whole adoption process, my dream was to take our whole family to Haiti to get Jordany. My hope was for each of the children to know and witness the birthplace of their little brother; to see the inner beauty of the Haitian men, women, and children amid the ashes and rubble of its poverty; to see the faces of a beautiful and strong people against the backdrop of Haiti's rolling green hills, misty mountains and clear blue seas; to meet and thank those who have dearly loved and cared for our son; and to appreciate, in some small way, the sacrifices of time and energy and unconditional love that were made to bring sweet Jordany into our lives and family.

While the expense of six outbound flights and seven inbound flights was out of the question for us financially, a dear friend of ours rose to the occasion. He approached Don and told him that he had more airline miles than he could possibly use, and he offered us five award tickets. With the gift of these five seats, we were able to bring all four of the kids with us to Haiti and our quiver of five home to Franklin. Talk about humbling. Talk about receiving. People gave and gave on behalf of Jordany.

On April 6, 2014, our trek to Haiti began. All six of us boarded the plane, hardly able to contain ourselves from the excitement, and flew the first leg of our journey from Nashville to Miami. We had a layover in Florida, and while we waited to board our next plane, our flight to Haiti was canceled because of weather conditions. *No!* At this point, we were *so* close to seeing our little boy, and yet our patience was being tested again.

Of course, the airlines took care of overnight accommodations. We all slept fitfully in the airport hotel, but we woke up with adrenaline and could hardly wait to see Jordany. Finally, we boarded our Caribbean-bound plane and arrived in Haiti on April 7, 2014. Originally, we were to spend two nights at the guesthouse with Jordany, but because of our flight delay we only stayed one night.

When we had finally arrived in Haiti, the scene was pretty much the same as it had been the last two times that I had been there. We had a van waiting to take us to the creche and up the mountain we went. As I watched the kids take in the sights, scenes, sounds, and smells around us, I knew that bringing them was the right choice. They needed this experience. They needed to know of Jordany's homeland—the good and the not-so-good. Perspective is important. This trip accomplished that.

Arriving at the compound, we were escorted into the guesthouse and taken to our family room where we had two queen beds, a twin bed, a king bed, and a bathroom. The setup was designed to create a sense of togetherness and connectedness for your adopted child. There was plenty of room for all of us—nothing fancy, but everything was comfortable and offered the necessities.

We waited anxiously to see Jordany and stepped out into the hallway to take a look around. There were some other guests there, folks who had arrived with church missions and medical groups to minister to the children in the creche. They got wind that we were there to bring our son home and were immediately enthralled and excited for us. I lingered in the hallway, and just as I turned around, Jordany's nanny appeared holding Jordany. As she handed him over to me, I could see a pained look in her eyes. I could tell that she loved this little boy, and it was hard for her to let him go. This time, though, Jordany didn't cry.

I hustled to our room, opened the door, and five sets of blue eyes landed on Jordany. Everyone was mesmerized. Seeing Jordany in person was no less than amazing. He was naturally overwhelmed when we stepped into a room full of his new family. He didn't really know any of us. Perhaps he recognized Don and me from our trip last year, and maybe the photo albums I had sent him with pictures identifying each of us by name, gave him some familiarity with us. Nonetheless, he had a lot to take in.

Despite having such a short amount of time in Haiti, we accomplished a lot. We made up a game to help Jordany learn our names. The seven of us sat down in a circle on the basketball court and set a soccer ball in the middle. One-by-one, we rolled the ball to one another. Each recipient of the ball said his or her name aloud to Jordany who seemed to love the game even though he didn't speak English. He did, however, seem to understand. Once we tired of this game, Brennan popped Jordany up on his shoulders, and we walked up the stairs to the overlook at the guesthouse, mountains in every direction.

Baker played peek-a-boo with a blanket and Jordany giggled the cutest giggle ever. We gave him coloring books that he, Eliza, and Cara colored in for hours, and he took cues from his siblings and warmed up to Don (remember that male figures were few and far between) as he felt a sense of safety. In the evening, we snuggled up in the beds. Each of the kiddos claimed his or her spot, and Don, Jordany, and I snuggled up together on the king bed.

Because our trip had been cut short by a day, we didn't have a lot of time to fit in what had been planned for us. So, Dr. Bay helped us figure out how to do as much as we could in a condensed amount of time. We woke up the next morning, packed up quickly, said our goodbyes, and walked out to the van waiting for us in the courtyard. Just as we loaded up, Jordany's nanny stepped out of the guest house and walked over to the van. She didn't say anything. She didn't need to. Tears glistened in her eyes. A sad smile tilted the corners of her lips slightly upward. The love she felt for Jordany was clear, and I'm convinced that her attachment to him helped him attach to us. We waved goodbye and drove out of the giant, wrought iron gates for the last time.

We took a whirlwind trip up to the overlook and visited the many craft huts. Everyone got a souvenir to bring home, including rain makers embossed with the word "Haiti," machetes fitted in embossed, leather sheaths (I don't know why we got these or how they made it through customs, but they did), paintings of tap taps, wooden boxes with "Haiti" etched in the lids, and more. We took photos to memorialize our time together, hopped back in the van, and went down the winding mountain road.

Our van wove in and out through the god-awful traffic in Port-au-Prince. Nothing had changed. In fact, if it could have been worse, I think it was. At one point we were at a very large intersection with four to five entry options that all converged in the middle. There were no traffic lights, no stop signs, no hint of a traffic pattern. Hence, there was no rhyme or reason to the traffic flow, or lack thereof, and it ended with cars juxtaposed at every angle in the middle of the intersection. Really, there was no way out of it. Horns honked relentlessly, people yelled, and craziness was everywhere. Finally, a man got out of his car and began motioning one car one direction and another the other direction until the web of automobiles was untangled enough for us to make our way on to the airport.

On our trip home, we stopped again in Miami, but this time with a planned overnight stay there. When we deboarded the plane, we were all starving, and we headed to the food court where we introduced Burger King French fries to Jordany. After our bellies were full, we went up to our adjoining rooms in the airport hotel, slept as best we could, and woke the next morning excited to get home.

Each time the seven of us boarded a plane, we were quite the sight. On the return trip to Nashville, one of the flight attendants asked to hear our story and Don and I shared it with her. After talking for a little while, she brought us a little bottle of champagne to celebrate. When we finally arrived in Nashville, everyone was understandably exhausted yet also thrilled. We did it. We brought our son home. It took three years; yet here we were a family of seven walking through the Nashville International Airport into the arms of throngs of loved ones who greeted us with welcome home signs, colorful balloons, and tender hugs.

As much as I wanted to adopt a child, I also think that I wanted to prove that I could do something hard, really hard. Raise four kids? Yep. Raise four kids simultaneously aged four and under? Yep. Add a fifth child ten years younger than the last biological? Yep. Was I trying to impress? I guess, in a way. I know from looking back on my life that part of my nature, or learned tendencies, were to please, to receive accolades. While there may have been selfish motives, the core of my being wanted to bring home a child from Haiti and doing so meant a lot of letting go of self.

The process required an enormous amount of work and just as much patience. I did this, but it was only the beginning.

HOW WAS I TO KNOW?

One thing I've learned is that I hardly knew anything about adoption until Jordany became a permanent part of our family. Don and I read books in preparation for Jordany to come home. We attended a bold, no-holds-barred seminar about adoption, both its beautiful side and its horrific side, and yes, there is a horrific side.

We learned that when adopting a child, you do not know what underlying issues are coming with your child; they vary from one extreme to another. There may be an inability to attach or a strong attachment instinct. Perhaps they'll be a violent child, one who might set your house on fire. Or, they may be a tender, loving child or a depressed boy or girl who experienced abuse. There are so many unknown variables that you cannot control or contend with until your son or daughter is home with you. Regardless, there are no adoptions, domestic or international, where the child has not experienced some sort of trauma.

We also dealt with occasional insensitivities from people who told us, "You knew what you were getting into." Well, that's like telling a first-time pregnant woman that she should know how to be a mom while she's carrying her baby in her tummy. Both adoption and biological births are beautiful. They have analogous traits, but they are different.

Books help, seminars help, friends who have experiences of their own to share help the most . . . but at the end of the day, you have to learn how to parent your child yourself. You have to know yourself and get to know your child–and in the learning comes the only true way to gain experience.

There is plenty that is misunderstood about bringing a child home (adopted or not). Often, I was asked by well-meaning, loving people, "Are you just in heaven?" My response was usually, "We are so happy to have Jordany home, but truthfully, I'm tired to the bone." We had missed the first four years of Jordany's life, which meant there was a lot of catching up for us to do and even more adjustments for Jordany to make.

Thankfully, Jordany never had violent tendencies. He attached well (which says something important about his birth mother and nanny at the creche). The adoption was not without trauma, though. There were blank stares to contend with and work through, and temper tantrums like I'd never seen, both Jordany's and my own, to be honest.

This process was not easy. It tested me as a mother. I lost weight. I experienced urinary retention where I could not pee. It was so excruciating that my best friend, Traci, took me to the emergency room. Stress can wreak havoc on your body. There was one particularly intense time when I could not get Jordany to calm down. One book that I had read recommended a way to settle your child. I recalled this method, and I followed its advice. I wrapped up Jordany in my arms with the intent of giving him a sense of safety. I tried to gather him into a hug while he was flailing about. I spoke softly and soothingly to him, but he fought me hard. So hard that he pounded on my chest and arms and bit me on the head.

Needless to say, I was beside myself with what to do, and I completely fell apart in heaps of tears and cried in my closet. I never tried that tactic again until more trust was established between the two of us, and eventually, hugs worked well when Jordany was open to receiving them.

Events similar to this went on over the next few years, but the traumatic episodes and temper tantrums continued to get better, and despite the hardships, Jordany attached well to me and to the family. Attachment helps; therapy helps. Patience runs thin, but it's needed to survive, and we did that and then some.

The first year Jordany was home, he grew five inches! That's what nutrition and love can do. Jordany is a handsome, beautiful, healthy child. He is full of life and joy. His temperament is good, and his smile stretches from ear to ear. Jordany's adoption story and our journey to bring him home could be a book in and of itself. Perhaps I will write that one next.

Through the process of morphing motherhood from biological birth to birth by adoption, I learned a lot about myself and how to love unconditionally. Being raised loving God and believing in Jesus, my maternal nature gave way to a fresh, new understanding of sacrifice. Knowing I am loved with an everlasting love, despite my nature, gave way to a new-found expression of love, and I am proud of the growth that I experienced during those first few years (more would certainly come).

CHAPTER TWENTY-SIX

MOM, MD

My instinct to nurture my children carried with it the responsibility of healing hurts, binding wounds, being compassionate, and expressing sympathy. Children are destined to get injured in one way or another, and mine were no exception.

As the kids grew, my mother's intuition was impressively strong with regard to knowing what to do when someone skinned a knee, hit their head, felt anxious, had a fever or a runny nose, experienced a stomachache, or whatever the ailment may have been at the time. I also was gifted with the ability to remain calm in an emergency. I can hear myself now repeating to one of the kids after an accident, "It's going to be okay. You're alright. Mama is here. You're okay." I said these words over and again into the ears and over the hearts of my hurting ones. My mom modeled cool-headedness and used similar comforting phrases to my brothers and me. This gift is part of who I am, and I'm grateful to claim it and recognize its importance.

HITCH IN THE GET-ALONG

When our son Brennan was eighteen months old, he began experiencing pain in his leg. He had been less active than usual and complained that his leg hurt. He hadn't taken a fall, and there were no physical signs of an injury. We figured he was experiencing growing pains, but one afternoon while he was at recess at Mother's Day Out, Brennan did not want to go to the playground. A couple of the teachers tried to coax Brennan to go play, and after a lot of nudging, he got up and headed to the swing set. As he toddled across the grass, the teachers saw a noticeable limp and alerted me to it when I came for pickup.

Once the schoolteachers told me what they had observed, I felt terrible. Brennan wasn't just experiencing growing pains like I had thought. He wasn't being defiant, and he truly was in pain. I called our pediatrician, we went to see her, and she ordered some imaging and blood work. After our appointment, we went home expecting to wait a day or two before hearing back from the doctor. However, the results came back shortly after we arrived home, and his white blood cell count was low, which indicated an infection, and there was a dark spot on Brennan's hip bone. When the doctor called us, she gave us the report and sent us straight to the ER. Scary.

While there, Brennan had more imaging done, more blood drawn, and various other tests taken to see what was going on in his hip. The MRI and blood work revealed a bone infection in his hip joint with no known cause. It seemed as though a typical cold had moved from his head and chest into his hip. The lab cultures that were taken could not identify the culprit, and, so, the infectious disease team was called in—very unsettling amid the already unknown.

Brennan was admitted to Vanderbilt Children's Hospital where he underwent more testing. With Vanderbilt being a teaching hospital, it was not uncommon for residents to observe and diagnose if called upon. Throngs of white-coated men and women came into our room multiple times a day to discuss Brennan's case and its elusive diagnosis.

Although we were in one of the best children's hospitals in the country, it was in dire need of an overhaul. Our room was stark and sterile, both literally and figuratively. There was no personality to the room with just a lone crib and two hard backed chairs for visitors.

The coldness of the room was magnified by the jail-like, steel-barred crib that reminded me more of a cage than a crib. I felt like my child was in his own little prison cell. I hated seeing Brennan "locked-up and behind bars." It was so hard to reach him through the slats or over the height of the crib. His pain was a level 10, and I loathed having him subject to so much trauma.

I became increasingly frustrated with the barrier between us. So, despite its limited sleeping capacity, I scaled the bars and climbed into Brennan's crib whenever I could. We slept together, him in my arms, my heart breaking. Multiple times a night, a nurse came in to check his vitals and draw blood.

However, the vitals weren't done in his room as you would typically think. Instead, I carried him into a room down the hall—It was so bright in there, I can still feel my eyes squinting from the glare. Honestly, it felt like we were going into a torture chamber, especially given what would come next. Sweet, little tow-headed Brennan was strapped down on the table, arms and legs in restraints, while he was poked, prodded, and pricked, all the while screaming and crying that toddler "help me" cry. I felt utterly helpless to help.

This experience was horrifying, and I know it was only a very small taste of what so many families suffer who have seriously ill children. Nonetheless, the trauma of the whole experience was real.

None of the cultures came back definitively. So, over the course of the next five days, the doctors treated Brennan with a high dose, broad-spectrum antibiotic administered through his IV. Because we were in a children's hospital, children were allowed to visit. Don brought Baker and Cara to visit, and when Brennan saw them, he squealed with delight. When I witnessed their pure joy, tears came to my eyes. They were so used to being together all of the time that being apart wasn't natural. Thankfully, after the fifth day of being in the hospital and on antibiotics, we were finally sent home with a liquid, bubblegum flavor, antibiotic that Brennan took over the course of the next three months.

With different illnesses and ailments, I packed my mental medical book with all types of information and remedies. I quickly learned not to panic at anything slight. More times than not, I was able to treat the kids at home as opposed to lugging four toddlers to the doctor's office where there were all the more germs to spread and bring home.

Over the years, we went to the hospital for many minor incidents, though.

SAVING FACE

Since Baker was quite young, he wanted to play football; however, we didn't let him play until he was in sixth grade. He played for a local league, then he played in middle school, and later in his high school years. During the first year he played for our town's local league, Baker got knotted up in a tackle that was bad enough, we had to leave the game and take him to the ER.

The odds were against this particular injury ever happening, but it did. Baker had a freak accident with another player. As the two wrestled to take each other down, the defendant slipped. His leg went out from under him, and his cleat managed to shoot through one of the openings in Baker's helmet. Not only did his foot defy the barrier of Baker's face mask, but it also pushed all the way through, puncturing Baker's cheekbone.

We left the game and headed to the emergency room. With Baker's head on my shoulder, he, Don and I waited in the children's ER for what seemed like hours. Despite the ice pack Baker held to his cheek, we witnessed it swelling and turning blue as we longed for someone to retrieve us and give Baker the care that he needed.

We were finally taken back to triage. The rooms were full, and extra beds lined the hallway. The nurse took us around a corner to a bed against the wall while we waited for an attending to oversee Baker's care. When the doctor arrived, he examined Baker's cheekbone and ordered an X-ray. An orderly came and wheeled Baker to the imaging center, and I followed along right beside him. The results of the X-ray revealed a fractured cheekbone. Apparently, the blunt force of another sixth grader's cleated foot was small enough to defy the facemask and powerful enough to puncture the cheekbone.

As the years passed and Baker continued to play football, there were more accidents that sent us back to the ER more than once. Baker suffered a minor concussion in middle school. In high school, however, during a pre-season scrimmage, he was hit so hard by another player that he blacked out for a split second. At first it wasn't apparent that Baker was injured because he got up fairly quickly. As he was walking off of the field, Baker turned to one of his buddies and said, "When are we starting the game?" Immediately his friend knew that something was up. Baker didn't know that he had been hit, nor did he recall the play. So, we followed concussion protocol until he could play again.

Injuries weren't reserved for our hometown, though. Inevitably, we found ourselves in one emergency or another. From the ocean to the mountains, some family trips were not complete until we visited an urgent clinic or an ER.

SNOW PATROL

On a trip to Florida, we met a special family. Their four kids were close in age to our four kids, and we bonded with the couple quickly. After exchanging contact information while at the beach, we vowed to stay in touch. Not only did we stay in touch, but the following winter we were also invited to join them on a family ski trip in Colorado. So generous and kind, they arranged a lovely stay for all of us in the beautiful Rocky Mountains. Our condo was set in the Vail Valley in the ski community of Bachelor's Gulch where the views of the snowcapped mountains are second to none. Our room came with six lift tickets for every day that we were there. I think we skied more on that trip than any other past or present.

One day, about half-way into our seven-day stay, Cara and I were skiing together and having a little mom and daughter time—as much as you can while traveling down a mountain. At any rate, we were on a more difficult run than usual and needed to be extra careful. As we commenced down the slope, we had not gotten too far when Cara fell. Just before she toppled over, I passed her on the slope, but as was my habit when I got ahead of anyone, I stopped, turned around and looked for her. She wasn't on her feet. She was lying in the snow. I was downhill a ways, but I managed to sidestep my skis up the mountain until it dawned on me that I could take them off which I did, and I made my way up more efficiently.

When I had finally inched my way up the snowy bank, Cara was in tears and had her arms wrapped around her knee. It was obvious that she was not going to be able to get down the mountain. Having had a similar experience with my mom when I was younger, I knew the protocol for getting help. I picked up one ski and shoved it into the snow at an angle and then did the same with the other so that when crossed, they formed an X which was the signal for help. Many folks stopped to check on us on their way down the mountain, and someone kindly reported our accident to mountain rescue.

Once the ski patrol arrived, they assessed Cara and determined that it was okay to move her. A medic picked Cara up into his arms and loaded her into the toboggan that trailed behind their snowmobile. From there, we headed to the urgent care center just down the mountain.

Propped up on a bed in the clinic, ice on her knee, and lots of attention, Cara went for an X-ray so the doctors could determine the extent of her injury. It turns out that she only had a sprain, but it was enough to keep her off the slopes for the rest of the trip. Honestly, Cara was not that upset about missing more skiing and was quite content sitting by the fire and drinking hot cocoa!

EXERCISE CAUTION

For several years I wanted some indoor exercise equipment. I eventually made that a reality when I found an affordable treadmill and purchased it. Because we had four littles, I made sure that there was a safety mechanism to keep the children from getting injured. In order to operate my treadmill, you had to have its key; otherwise, it would not work at all.

I used the treadmill successfully for a couple of years with no incidents. We did keep it in the playroom, but there was plenty of space for it not to get in the way of the kid's toys, books, and games. Albeit big and bulky, I anchored it on a diagonal in an out-of-the-way corner, and after each walk, I made sure to take out the key and hide it. Our playroom had a built-in counter with cabinets below and cabinets above. I would get up on the counter, stand on my tiptoes, and tuck the key on the highest shelf that I could reach, where it was safely out of reach from the kids (or so I thought).

Just like any other evening, when it came time for bed, Don and I sent the kids up the stairs to get on their pjs and brush their teeth. Sometimes there was complaining, but for the most part, the children would head upstairs without a fuss. Once they were in bed, Don and I made the rounds from the girls' bedroom to the boys'. We read stories, sang songs, said prayers, and gave lots of hugs and kisses. This particular night, however, was not a typical night. It was a nightmare.

Unbeknownst to Don and me, the kids had made a detour from our nightly routine and headed to the playroom instead. Our playroom was located above the garage, and our bedroom was on the opposite end of the house on the first floor. Even though the kids went to bed fairly early, Don and I tended to get in our comfy clothes (if not pajamas) while the kids changed. This was a typical night for us, and Don and I headed to our bedroom to change. Neither of us noted any unusual commotion, but that would soon change.

Once I was comfortable, I headed to the kitchen to clean up dishes from dinner, load the dishwasher, and wipe down the counters. I had hardly begun, when all of a sudden, I heard shrill screaming coming from the playroom. I bounded up the stairs, skipping every other step to get there faster. I came through the door and found Eliza stuck in the corner behind the still-running treadmill. My whole body lurched in horror as I scrambled to turn it off and gather up my baby girl whose hip was burned and bloodied, skin rubbed away by the belt of the treadmill.

When the kids were supposedly headed into their nightly routine, Eliza had followed along in a t-shirt and her diaper. Once upstairs and in the playroom, one of the kids had wedged a small footstool between the back end of the treadmill and the corner of the diagonal where it was positioned. To Eliza this looked like a great place to sit down and watch her sister and brothers.

While she was content on the stool, the boys had begun to scramble up onto the counter of the bookshelves. Little did I know that they knew where I hid the treadmill key. Of course, neither of the boys were as tall as me. So, the likelihood of them reaching the upper shelf was unlikely. However, I didn't take into account that they might have put a stool on the counter to reach the key, which is exactly what they did.

The details of what happened next are sketchy, but the best I recall is that while Eliza sat behind the treadmill, the boys had climbed off the counter, stuck the key into its lock, and turned it on. In the blink of an eye, the belt of the treadmill caught the edge of the stool and tipped Eliza over. She got pinned between the stool and the running belt, and the racing, rough turf began spinning and rubbing up against her thigh. With only a diaper covering her bum, her sweet, little legs were exposed, and her right hip was ripped bare.

As I grabbed Eliza screaming and wailing from the pain, I shouted out for Don and ran down the stairs with my shrieking baby in my arms. My gosh. It was awful. Her tender skin now raw and torn, exposed and bleeding. I could hardly bear to look at it. My poor girl. Horrified, Don called 911, and the EMTs who were just a quarter of a mile from our home were on the scene quickly.

Both a fire engine and an ambulance arrived at our house. Firefighters and medics ran up our garage stairs and into the family room where I was holding Eliza still crying and in so much pain. Her hip and thigh area were assessed, and the medics determined that she had suffered second-and third-degree burns. We were sent straight to the ER where Eliza was cared for, given medicine for pain, and her wounds cleaned and dressed.

My heart just broke for her. I remember my own body feeling raw. As any mother with an injured child, I wanted to take the pain away from her. I felt helpless and at the same time grateful that it was not even worse than it was. Thankfully, we didn't have to spend the night in the hospital. When we were discharged, I took Eliza to my parent's home to care for her in a calm atmosphere. As is her nature, my mom took care of her baby girl while I took care of mine. Mothers mothering mothers and daughters. My mom. She was always there to help.

Once the wounds were healed, the burns left behind scars on Eliza's hip. As she grew, we told her that she could have plastic surgery to reduce the scarring, but she always declined. She told us that the leftover remnants of the burn were part of her story, and she saw them as a badge of survival.

YES, THE DOG BITES

Jordany had been home less than a year, when the unthinkable happened. At the time, we were spending a getaway weekend with my parents in our family cabin. Going to Rock Island, Tennessee wasn't part of my childhood, but it was a part of my children's tweens, teens, and early twenties. Always a respite and welcomed change from the "busyness" of life, this trip was an exception.

Jordany was five. The seven of us, my parents, and their dogs were all gathered in the great room watching television. Jordany, uninterested in the show on TV, climbed down from the couch onto the floor where my dad's boxer, Buddy, was resting. We had not had any problems between Jordany and Buddy or either of our dogs, but this evening was different.

Naive to the risk and given that Jordany had never been bothered by Buddy, he made his way closer and closer to the dog. Jordany was still savoring a morsel of food from dinner. It was common for him to keep food in his mouth for a while. At any rate, it seems as though Buddy smelled the food, and misinterpreted Jordany's encroachment of his space as being aggressive. Then he lurched forward and bit Jordany right on the apple of his cheek.

I was just a few steps away in the kitchen when I heard the heart-wrenching scream of my five-year-old. I turned around at the sound and watched someone scoop Jordany off the floor, while blood poured from his soft face, skin ripped and gouged.

GOOD GOD ALMIGHTY!

My knees wobbled, my stomach turned, and I let out a stifled scream inside. I had flashbacks of Eliza's treadmill injury and of the rawness of it all in every sense of the word. Someone needed to be calm, and I was that someone. As a mom, I had the ability to set the tone in the room, hysterics could make the situation entirely worse. There would be time for hysterics later. What my son needed now was help.

With a gulp of air, and my breath held, I rose to the occasion of Dr. Mom. I gathered my bloody-faced boy into my arms while he screeched and howled his little lungs out.

Panic was everywhere in the room. It was Sunday night in a very small, Southern town. We were far from a local hospital or ER, but thank God we did have a friend who was a doctor, and he eagerly agreed to meet us at his office.

Like I've said before, no one wants to see their child suffer in any manner—helpless littles at the mercy of their caregiver can be too much to witness—but all of this is part of motherhood and caring for your children. I gathered my composure as best I could, put on my "It's going to be okay" face, and raced to the car. We couldn't get there fast enough. I held pressure on Jordany's cheek with a towel, and he calmed down as we drove. He really had no idea what had happened.

When we arrived at the doctor's office, he let us in through the back and took us to an examination room. Sometimes, the necessary methods for preparing a wound to heal are just as painful, if not more so, than the episode itself; both can be traumatic, and that's how it was for Jordany.

Stitches were definitely needed, but there were torn parts of his skin, some of which needed to be clipped away and others to be stretched together to cover the hole in his cheek. Because this would be terribly painful, the doctor had to numb the area with two injections into Jordany's tender face. It's hard to convey my own feeling of numbness as I held my little boy; I was helpless to do anything for the pain other than be his mom. I held onto him for dear life whispering words of comfort, "It's okay. It's going to be okay. Mama is here. I love you. *Shhh*. It's okay, sweetheart." Of course, it's technically not okay. He's hurting, and I have no balm for healing.

In spite of the horror, we made it through six stitches—less painful thanks to the lidocaine injections that Jordany suffered through—painful, nonetheless, in every other way. The doctor dressed his wound and gave us instructions for his care while his skin mended itself.

Jordany missed several days of school, and after time, his wound healed but not without a mar on his beautiful skin. He's now fourteen, and the scar on his face has diminished considerably. Ironically, he has never stopped loving dogs, but he is also known to be cautious around dogs. He knows to ask permission to touch someone else's dog, and he respects the boundaries of pets.

Experiencing trauma of any kind with your kids is nothing that a parent would wish for; however, through those physical and emotional struggles, we grew into better parents and into a stronger family.

Looking back on these stories, I can see where I was stretched and thinned, but that's to be expected in any human condition. Suffering is part of living. What you do with the pain, though, changes your trajectory for the better or for the worse; either way, though, both produce growth.

The Dr. Mom type of mothering that I was doing was *not* codependency. It was a crisis and needed intervention. My children had a necessary dependency on me, and I had the duty to fill because of my love for them and desire for them to heal, grow, and thrive.

I am grateful that motherhood is part of my story. Caretaking has long been a role that I have risen to, sometimes to a fault and to my own detriment. When I look back on the early days of mothering, I can see where I lost part of myself, especially to the immediacy of my own circumstances—four kids aged four-and-a-half and under. There was little time for me, for self-care.

Mothers who stay at home and mothers who have an additional job outside of the home have traditionally pulled quite the load of responsibility. It seems as though things are changing now, and that is good, but my reality was that I was doing a lot. I recall times that I wished I could get just sick enough to go to the hospital so that someone could take care of me. Why? Well, there wasn't anyone who could do my job, not all of the things. If I had a legitimate reason, non-life-threatening, to go to the hospital, then someone else could make all of the arrangements for the kids, take care of whatever needed to be done at home, and I could have a break while I was nursed back to health.

As crazy as it may sound to give this feeling a voice, I would venture to say that I'm not the only one who has felt similarly. What about you? Did you have those days that you wanted Calgon to take you further away than the bathtub? Maybe you were better at self-care than I was, but even with that, being the caretaker requires a tremendous amount of giving, self-denial, and life interruption. It is easy to lose sight of who we are.

Forgetting who we are is common. Retracing our steps, though, and rediscovering ourselves is critical. Where did I lose myself? How can I find myself so that I can answer the question, who do you think you are?

CHAPTER TWENTY-SEVEN

TRAPPED BY GRACE

Religious institutions far too often fail when it comes to caring for the wounded. As I've told you earlier, I grew up with lots of love but also in a school and church environment with loads of legalism. I felt like there was very little room for grace, at least not for the "heavier" sins like sex before marriage, adultery, pregnancy out of wedlock, abortion, gender diversity and neutrality, LGBTQ+, addiction, and, of course, murder. Even with murder, though, it seemed like the ministry rose up to the incarcerated and gave them, at least, some grace. The "sins of the flesh" were kept hush-hush or if they were revealed, the same that came with confession failed in comparison to what unconditional love could have done.

There was hardly a place for vulnerability in the constraints of my religious background. Sure, there were opportunities to come forward and ask for forgiveness, but the church community lacked, was afraid to extend, or did not understand the open arms of the love Jesus demonstrated in the Bible. Don't misunderstand, though. There was certainly love, and my church congregation was loving. It's just that legalism bred conditions that were impossible to live up to.

Unfortunately, there was (and is) a very distinct difference in the way that love looked. Religion, legalism, and any type of rules-oriented, performance-based love is a poor disguise for love. Yet, society has managed to mold "love" into simply, "to do" and "not to do."

Why? Because there is such a dominant need for control and identifying "right" and "wrong" beyond the code of "love your neighbor as yourself." When a ruling body gets to control the narrative, and you do not get to have a say, be careful and evaluate if you are in a space where you can be you and others can be their own authentic selves.

The reason that I remain attracted to the Love of Jesus is that he did not discriminate, ever. He always held space, honor even, for the wounded and the broken-hearted. He beckoned everyone to come to him regardless of race, religion, or sexual preference, and they came to him because he was safe, and he loved them. Period.

Great confusion exists amongst religious sects when it comes to the foundational principle of loving like Jesus, *but* the misunderstanding isn't because the principles in the Bible are difficult to grasp. Rather, the confusion came of the confinements that have been imposed by the patriarchy since the Bible's first interpretation from its original text. The whole point of the Gospel is skirted when love and acceptance is offered only when one meets said boundaries and is able to tick "yes" to each box. There is only one box, if you even want to call it that. The universe was created in love, and we should return that love with our own best version of love. Perhaps, that is harder to do than to abide in any rules-oriented system.

From my early dating years with Don, up until this very moment, my views of man-made constraints in church culture are ever evolving further and further from the box-ticking manifestation of the Bible. Instead,

I continue to move toward love and kindness, acceptance and grace, mercy, and goodness. I honestly believe that the Bible's sole purpose is to extend love without condition and with compassion. I believe that the point of turning to the Bible is for this very reason–anything that looks less than love, *is* less than love.

In my mid-twenties, my mom introduced me to Henri Nouwen, a Dutch Catholic priest, professor, theologian, and writer. Nouwen had an amazing ability to relate to people both in person and through his books. He was not afraid to be vulnerable, and he saw vulnerability as a conduit to community and compassion. Once I started reading Nouwen's works, I better understood the unending "belovedness" that God has for everyone, even me. This was a revelation, a tipping point for me. Nouwen writes in *You Are the Beloved: Daily Meditations for Spiritual Living*:

> "Compassion asks us to go where it hurts, to enter into the places of pain, to share in brokenness, fear, confusion, and anguish. Compassion challenges us to cry out with those in misery, to mourn with those who are lonely, to weep with those in tears. Compassion requires us to be weak with the weak, vulnerable with the vulnerable, and powerless with the powerless. Compassion means full immersion in the condition of being human."[2]

Nouwen's journey of faith and interpretation of living like Jesus resonated with me like nothing I had experienced in my past. I craved that freedom for myself and longed to love in such a compassionate way. Once I explored the art of compassion and dove deeper into Nouwen's writing, I discovered other theologians who were on similar journeys. One of the more profound writers I was introduced to was Father Richard Rohr.

Rohr, an American Franciscan priest, is also an ordained priest within the Roman Catholic Church. (Scratch any uncomely image that a "Catholic priest" may invoke—that is not Rohr.) It was natural that I was wooed by Rohr, as his mentor was Henri Nouwen. Rohr's writings often focus on inclusion, diversity, acceptance, and living a life that manifests love instead of one that regurgitates orthodoxy.

I am mentored by the work of Rohr, who is an evolutionary thinker, a mystic, a dynamic outward expression of love, and a lover of the Divine. While I have read several of his books, one that had a profound effect on my life during a critical time in our family history is *Breathing Under Water*. Within its pages, Rohr explores the truisms and lack thereof between biblical theology and the twelve-step program of Alcoholics Anonymous. I experienced many *ah-ha* moments reading this, recalling a life of trauma that had included addiction. Some of my favorite excerpts from Rohr's *Breathing Under Water: Spirituality and the Twelve Steps* include:

> "Religion is lived by people who are afraid of hell. Spirituality is lived by people who have been through hell."[3]
>
> "How you do life is your real and final truth, not what ideas you believe."[4]
>
> "Only love affects true inner transformation, not duress, guilt, shunning, or social pressure."[5]
>
> "And to be fully honest, I think your heart needs to be broken, and broken open, at least once to have a heart at all or to have a heart for others."[6]

There is a glaring dichotomy between religion and recovery, and what Rohr makes shockingly clear is that the people in the recovery groups meeting in the basements of churches act more like a transformative "church" than the routine Sunday morning congregation in the sanctuary. Church-*life* happens in brokenness not in perfection, as if that were even possible.

Our focus should be on love and "belovedness." One does not cause us to earn salvation or lose salvation. There are no requirements to pray harder, read more scripture, or whatever, in order to be loved. We all miss the mark. We always will, but that's why grace and love exist. Rohr says, "God has trapped us all inside of certain grace and enclosed all things human in a constant need for mercy."[7] In other words, within the perfect Love of the Divine, grace surrounds us like a fortress, an unending wave, a sanctuary. And inside this web of grace, we are still human, and, thus, we remain in a state of being that is always needing mercy—we are imperfect. The gift of imperfection revels in the grace that we cannot escape.

If you're interested in exploring this quote more, listen to the December 28, 2022, episode of Brene Brown's podcast, *Unlocking Us*, in which she interviews Rohr both about *Breathing Under Water* and another of his books, *Falling Upward*.[8]

My release from the grasp of religious institutionalism is, in part, credit to both Nouwen and Rohr. Their enlightenment and grip on the foundation of love also contributed to my ability to walk through hell and out on more than one occasion.

Who do I think I am at this point? I am liberated. I am free to love, unhinged. Trapped by certain grace. Held in the need for mercy. I am beloved. I am evolving.

Scales that once covered my eyes are being shed, and I am seeing what true love looks like and understanding how true love behaves.

CHAPTER TWENTY-EIGHT

PRO MOM

The story of my parents' trauma and separation was one of the most significant catalysts of change for the better in my life, and, while there are multitudes of lessons gleaned from living life, there is another story that I want to share about crisis and transformation.

Before I tell the story, it's important that you, as a reader, understand that every life event that any of my children had while they were being raised, shaped me as a mom.

It seems to me that, as would be the case for any life's work, you don't become a "professional" until the end. Even then, I'm quite sure there are no experts in parenting. However, there are those of us with loads of experience to draw from, and it's those experiences whether joyful or traumatic—more than likely both—that revealed more of myself to me both as a mom and as a woman.

With my dream of becoming a mom alive and well, no one could have prepared me for what lay ahead. I do remember couples ahead of us in age telling us to enjoy the days before puberty. I would often hear something to the effect of, "If you thought you didn't like changing diapers, inevitably, a circumstance will rear its face, bring you to your knees, and make you wish it was all as simple as wiping a baby's butt."

While some may feel as though they really never went through a crisis with a child, no one is immune to upheaval in one form or another. We do, however, have choices: We can push our struggle under the surface, refusing to acknowledge it and hoping it will go away. We can deny it and pretend everything is fine. We can hide. Or we can face reality head-on; we can walk through the struggle, do the work, and pray that we will make it to the other side.

I know that there is nothing that I did or that Don and I did as a couple that was perfect— far from it, but isn't that part of the learning curve? Isn't that where growth happens? In the depths of despair, in the slippery slope, in the hard work?

In the dark times, did I not know that these life events were shaping me, helping to define me, and seeking to challenge me? Sure. Training me? Absolutely. In order to do the work, you have to take the class, go through the course, do the hard things, and finish the test. Being a mom or a stay-at-home caregiver is no different.

Perhaps, I did not know who I was amid the struggle, but looking back, I was resilient and strong. I managed to put up safe boundaries for myself because of what I learned in earlier crises. I didn't do it perfectly, but I did do what I could to get to the other side, to heal.

When I thought I wasn't enough, I was.

When I thought I'd never make it through the hell, I did.

When I thought I was weak, I know that I was strong, because I allowed myself the opportunity to be weak. For when we are weak, we are strong.

With those ideas in mind, I have retraced my life as a mom and a woman in both the good and bad times, in the joyful and sorrowful periods, and in moments of weakness and strength. Each story that follows is related to experiences with one or more of my children.

The story is the work; the ending is the strength; together, they produced growth.

So, here we go . . .

CHAPTER TWENTY-NINE

CRISIS MANAGEMENT

Whenever I'm approached by someone who says, "I have something I want to talk to you about," butterflies stir in my stomach and my heart begins to race. My natural fear instinct sets in, and I assume that the topic will cover something that I won't like to hear about something I or another person did. I know that phrase is also used to introduce good news, but I'm inclined to go negative with this particular set of words.

At any rate, in 2012 Don and I experienced a seismic shift in parenting when one of our children came forward with a confession. It was a Wednesday night, and we had picked up the kids from their youth group at church and headed home. Our car climbed the hill nearing the house, and we pulled into the garage. Three of the kids got out, and one of them lagged behind and asked us to stay in the car; there was something that needed sharing.

While Don and I braced for something, we had no idea what was coming next. And just like I said earlier, anxious butterflies swirled in my stomach, and my heart began to pump faster as I prepared for the news.

In our family, though, we tried hard to provide a safe space for the kids to come to us with anything. Our goal was to pose no judgment, assure each child of our love for them, remind them that nothing could dissolve that love, and try our best to be available and present.

As we sat there waiting, none of the pounding in my body stopped. It just increased as we predicted the worst, whatever that meant. However, this scenario was a perfect picture of how we'd raised our kids. Despite the difficulty of the situation, this child felt safe enough to share. The miracle was that we were being trusted with something that felt like shame to them—but the need to release the burden was stronger than the risk of discomfort. It took a little time for the confession to be articulated. In my head I'm thinking, *Out with it. I can't wait any longer.* Then our child began to tell us that they had been offered a joint in the bathroom at school. Inside, I was mortified. I began to gaslight myself with inner talk like, *"You failed."* In anxious situations with the kids or friends, I was usually the one with composure and calm. This time was no different. Even though every ounce of me wanted to scream. I knew that a response like that would inhibit difficult conversations in the future.

With the engine turned off and the other kids inside, we spent some time talking over what had happened. This was a perfect example of peer pressure and a great time to lean on Nancy Reagan's "Just Say No" to drugs campaign that I grew up with—whether it was successful across the country, I don't know. What I do know is that it worked for me, at least in one instance.

When I was a junior in high school, I went to my first prom, at another school, of course, because, as you may recall, dancing leads to sex. I digress. My date and another couple pulled up to my house in a black limo. I climbed into the car in my rose-colored prom dress, which had belonged to my grandmother. (I think this could have been a scene from a movie. I either looked ridiculously out of style at the dance or I somehow pulled it off). I lifted the skirt of my dress so as not to step on it as I climbed in. My date helped me up, and I sat down on the wraparound couch inside the car. Just as I sat down, one of the guys in the car leaned over to me and said, "Hey. Look." He showed me his cup. "I brought beer for everyone."

He knew full-well that I didn't drink, smoke, or do drugs—a real-life Sandra Dee—so, for him to shove a beer in front of me, the affront was at the least mean. He wasn't joking though. His goal was to get me to drink that night. The harder he pushed, the more adamant I was against it. The peer pressure was suffocating—so much so that I got really angry and carried a grudge against this boy for the rest of my high school years.

Back to my child's confessional: While it was a difficult night for all of us, it was also a chance to exercise our promise and put our money where our mouths were. Don and I were supportive and loving, concerned and heart-broken, but relieved by this child being able to share something so vulnerable.

Turns out there were other things this child needed guidance with, and we took the opportunity to begin counseling at a well-known, respected counseling center that was completely focused on kids. Our child had a good therapist. We went weekly for a while and then dropped to every other week until we petered out altogether. While the therapist was knowledgeable and helpful, none of us were skilled with sniffing out manipulation—far from it! We thought all was going well, but unbeknownst to us, everything was falling apart.

GASPING FOR AIR

Another chapter of acting out unfolded, and I began asking myself confrontationally, *"Who do you think you are?"* Any false sense of Super Mom that resided in me was whisked away with one swish of the broom, and I began gasping for air over the next few years. I was not who I thought I was—confident, cool under pressure (for the most part), attentive, loving—I became completely unhinged.

As a thirty-something mom of a tween and three teens, I herded quite the amalgamation of hormones, peer pressure, middle school, and high school and all that goes along with the lengthy stages of adolescence. Some kids have it easier than others. Some have tough roads to hoe. Parenting is no different. Kids from the same household aren't the same. Even twins aren't the same. Pick four people anywhere, put them in a room, and you'll get a combination of personalities and ways of doing things—none identical to the other.

I knew this about my kids. No one of them was the same—each distinctly and beautifully different from the other. Did I anticipate anything like this? Maybe a little, but not too seriously. A lot of parents assign, both seriously and in jest, labels to their children—"She's gonna be the drama queen. He's destined to be a class clown. She'll be one to raise a raucous. He'll be a career criminal. (Ha!)"

Was I prepared for the long road ahead? No. I did have somewhat of a foundation with regard to counseling and therapy language. I did not have any tools as a mom feeling desperation and no control of the situation.

CHAPTER THIRTY

NAIVE IS AS NAIVE DOES

The fall from the cliff was a slow one. There were lessons for me to learn along the way. I was still quite trusting, and I always opted for the benefit of the doubt when it came to the kids, but not long after the car confessional, odd things popped up. I discovered clues to misbehavior, but there was always an ever-ready explanation. True to myself, I saw each excuse as quite plausible.

Silly me.

These discoveries weren't for just one child. No kid was immune to my suspicions. One day while cleaning out a kid's closet, I came across what looked like a pile of blue jeans. As I untangled the chambray mess and pulled out the jeans, I tugged and tugged and watched in dismay. The jeans were all connected. One pant leg knotted on one pant leg, and on it went, one after the other. What I thought was a pile of soon-to-be hand-me-down clothes, took shape to be something entirely different. Five or more pairs of jeans tied together made one pretty interesting discovery. These weren't just jeans: This was a rope!

I confronted my child about this odd unearthing, and I was told that the "jean rope" was used for a friend who had spent the night and needed to leave early the next morning. However, being sensitive, this friend did not want to set off the exterior door chimes that might wake Don and me. So, the "in-jeanous" escape rope was launched out of the second-story window and tethered to something in the room to secure it from falling. This explanation made enough sense to me. I was a bit skeptical, but I took my child's word for it. I wanted to show trust.

At this point, the person that I thought I was at the time was a mom who knew her kids well. I often extended the benefit of the doubt and let out a long, metaphorical, not blue jean, rope of trust to all of the kids. My trusting nature, though, was naive and perhaps enabling. However, as I think back on the young mom that I was, I love her. I berated myself for so many blind trust issues, but, you know, how else was I going to learn? The education comes from the circumstances, and what you choose to do with them when you find out you missed the obvious.

Enter growth . . .

This wouldn't be the only time the wool would be pulled over my eyes. Not too long after finding the jean rope, I found an unopened six-pack hidden in a closet. I also uncovered some airline size bottles of vodka under a sink. When I confronted the would-be-perpetrator over these discoveries, I got an apology, and a classic response, "It won't happen again." Was I too trusting? Yes. Was I in denial? Probably, but the denial was clothed in my desire to believe.

Unbeknownst to us, some of these issues were brought up during church youth group. The kids were all involved in small groups, each equipped with a leader to help navigate the rough waters and challenges of middle and high school. The leaders were trusted individuals who lived the gospel message by example and provided an environment of safety and help. It was not uncommon to seek out your group mentor for comfort, direction, sympathy, and understanding.

There were, understandably, ups and downs in small groups. Some advice given was from experience and was well-founded. Other direction was well-intentioned, but, perhaps, untested. It wasn't uncommon to be told that more prayer, more scripture reading, and more faith were the keys to transformation and doing the "right" thing. I experienced these same well-meaning, but inadequate box checking steps in my own youth group growing up.

Unfortunately, praying more, praying harder, and reading the Bible more didn't (and doesn't) translate to perfection, and may not even lead to turning a corner. It can certainly be edifying to pray and read the Bible, but those acts were not practical solutions. Our kids knew how to pray, and they prayed. They also knew the Bible and had many stories and verses memorized. Sadly, giving a child advice like the aforementioned, setting them up for failure when praying harder and reading the Bible more didn't solve their issues. These internal feelings then led to shame.

As a mom, I was faced with the challenge of steering my kids in the right direction without shaming them. I know that I failed many times, but I learned a lot about the destructive nature of shame and the havoc it can wreak–short-term but also, inevitably, long-term. If only I could have read minds. If only I had the privilege to know the pain that was being carried.

STOP RIGHT THERE.

How does one pray harder? How does reading more scripture evoke change? These options may be helpful to some, but they are not solutions. Answers like these to a hurting, struggling child were poor choices at best, and detrimental at worst. Implementing change requires a safe space for vulnerability, honesty without judgment, and a hands-on, caring approach.

At that stage of my mothering career, I didn't have enough experience to know to ask some of the key questions of men and women leading and directing my children. I learned, though, to check with the kids to see how their small groups were going. I knew to ask about the leadership style and advice that was being given. I knew to check to see that they felt heard, especially at home.

As you can imagine, no amount of prayer or scripture was going to change the behavior. Instead, it only got worse. Think about this for a minute. Spirituality is great, but it is not a "fixer." Knowing how to talk to God, what to ask, and where to find encouraging words are great skills to have. However, whether you are thirteen or fifty-three, if you don't have the tools for change, if you don't want to change, or if you feel hopeless and alone, being "more spiritual" will have little, if any effect.

I didn't have first-hand experience with drugs or alcohol as a young person. I was naive to the signs of manipulation which perhaps put me at a disadvantage in the months that were to come.

Don and I were oblivious to any dangerous behavior beyond experimentation.

After youth group one Wednesday night, the kids came home and fell into their regular routine. Once they finished up their homework and eventually went to bed, Don and I followed our own ritual, put on our pjs, and went to the library to watch TV.

Positioned under the west-facing picture window in the room, there was a large, brown leather sofa. On either side of the couch were club chairs with ottomans, and on a right angle, there were two sets of French doors. One set had windowpanes from the top to the bottom and looked out into our front entry hall. The second set of doors was solid, opened into our bedroom, and could be closed for privacy.

COMING CLEAN

After a little television binge, Don and I headed to our room to get ready for bed. We closed the doors to our bedroom, brushed our teeth, and climbed into our king-sized bed. Don read on his iPad before going to sleep, and my head hit the pillow eager to drift off to dreamland.

Our room was on the first floor, and the kids' bedrooms were upstairs. It was unusual for any of the kids to come down to our room once our lights were out. However, right before I fell asleep, I noticed our main bedroom door open and softly close. About the same time, one side of the French doors slid ajar and closed quietly. Before I knew what was going on, two of the kids propped themselves up on the end of our bed in the dark. The sneaky nature of their arrival was unsettling. I sensed something was off.

To say the least, we were not prepared for what was to come. They both were equally and justifiably concerned about their sibling and told us that there were a whole lot of things that we did not know. Once we promised to keep this meeting a secret, details began to unfold. These two kids had been carrying a burden of genuine concern for the safety of one of their siblings. Telling us was their last resort, but they knew it was the right thing to do even if it felt like a betrayal.

Remember the jeans? Well, yes, they were knotted together as an escape route but not for a friend who was being polite and sensitive by lowering himself out a window so as not to disturb anyone. No. The jeans facilitated an opportunity for dangerous behavior.

We were told that their sibling had been sneaking out of the house, driving Don's SUV (at age fourteen) across town to a friend's house, partying into the night, and then returning home intoxicated, so much so that one night they'd hit a deer. The collision hadn't left much of a mark, and we had not noticed it.

While acting out isn't abnormal for teens, it was the first time that we had been faced with it as parents, and we feared for the safety of our child—not to mention the potential for a DUI, a stint in juvie, or, God-forbid, a tragic accident. As the four of us sat there in the darkness on our bed, we talked at length and asked questions. Once enough had been uncovered for the evening, the two kids snuck out of our room the same way they had come in and headed up to their own beds.

To say that Don and I were shocked would be an understatement. Did it seem plausible, though? Yes, it did, and the puzzle pieces began to come together. Had we been ignorant or provided some subconscious enabling, for instance, had our forgiveness been viewed as permission? We not only needed new boundaries, but we also needed an intervention.

I called the counselor who had been working with our child, gave him an update on the escalated acting out, and asked for help and direction. In his professional opinion, he suggested that we seek out some sort of treatment program. A wilderness program was what the counselor thought would help the most. I held myself together on the call, but inside I was nauseous and filled with anxiety.

The counselor also advised us to give our child the opportunity to come clean without our being accusatory or using language that would evoke a defensive or manipulative response. The next day, Don and I called our child into the library to talk. Being called into the library often put the kids on high alert wondering what they had done wrong. It wasn't always to talk about misbehavior, but if only one of them were called, more than likely, something was askew.

The three of us gathered in the room and closed the doors for privacy. Don asked our child, "Is there anything that you want to tell us?"

"No," they responded.

"Are you sure?" I asked. "We've heard there are some things that we need to be concerned about."

"I'm not sure what you're talking about," they said. So, I brought up the knotted jean rope, and then the story began to unravel.

Trying to get a kid to be forthcoming about something that they know is going to have negative consequences isn't always easy, and our situation played out similarly. After a few rounds of questions, we were able to get a lot more information. It was an opportunity to come clean, and many circumstances were shared with us. Some stories weren't a surprise. Others were. There was anger. There were tears. There were hugs, followed by our child asking for help.

We talked about options, and all agreed that we should look into a wilderness program. So, I researched many varieties of offerings and called facilities and camps all over the country—talk about phone calls that I never thought I would make. Each chat was gut-wrenching. I talked to a few parents who had been in similar situations. I gathered as much info as I could and at the same time thought, *How could I possibly be doing this?* All of it was surreal, and I felt disassociated, like I was floating above myself watching as I went through these foreign motions.

Don and I were at the point where we feared the worst. Not only was there immense anxiety over what could possibly happen but there was also anger, toward ourselves for "poor parenting" and toward our child for putting us through what felt like a nightmare. I looked at the wilderness program from the standpoint of "What else could we possibly do?" The way that the counselor guided us, we felt that some dramatic action needed to be implemented soon or we were doomed.

I want to pause here to say that I'm not telling this story to shame my child. The reason that these events are in here is because of what it took for me to deal with it and get through it. None of us wants to do the dirty work. I didn't want to be a mean parent. Our child didn't want to experience the consequences of poor decisions, but this is real life.

Our situation is mimicked in some form or another every single day. Parents are faced with tough decisions. There are no perfect ways to handle anything. Some are better than others, and we did the best that we could with the tools that we had. As a mom who chose to send her child to the wilderness for rehabilitation, I honestly did not know who I was in all of this. I did not know who I was that I would have to make such a decision on behalf of the welfare of my child. The fear of failure was hanging in the balance. The "what ifs" hung like weights around my neck. In the back of my mind, I understood the importance of going through the valley, but in the forefront of my circumstances, I was scared to death. What I know from looking back and from learning along the way, is that we were all setup for change, for transformation, and reconciliation. That's the beauty of the struggle, even though the struggle itself does not look so beautiful at the time.

GOING TO CAROLINA, only not in my mind

Unfortunately, this trip to Carolina was not a dream. It was for real. Tearfully, we landed on a camp in North Carolina. We chose this one for many reasons, two of which were, I had a faint connection to the admissions counselor and liked the rapport we had over the phone; the other being that we talked to some families whose children had gone to this same program. The overarching theme, if you will, of making this decision was that the younger we started, the better the chances of recovery into adulthood.

Naive, green, and unskilled in this area, Don and I did the best that we could in the circumstances and drove six hours to North Carolina, our child in the fetal position in the back seat for most of the trip.

Our mostly silent drive through the beautiful Blue Ridge Mountains was not reminiscent of any trip to North Carolina that we had taken in the past—trips to the majestic Grove Park Inn gloriously built just above Asheville, tours of the grandiose Biltmore Estate perched in the mountains with views of its property for miles, and my own childhood memories of attending Camp Greystone when I was a young teen.

This journey was laced with anxiety instead of anticipation, loathing instead of excitement, and pain as opposed to joy. Silence hung stale in the air of the car. It cloaked our shoulders and weighed on us as if we had put on a fur coat while sitting in the desert sun. There were not any appropriate jokes or light-hearted conversations.

Our car moaned and groaned up the mountainous incline; it whipped and turned, slowly zig-zagging. We rounded corners again and again and again. I felt dizzy and car sick. Our stories fell flat as the echoes of what lay ahead lurked in our minds and in our bodies—mostly it was torturous. I ruminated over whether or not we were doing the right thing. I didn't know, and I felt empty of options. How would we know unless we tried?

Upon arriving at the camp, we drove down a long, gravel, tree-lined driveway. We passed horses grazing in the fields and cattle lolling around, eating grass and grub. As we rounded the last turn through the golden Aspen of fall, we came upon a lodge-like cabin that turned out to be the intake center, ominous despite its ruse to feel like summer camp. Summer camp it was not, anything but.

There was no one about. No one to greet us. No one to point us in the right direction. We followed the signs and drug ourselves up the pebbled path, climbed the wood plank staircase, opened the squeaky screen door that slammed behind us and walked into the reception area. My stomach lurched. I wanted to throw up–not because the building was inhospitable, but because it poked the already tender bruises on my heart. I could only think, *Let's turn back. I've changed my mind. We can't do this.*

We did do it, though. We were greeted warmly, offered snacks and water, and taken to a conference room of sorts to begin the paperwork. I don't remember the exact moment, but at some point, early on, someone came to get our child to do an intake in another cabin quarters on property. I can still feel the horror that spun through my insides.

WTF were we doing? The best and weakest answer that I have is that we were doing the best we could with what we had, what we knew, and how we were counseled. Our urgent sense to save our child surpassed any other thought.

As we wrapped up the questions, note taking, and emptying of college funds, we stood, shook hands with the intake counselor, and said goodbye. We walked toward the door, and all I could feel was a hollow, gouging void. Still questioning if we were doing the right thing, we numbly took the stairs down to the gravel driveway, and just before heading to our car, we got to see and hug our child.

Right this minute, as I type these words, I can still feel all of the pain of that day. The wilderness program seemed like our only hope. I wanted to wake up from the nightmare. Yet, I was not asleep. I hugged my child, and gave reassurances; yet, all the while, it felt like a terrible betrayal. This event was the worst consequence that we had ever imposed, and I loathe recounting it.

Our only communication during the next six weeks was handwritten letters courtesy of snail mail. We spoke to the appointed counselor once each week and were caught up on progress and updated on behavioral changes. A few weeks into the program, Don and I attended a parent's retreat of sorts—retreat is not an appropriate word because it was not a retreat. It was torture. We traveled back to North Carolina and participated in small group discussions, workbook engagement, and camaraderie with others in similar situations.

One of the saddest parts of this parental retreat was the number of parents who had not told anyone else—not family, not friends, no one—that they had sent their child to treatment, and, on top of that, most of the teens that went to this program were taken by surprise, usually during the night, and escorted to the camp by counselors. As awful as it sounds and as harsh as it felt, the fact was that each of us was doing what we thought would help the most.

THE LAST LEG

Our third trip to North Carolina was the final one in this journey. We joined other families for an experiential weekend with our children that concluded with a graduation from the program. I will never forget seeing my child for the first time. As a group, we hiked with counselors up to an open area on the mountain. We waited here for the kids to arrive from beyond the trees and out of the woods. My heart raced and raced and raced. I so feared that my child would be terribly angry with me, but as the kids emerged, backpacks on their backs, they looked weary but happy, and my child came running to Don and me. We hugged so tightly, with tears, compassion, and relief.

The reunion weekend consisted of the parents participating in some of the activities that the kids had experienced themselves. We did group and individual therapy. We slept in cabins, ate food cooked by the kids, and participated in family games and learning. While we could hardly wait to leave, we did take tools with us that we used to the benefit of our whole family, all in an effort to improve communication, extend unconditional love, and provide an orbit of constant grace to all of our children. This story has a redemptive ending and a resurgence of trust, which is not easily restored.

One of the counselors from the wilderness program had said, "Trust is earned in drops and dropped in buckets." Think about that sentence. Imagine you have a large bucket filled to the brim with water. All is well. However, just as you think everything is hunky-dorey, someone comes along, dumps out the water, and leaves you holding a now empty bucket. There are no rivers or streams, no wells or lakes. Your only source of water is a slowly dripping faucet. You have no option other than to wait for each drip to slowly refill your bucket one tiny drop at a time—a very slow process. You're grateful, though, to have the water; however, in a split second, another mishap comes along, and your bucket gets turned over and emptied again. You have to start over, but this time with more trepidation.

As a mom, my tendencies were never to over-worry about my children. I wasn't a helicopter parent. Don and I encouraged the kids to advocate for themselves at home, at school, and with their friends. While we maintained our intent, the experience of having a child's mental health, well-being, and life in the balance, caused me to be highly anxious.

CHAPTER THIRTY-ONE

I CAN'T FIX IT

When we brought our child back to the atmosphere that started the collapse of trust, the reality was extremely difficult for me. I found myself on edge all of the time—worried, scared, I kept my eye on Find Friends way too much. If someone were not where they said they'd be, my heart raced. Looking back, I really don't know how I would have endured the situation differently. My heart longed to make everything okay. My "fix-it" nature wanted to wrap the package neatly and tie it with a bow, or to maybe use a lock and key to keep things from unraveling. Of course, this situation was out of my control. I could not fix it. I could not bar any of my children from eventually doing anything they wanted.

My heart landed in trust, trust in the promise that I believed—only God could protect them—not from hurt, because being hurt is the nature of a broken world. Not from poor decisions, because we have free will to make the choices that we want to make. But, instead, I trusted in the type of protection that God gives all of us—safety in his love and in his promise that we are never forsaken. If we don't have faith, what do we have? Eventually, I had to lay myself bare and walk through the process.

Given my worry and anxiety, the "trust bucket" was hard for anyone to fill. I was skeptical of everyone's moves. I imagined the worst. I drove myself crazy trying to control everything. One day, though, I'd had enough—enough of my own effort to try to return us to the way things used to be or to the status quo, whatever that was. I gave up on my ability or even capacity to guide life's thread through my needle of perfection.

Once I let go of the reins, I was able to turn to myself. I was the only one that I could control, and I worked hard. I wasn't the only one to plug away at change. All of us did. Through months of counseling, outpatient treatment, attendance in twelve-step programs, family meetings of honesty, and questions, there was beautiful, transformative healing unlike anything that I could have imagined, either manipulated or controlled.

I did not know the depths of my own ability to recover. I felt desperate. Alone. We waded through muddy waters and did the best that we could as parents. Imperfect but actionable and healing. Never did I consider going through a crisis like this, much less gain a new, improved form of communication for our whole family.

Were it not for grace and mercy, there would have been no healing. I am grateful for a God that is not a raging Zeus in the sky, but is, instead, one of compassion. One who offers not only a fatherly role, but also a maternal love that I believe is significant in the persona of the all-encompassing Love.

Crisis will change you. Any crisis. Great or small. None is to be diminished. Each has value. Each is to be honored because of what they offer us when we traverse the desolate plains and climb out of the hellish valleys. My crises have created an empathetic side to me, not because I understand everything that someone may be going through, but because I can, at the very least, empathize with the pain of life's challenges. The difficulty of walking through hard times with a child has shown me the importance of vulnerability and thoughtful communication. I view myself as more relatable, and I see a woman, a mother, who did the best that she could to help any of her children through a crisis.

CHAPTER THIRTY-TWO

FLYING THE COOP

As the kids grew and my role in their lives changed from their dependency on me to their independence of me, I've witnessed a shift that not only encompasses motherhood (once a mom, always a mom), but also invites a newfound friendship, an adult connection, and even mentorship.

At the time of writing, we still have a fourteen-year-old at home. So, we are not empty nesters, but with the growth of our kids into responsible adults we have been exposed to some of the feelings and newness around kids flying the coop.

While there was the traditional nest emptying that included the kids going off to nearby colleges and moving into apartments not far from home, it wasn't until they actually began moving out of the state and became self-sufficient that I suffered a crisis of identity—not for the first time, but perhaps it was the most poignant given that I was separating from a significant part of myself, one that had been part of my identity for more than twenty-five years. While my dream of motherhood wasn't being extinguished, its landscape and scope of need was drastically changing.

BROOKLYN

In 2018, our oldest son Baker was the first to fly the coop. At age twenty-two he moved from small-town Knoxville, Tennessee where he had attended college (Go Vols!) to big-city Brooklyn where he had landed a new job. From the physical move to apartment hunting, finding roommates, and embarking on a life of independence, he managed all of it on his own.

I think the distance of over nine hundred miles was the first significant impact on me; whereas prior to moving, he had only been a few hours away, and we saw him often. Now, however, coming home wouldn't be as easy as it had been; nor could it be as spontaneous. Instead, a trip to Tennessee now required pre-planning, keeping an eye on flights and fares, and making transportation arrangements to and from the airports. While the flight time to New York was less than the drive time to Knoxville, there were a whole lot of other factors to consider on each end, and soon, the distance began to feel expansive to me.

Our busy house got quiet. It was odd, unfamiliar. The number of cars that used to stack up in our driveway diminished. With one less child in the house, fewer friends stopped by. Not as many teenagers rumbled down the stairs. Our back door no longer opened and closed as much. One less person asked, "What's for dinner?" (Honestly, that was fine.)

The ambiance of our home changed. Each time one of the kids moved, a part of me moved, too. Their leaving took more and more of my identity as a mom away, opening spaces in me that I had long forgotten. There was no rush of chauffeuring kids to and from activities, no parent teacher meetings at school, no one to tuck in at night, and, while I didn't know it at the time, little pieces of me began unraveling. The unraveling turned to stitch cutting, and little pieces of momhood drifted away in the breeze—a slow tumbling at first, and then faster than a snowball downhill, the question of "Who am I?" became louder and louder.

Little did I know that these new adults would keep flying farther from home as our nest seemed to rapidly empty. In mid-2019, about a year after Baker moved to Brooklyn, Brennan received a job opportunity in Manhattan, which he eagerly accepted.

BROOKLYN: PART TWO

Brennan had been living in an up-and-coming area in East Nashville. He had two great roommates who weren't easy to leave, but being in the prime of life the allure and opportunity waiting in New York was too hard to resist.

While Brennan didn't have loads of furniture, he did have enough to rent a U-Haul. Once the U-Haul was full and loaded, I hopped in the passenger seat of the truck. We took to the highway and headed north to New York City.

Brennan drove the whole way, but I provided entertainment and support. As the crow flies, we traveled about 910 miles over the course of two days. I wouldn't trade that experience. I'd do it over and again. The memories, the laughs, the contented silence, the serious discussions, it was all worth every mile marker and more. In the passenger seat of the U-Haul, I looked with awe at my middle son.

On our second day of driving, we finally came upon the Holland Tunnel just outside of Manhattan. As we approached the tunnel, traffic slowed down, and the overhead signage forewarned drivers that there was a toll due ahead. There were warnings that credit and debit cards were not payment options. Cash was the only option. Given the fact that it was 2019, and people didn't really carry much cash anymore, we weren't any different. Granted, we had a few dollars and some change, but from looking at the signs, we couldn't work out what we were going to owe. We were both a little panicked and nervous, but we felt like we could manage. We were wrong.

As we inched toward the toll booth, a woman stepped out and said, "That will be forty dollars." My brain snapped *What?* My palms began to sweat. We didn't even have five dollars cash. Thankfully, and opposite the stereotypical New Yorker, this woman was very kind and was ready to help us. As we looked around, though, neither Brennan nor I could figure out how in the world we were going to get out of the toll booth area. We certainly couldn't back up. We couldn't go through because we were unable to pay. What were we going to do?

Lucky for us, as it turned out we weren't the first ones to have had this problem. There was an exit for unprepared people like us. Before we turned around though, the teller told us where there was an ATM where we could get cash, and then she explained how we could come back through. (I imagine that ATM gets a lot of business!) Brennan pulled the U-Haul truck forward, through the "gate of shame" held open by a policeman, and we headed to get our cash.

We followed the directions to the gas station, and, as we approached, we could clearly see that there was barely room for our big rig. However, Brennan managed to squeeze the truck in on the side of the lot while I went into the tiny mart to the ATM. I felt a little less than comfortable withdrawing money in such a tight, crowded space, and with my anxiety rising, I could not remember my PIN. *Ugh.* I tried and tried and tried. I began sweating and getting nervous. I just wanted out of there. Finally, the number came back to me. I grabbed our cash and jumped back into the U-Haul with Brennan.

Once I was buckled in, Brennan turned the truck around, and we headed right back to where we had been moments earlier, the toll booth at the Holland Tunnel. Intentionally, we picked the same teller to return to and thanked her for her help. She raised the gate and we drove into the Big Apple and headed toward Brooklyn.

Brennan managed to get us through the city with all of its traffic, horns honking, and drivers yelling. Once on the other side, we took the Brooklyn Bridge and went to Baker's apartment in Williamsburg.

Looking back, I cannot pinpoint the undoing of self in the moment. I believe as I mentioned earlier that the unraveling starts slowly and then spirals. I was present in the moment, and I was excited for both of my sons and their new lives in the city. I marveled at sleeping over in Baker's apartment, seeing him in his element and knowing that Brennan would claim his new identity and independence in "The City that Never Sleeps." My thoughts were abuzz and I had mixed emotions of loving and leaving. Two parts of my heart left to fend for themselves, if you will. Me? Eventually, I, too, was left to fend for myself.

Within a day or so of our arrival, Don drove to New York and joined us for apartment hunting. Over the span of just a few days, Brennan found an apartment in Bushwick and a roommate to boot. However, about six months after he moved, 2020 came in like a lion, and the Pandemic hit hard in New York. Brennan's company closed indefinitely, and he traveled home to spend the next six months with Don and me. Baker stayed behind working from home in Brooklyn.

CHAPTER THIRTY-THREE

SHUT IT DOWN

As Brennan returned home, in-person classes at schools and universities shuttered their doors, offices closed and took to meeting over Zoom, people sheltered in place, and the world became very unfamiliar.

Our daughter Cara, Brennan's twin sister, was in her last year of college at The University of Tennessee (VFL) when the world stopped spinning. All of her classes moved online, and she and her roommates decided to stay in Knoxville in their apartment until the lease was up; however, Cara got COVID. She was the first of us to officially get it.

However, both Baker and Brennan had been terribly sick in early 2020. Knowing what we know now, they both probably had COVID, but it was before there was a name for it, much less quarantine protocols, masks, or tests.

With Cara being so sick, our immediate inclination was to have her come home, but then it dawned on us that if she were to come home, then Don, Jordany, Brennan, and I would all be exposed. That would mean that Don couldn't go to work, and after that, a domino effect upon many dynamics would cause a lot of stress.

I hated telling Cara that she couldn't come home. She had packed her car and was ready to go when all of the COVID consequences struck me. Imagining her staying in her apartment, sick to the degree she was suffering was excruciating to me. Close to needing hospitalization, it was painful for her for obvious reasons and painful for me because I couldn't get to her to take care of her. Living in an apartment situation with COVID is less than ideal especially when you're the only one. Cara stayed in her room, wore a mask anytime she needed to grab something to eat, and suffered pretty much alone.

She cried when I called her back and told her that she couldn't come home. I felt awful. I cried, and all I wanted to do was go take care of her, but that wasn't an option. After a few more days of being miserable, she and her friend, who also had COVID, figured out a way to get to Franklin and quarantine together. Thank God. Given the situation, it was as ideal as it could have been.

Once Cara no longer tested positive and after the recommended quarantine period, she was finally able to come home. As the last few weeks of school rushed along, a decision about graduation hung in the balance—not just at Cara's school but all across the country and the world, for that matter. For some, walking across the stage, receiving your diploma, and celebrating with your graduating class may be of little consequence; however, I'd say most graduates wanted the pomp and circumstance and public acknowledgment of a job well done.

Cara was in the latter group. She had dreamed of her college graduation. Understandably, she wanted all the bells and whistles that a traditional ceremony would hold, and there was a lot of nervous energy around what decision the university would make. Hearsay and conjecture forecasted a fall ceremony, but as COVID got worse, and the outlook of the fall semester was in jeopardy, the university eventually made the call and canceled graduation altogether.

All of us were devastated, but none more so than Cara herself. It seemed her tears wouldn't stop, and there was little, if anything, that I could do to make the situation better. It was out of the control of any of us.

But what wasn't out of our control was the ability to make the very best of the situation as possible. So, Don, Cara, and I began thinking of ways that we could create a memorable graduation full of fun and celebration. Given the nuances of the pandemic, we had our work cut out for us. What we determined first, though, was that the ceremony should be at our home, in our backyard on our hilltop, stamped with many of our family's momentous occasions like birthdays and holidays. With the setting agreed upon, we began planning.

Cara, like friends before her, wanted a special graduation photo shoot poised in her graduate attire and traditional white dress. Ordinarily, she would have had this done on campus, but that was not an option. Instead, Brennan and Cara set out for downtown Nashville where Brennan snapped wonderful photos of Cara tossing her mortar board while a policeman kindly stopped traffic on Broadway. With the lights of Nashville's honky-tonks shining in the backdrop, she struck pose after pose in her personal photoshoot which also included shots of Cara popping champagne on the Pedestrian Bridge.

Meanwhile, back at the ranch, we worked hard on plans for the graduation. There are plenty of situations where Amazon has come in handy for me, never more so than on this occasion, though. Given "stay-at-home" orders, once again, Prime was a lifesaver for what we needed.

I spent days planning, ordering decorations and supplies, and crowning our house with signs and banners celebrating the graduate. If you were to have driven by our home at this time, you would have had no doubt about what was happening in our household. Don created a dreamy backyard setting on the hill behind our house. He hung string lights from the trees, set up chairs six feet apart, rigged a sound system, and cleaned and mulched the whole hilltop for our guests to enjoy and still be comfortable attending.

We invited some neighbors and family and had a great return of positive replies. Not only did we have guests coming, but we also had secret plans for speakers and for a commencement speech from a surprise guest. Once the streamers and banners were set and the flow of the ceremony determined, the big day arrived.

On May 9, 2020, my parents, my brother Rob and his wife, Jenny, and their girls, Ruby, Lola, and Phoebe, joined our family, friends, and neighbors to celebrate Cara. The guests mingled six feet apart and sat at equal distances per COVID protocol.

"Pomp and Circumstance" played over the stereo speakers as Cara climbed our backyard hill decked out in the regalia of a graduate with a robe, mortar board, tassel, and all. Seeing her walk up was beautiful. The image of her being escorted by Jordany through the imaginary partition between two trees will be a memory forever etched in my mind. Under the glittery, dangling numbers of 2, 0, 2, 0 and with guests settled behind her, Cara sat down, and our service began.

As he stood atop the hill with western valley views for a backdrop, Don welcomed everyone to our unconventional and exciting graduation, and I thanked everyone for taking the risk amid the pandemic to join us.

Because Baker lived in New York, and with all of the travel restrictions, he wasn't able to join us. However, he did get to "attend" live on Zoom. He greeted Cara from the screen of Don's iMac, gave a heartfelt tribute to Cara, and stayed with us throughout the ceremony.

Brennan spoke to Cara from behind the black music stand (our makeshift podium) facing the crowd. He delivered kind and tender words with a love that only twins can share.

The commencement address was pre-recorded, but very personal, as it had been sent by a very dear friend of ours who was working in London at the time. We all shed tears of joy as the sun sank lower in the sky and the twinkling bistro lights began to glow above us. Cheers and toasts from the crowd came one by one, each heartfelt and beautiful.

While I know that our homespun ceremony could not have stood up to the grandeur of a college campus graduation, I also know that this service could not have been more personal, intimate, and celebratory of our sweet Cara.

Not long after her stay-at-home graduation, and despite the pandemic, Cara got a job with a social media startup out of Arizona. She was able to take the job and work from home. Ideally, Cara would have gotten a work visa and moved to London, but that dream had to be put on hold.

As the summer moved along, Cara's job went well, but she really wanted the experience of living and working in another city. She was looking for an adventure, a challenge, a fresh perspective, and a new view–literally a change in landscape. Lucky for Cara, one of her best friends was planning to move to Arizona, and so the two of them got together and found an apartment near Tempe.

For some reason, I earned the title of "Primary Moving Partner," having moved Baker to college, Brennan to New York, and Cara from dorm to sorority house to apartment. Once again, I was honored, if not a little anxious, to be nominated to drive with Cara to Arizona.

CHAPTER THIRTY-FOUR

GO WEST

With an apartment chosen and a plan in place, Cara sorted through her clothes, tchotchkes, photos, books, furniture, and whatever else she wanted to bring to help get her started in her new home and new state, physically and mentally. My mind was boggled that my eldest daughter was going to move across the country. I was excited for her, but I knew that another piece of my heart, and my long-held identity as Mom, was perforating and tearing away. I was also well-aware that her move was part of her growth and would help shape the woman that she would become.

Once Cara decided what she wanted to pack, the two of us organized, boxed, and crated all of the various and sundry items she had picked out for her new adventure. In August of 2020, she and I packed up her beige Chevy Cruze, pulled out of the driveway, and waved goodbye to Don, Brennan, Eliza, and Jordany, and we started our thousand-mile-plus journey to Arizona.

Ironically, driving is not my thing. I get antsy and nervous with my hands usually at 10 and 4 or 9 and 3. My knuckles whiten, and my body tenses. This isn't to say that I'm not a good driver. I am. I learned from my grandfather, the car salesman, that when you drive, you should drive so that your passengers are comfortable. In other words, drive cautiously and defensively without sending your riders into cardiac arrest with speed and sharp turns. Jokes aside, driving at night or during the rain are both hardships on me. As long as I'm not going too far a distance I can manage, but I get halos, despite wearing my glasses, and an occasional mirage or two.

At any rate, you may recall that Brennan drove us to New York with me as the head cheerleader (and hopefully not too much of a backseat driver.) It was the same with Cara. Although I did volunteer to help with the driving, Cara wasn't really interested. I didn't blame her, and it was better for me anyway. In a way, we each had control of something—one of the steering wheel and the other of her sanity (which flip-flopped with the occasional, unavoidable anxiety caused by other drivers). All-in-all, I happily crossed the country with Cara as the designated driver.

Keep in mind, the lockdown was lifted, but COVID was still very much a concern. This was the first time either of us had gone out of state, much less across the country, since the pandemic. We had our hand sanitizer and masks at the ready and felt confident in our COVID protocol "training."

Over the course of the next two days, we spent twenty-four of those hours in the car. We watched the rolling green hills, farmland, and all fade into the distance as we left our sweet town of Franklin, Tennessee. The landscape flattened as we trekked west toward Elvis's Graceland, the best Memphis barbeque (or so I've been told), and home to the famous Peabody Hotel (*quack, quack*). From there we hung a right into Arkansas. I had taken some of this route in my past when I attended college in Abilene, only the drive to Abilene was a whole day shorter than this one would be.

Cruising toward Little Rock, then north in the direction of the Ozarks, and just past Fort Smith, Arkansas, we crossed into Oklahoma. Across Oklahoma, through Oklahoma City and bound for The Great State of Texas, the flat terrain began to get to us.

I'll tell you what. This drive was not for sissies. It was a helluva haul. We chased the sun and headed for Amarillo. We made it—not by morning, but by sunset!

Dear friends of ours with connections set us up in an oasis of welcome and rest. We pulled up to a lovely community where there was a cozy home for us to lay our weary heads. Exhausted, we showered and snuggled into the big king-sized bed, where we watched a little TV and drifted off into dreamland, or, that excited, light-deep-light sleep that you have when you're somewhere new and on an adventure.

ON THE ROAD AGAIN

We set our alarm for pre-dawn so that we could make the most of the daylight. We climbed into the car and watched as the August sun began to rise up from the dusty horizon. We were mesmerized as the first slice of orange began to blossom into pink, red, and yellow. Cara turned our car onto Interstate 40 West, and we hit the road again.

Leaving Amarillo, headed for Albuquerque, we spied markers for Native American reservations and watched as the road wound around through red rocks saluting us as they jutted up the sides of the interstate—a glorious, unfamiliar landscape. We still had miles and miles and miles to go.

To pass the time on our trip, we listened to several of Cara's favorite playlists, news reports, and a lot of podcasts. One that we probably listened to the most was

My Favorite Murder. Now, if you can handle all of the F-bombs, it's a great one for making a long trip seem to go more quickly.

Another podcast we chose had Michelle Obama as their special guest. The episode was promoting her new book at the time, *Becoming,* which I later read, enjoyed, and now highly recommend. If you don't know, Michelle is known for her motto: "When others go low, we go high." This First Lady holds a special place in my heart. There are many women who champion the power of those of us who are women, but I think Michelle struck a special chord with me because of her age (only a few years older than me) and her extraordinary circumstances—living in the White House and raising two young daughters.

I admire her as a woman of strength, dignity, and of major consequence. While I don't possess her stature and presence, I do hold her conviction of kindness first. This value is part of who I am and is non-negotiable in how I treat others—how I *desire* to treat others. I see that part of me, and hearing the same from Michelle, my convictions are reinforced, validated.

Her story from growing up on the South Side of Chicago to growing a beautiful family in the White House is wonderful. The challenges that she faced sometimes seemed insurmountable and many certainly were unfathomable, racist, uncaring, and mean. Michelle Obama carried herself gracefully and influentially as first lady, and she ushered change, diversity, and inclusion into the White House. Her goal was to bring "the people" to the people's house, and she did just that, especially with children. Some call her the "Forever First Lady." I tend to agree. Her mark on history is beautifully indelible and is stamped on my heart.

As Cara wound us round and round the mountain roads, we picked yet another podcast to pass the time on our journey. We landed on an episode called "The Baseline Killer." From the title, we knew it was, of course, a murder, but that was all we knew. As the podcasters began to tell the story, Cara and I were intrigued—up until we weren't, when our intrigue became horror as we learned that this ghastly assault and murder happened on Tempe, Arizona's Baseline Road, the very street to where I was moving my daughter.

As the recount of the events soaked in, we realized that the violence had happened a good ten to fifteen years ago, and that the murderer was arrested and convicted. We rested a little easier, but *what were the odds* that we would stumble upon a murder podcast, not only centered around right where we were headed, but also on the same road?

This unexpected reality slap stiffened my spine. Our ride thus far had been all fun and games, so to speak, but suddenly a dose of real life and the dangers of the world pushed its way into my thought patterns. I had to put those fears aside. Moving Cara to Arizona was part of the letting go process. She was the third of five to fly, and my role, my identity, continued to shift, even in that very moment. I saw myself emerging as a friend, encourager, confidant, and launcher.

Despite being shaken by the podcast, we knew our lives couldn't hinge on "what ifs," and we shifted toward positive thoughts as we entered New Mexico. Rolling through, tumbleweeds here and there greeted us, and in the middle of a blink, a roadrunner flashed right in front of us across the highway. New Mexico gave us a memorable greeting as we conquered its width and eventually crossed the state line into Arizona.

For some reason, our GPS kept us on I-40 West in the direction of Flagstaff. Despite my having been to Arizona many times, I had only ever flown, and neither Cara nor I were that familiar with the landscape. So, we put our trust in technology and followed the path laid out before us. It wasn't the wrong direction, but it was certainly not what we were expecting in the desert of Arizona.

In case you don't know, all of Arizona isn't flat. Yes, I'd heard of and been to the Red Rocks of Sedona and seen its splendor. I had also been to the Grand Canyon and knew that temperatures across the state varied widely. What we didn't have in mind was that we would actually be climbing pine tree-covered, green mountains—make that mountain after mountain after mountain. Once we took a left at Flagstaff, the landscape was anything but desert.

Cara and I began to get suspicious, but our GPS course couldn't be altered. We were at an elevation of over eight thousand feet, in the boonies, with no cell service. The mountains went on for what seemed like an eternity. Every time we thought we were done, we climbed another. When we hit the cute little ski town of Strawberry Park, we both busted out in laughter, sure that we were heading in the wrong direction, but we kept driving.

WIDE OPEN SPACES

We had no choice but to trust the compass which had us descending from the mountains, down into the plains, and to all of the wide-open spaces. Turns out, we had our Google Maps set for Phoenix, which took us over Tempe and through Phoenix. As the car rolled out of the mass of trees, The Chicks song "Wide Open Spaces" appropriately announced our descent into the desert. We watched the car's exterior temperature gauge climb right before our eyes. As fast as you could ski down the mountain, the thermometer raced to 100 and kept climbing until it reached 114 degrees. Man, it was H-O-T.

Don't get me started with the, "but it's a dry heat" nonsense. An oven gives off a *dry heat*, but would you climb into it because there's no humidity? Would it feel less hot? Nope. No way.

And so, it was for us, hot as hades.

As we reached the Phoenix area, we realized that we needed to update our GPS coordinates and enter the address to the apartment. Because we had put "Phoenix" as our destination, we spent a little extra time in the car and had to circle back around to get ourselves to Tempe.

About thirty minutes later, our countdown to touchdown was just around the corner on Baseline Road! With the apartment complex in view, we noted the southwest influence of the architecture—cream colored, concrete buildings, roofs adorned with terracotta, clay shingles that mimicked the dominant look of buildings and structures in and across Spain, Italy, Mexico, and across the Southwest.

Cara pulled the car up to the covered, arched entry way toward the black, wrought iron gate of what would be her new home. The gates were closed, and we didn't have a code yet. So, Cara used the call box to announce our arrival and requested for the gates to be opened, and they were. We scooted around different buildings labeled with single alphabet letters to distinguish one from the other.

Finally, we discovered Cara's building and pulled into a parking spot. When we stepped out of the car onto the pavement, it hit us that we had unwittingly climbed right into a 500-degree dry oven. Hot is HOT. We had no choice other than to get out, and as we did, the sun-baked blacktop whooshed up our legs and through our clothes as though we were standing Marilyn Monroe-style on top of a huge heater. The sun had zero mercy on us and thrust its rays upon us. Our skin immediately began to burn and sting. Keep in mind, this was August; Tempe had been heating up all summer long, and there was no relief other than air conditioning.

Not so lucky for us, we had a car full of apartment decor, cleaning supplies, clothes, and more to lug up Cara's new, third floor walk-up! Because of our excitement about arriving, we had adrenaline to get us started. Over and again, we climbed those stairs, arms full, energy waning, wilting, and withering quickly after each flight.

Soaked to the bone in salty sweat, we took a break to cool off in the AC. Once the car was unloaded, our mission was to head to Costco for supplies, essentials, and snacks from the coveted food demos peppered across the warehouse! Pulling up to Costco, we had a complete heat wave repeat—no less unnerving than what we had experienced earlier.

We got out of the parking lot as quickly as possible and trotted inside to cool relief. We scooted all over the warehouse and looked at every single thing in the store. Of course, we had to evaluate the need and/or desire for the plethora of offers afforded us. Soon want and need became indistinguishable (I'm sure our hunger alone didn't help), and we piled our shopping cart to the hilt.

Once we had our heart's desire, we loaded the car and got buckled in to head back to Baseline Road. The walk from Costco to the car plus putting all of the cart's contents into the trunk was enough to have us sweating bullets again, and we were ready to cool down again.

What we didn't realize, though, is that in heat like this, cars have a very hard time cooling down. Cara's AC struggled to produce any cool air. So, we rolled down the windows, but there was no breeze, only the hot air from the car's undercarriage moved in to mingle with the sauna in the car, which was now 117 degrees!

Once we got the goods to the apartment, we repeated the trek up and down the stairs until the trunk was unloaded and our Costco stash was in the apartment. I recall a self-initiated collapse on the floor—body prone, legs and arms shaking, this mom did not know how she was going to do this over and again for the next few days. There was still so much to do, to buy, to set up so that Cara could get off to a good start.

My reserves were spent. The heat was too much to keep up this pace, and I decided that from here on out, barring any "emergency" need, any and all purchases would be made online!

PRIME TIME

Prime rescued us and proved to be a much cooler way to shop. Plus, someone else got paid to bring the items up the stairs! Cara didn't have a bed yet, but her roommate had space for her, and I had hotel reservations nearby. After a lot of hard work that day, the girls drove me over to the all-suite, decent-enough hotel. When we drove under the porte cochere, I got my bags and hopped out. Looking around, the area seemed a little sketchy, but I went on anyway. I was so tired. I couldn't wait to get in bed.

Once I checked in and got my room number and key, I boarded the elevator. Just as the doors were almost closed a man slipped his fingers through the small opening, parted them, and jumped in. I'm fairly conversational and polite. So, I said, "Hello," and we chatted as the elevator inched its way to the second floor. As I got out, the man stepped out just after me. I gave him a friendly, "Goodbye," but before I could leave, he said, "You're so pretty. Do you like to party?"

My brain buzzed, *Umm . . . what?* Was I being hit on while by myself outside an elevator in a hotel in a strange area? I was uncomfortable, but in my best Southern kindness, I thanked him, and said, "No, I don't like to party." What else was I supposed to say?

He asked again, "Are you sure?"

Now I'm rattled. "Thanks for the offer, but no," was my comeback when I wanted to say something completely different; however, I also did not want to encourage any additional communication.

With trepidation in my spirit, I was determined to walk confidently down the hall away from the man and away from the elevator, and just over my shoulder, I saw several other men step out to join my "suitor." This made me nervous for my safety. As I proceeded down the hall, I intentionally passed my room and turned toward a room at the end of the hall that wasn't mine. I had my key and pretended to use it. Out of my periphery, I saw the men get back on the elevator and disappear.

When the coast was clear, I went to my real room, opened the door, rolled my suitcase in, and immediately closed the door. I set out the "DO NOT DISTURB" sign, turned the bolt, and flipped the extra security lock that makes the door almost impossible to open (unless you have one of those tools that security has—but I wasn't thinking about that). Still, I began to feel less and less safe. To help ease my fear, I pulled the sofa bed couch in front of the door for another layer of protection.

Truly, I was exhausted, and all I wanted to do was take a shower and collapse, but as I wandered around the room, I got increasingly anxious as I looked around. There were two queen beds. One for Cara in case she wanted to stay with me one night. I hemmed and hawed over which bed I would sleep in and settled on the one furthest from the door, which had the allure of safety by distance.

As most hotels do now, both beds were covered in white bedding—white everything—I guess so it can be easily bleached. Even though white can be cleaned fairly easily, some spills still leave marks and dark hairs catch in the threads of comforters and sheets. Unfortunately, both came to my attention on the bedspreads of each bed. The bathroom mirror had grimy hand marks down the front of it that made my spine tingle.

In my obviously uncomfortable predicament, instead of getting out of there right away, I thought, *Be a big girl. You're okay. Just lay down and go to sleep. You don't need to make a whole thing about this. Don't bother Cara. Suck it up.* This type of self-talk is such a perfect example of the pleaser in me. I'm willing to be afraid and alone rather than upset the "apple cart" of sorts. I don't want to bother anyone. Behavior like this is a fallback for me, a coping mechanism but one that isn't helpful for anyone.

Thankfully, this self-talk didn't work, and I thought better of myself and of the fact that I knew my daughter would not want me to keep quiet about my feelings. So, I picked up my cell phone and called Cara. Cara is calming and settling. She's rational and smart, and she said there is no reason for me to stay where I feel unsafe. So, she and her roommate, Caraline, left immediately to come get me.

Both Cara and Caraline are women who can hold their own and own it. I felt relieved that they were coming. I tidied up the room and got rid of any appearance that I had been there. There was a knock on the door, and through the peephole, I could see my saviors!

I grabbed my purse, wheeled out my suitcase, and stepped into the hallway. A nanosecond before we turned toward the elevator, Cara quickly changed our direction. Apparently, the group of men had returned and were loitering around the elevator. We walked to the end of the hall to take the stairs instead. When we opened the door to head down, the stairwell looked as though someone had turned on a fog machine—not too heavy but just enough to be suspicious. The scent of weed wafted through the air, and with heads high and quick on the steps, we passed one person after another on a "smoke break," not employees. Without incident we exited out the exterior door and were right by Cara's car.

We returned to the apartment. Cara and Caraline shared the bed, and I slept on the air mattress by choice. If you've ever slept on an air mattress, you're probably aware that your quality of sleep is at high risk of suffering. Any movement I made caused air to leak. The mattress got too soft. So, I added more air, but then it was too hard, and its grooves of plushness were less than plush. The night was short, but I was safe and sound.

The particular hotel that I had booked was fairly close to Cara, but I didn't know the surrounding neighborhoods, and I picked an area that was sketchy unbeknownst to any of us. Lesson learned.

There was another "lesson" that I had learned in the many years that I had traveled to the greater Phoenix area. You could never go wrong in Paradise Valley. So, I quickly booked a nice casita on a beautiful resort property. Because it was August and not many people come to this area in August because *it's an oven* and because travel was suffering from the effects of COVID, hotels, especially the nice ones, were hurting for business.

To my great surprise and delight, I booked this beautiful property for pennies more than my previous spot which did not seem to be suffering from the pandemic given our experience. At any rate, I had a lovely room with a king bed and a nice bathroom, and it was located just a few steps from the pool!

This time around, Cara *did* stay with me. Who could blame her? We spent the next few days ordering from Amazon and the next few evenings in the pool (which felt more like bathtub water, but it was still cooler than the air), drinking cocktails, and watching the sunset. Not too shabby.

Cara and I did the best we could to get her as set up as possible while I was there. We found a bed for her at IKEA—or, as Brennan would say, "the Lego store for adults," because everything has to be put together. Cara and I spent some sweet mother/daughter time together in Phoenix. We laughed and shaped memories to hold for a lifetime. When it was time for me to leave, Cara drove me to the airport, and what had been giggles and smiles was now a mixed melody of sad, happy, and proud tears. A familiar scenario raised its head again, and I found myself leaving yet another piece of my mother's heart and another part of my identity.

It was pretty strange to have Cara drop me off at the Phoenix airport knowing that she was going to turn around and begin a whole new life, and I was flying home to another version of myself yet to uncover. Discovering and rediscovering who I think that I am leads to more unraveling and self-revelation—some of which I was willing to look at and grow from. Yet other parts have been held until the writing of this book, the deep-seeded versions of me that I have long kept buried.

CHAPTER THIRTY-FIVE

KANSAS CITY, HERE SHE COMES

In May of 2023, Eliza graduated from college. She had finished her last two years of school living outside of the home but close by. This had meant the number of people living in our home was down to three, which was an adjustment for us.

Just before Eliza graduated, she and her boyfriend, and their two Chocolate Labs, hit the road and moved to Kansas City, Missouri. She had lived in KC for just two weeks before she came home to walk for graduation. It was great to have her home for a long weekend.

(Yes, Eliza *and* her boyfriend moved to Kansas City. They moved in together. And, yes, I was more than okay with it.)

Part of discovering myself at my age and stage was coming to terms with what matters most. I reasoned that although boyfriends and girlfriends living together was frowned upon by some, we were in a new generation and I'd moved on from a lot of "rules." I am an accepting person and try my best not to be judgmental. In these circumstances, I saw nothing but joy and adventure for two young people.

While I wasn't recruited to drive to Kansas City for the move, I did show up (invited) a few weeks after Eliza's graduation. With her boyfriend training for his job in a different state, being on her own in a completely new place had Eliza feeling a little down—insert Mom! I suggested to Eliza that a visit from her fun (at least I like to think so) mom was just what she needed, however, I didn't go without Eliza being in hearty agreement. My baby girl was gone on her own in a brand-new stage of life. She lived in an unfamiliar town and was alone with her dog, Scout, while her boyfriend and his lab were in Oklahoma for a couple of weeks. My heart raced to see her, and this seemed like the perfect opportunity.

If there's one thing that I enjoy, it's helping my kids in whatever (reasonable) way that I can. Part of who I am is being a nurturer, and I also love to help the kids set up their new spaces—whether rearranging their rooms at home, settling them into the status quo of dorm decor, or helping them design a new apartment. So, Mom, the nurturer and interior designer, boarded a plane for Kansas City.

On a cold, overcast, blustery day, Eliza picked me up at the Kansas City airport, and we couldn't have been happier to see one another. She and I had a lot of fun designing her new apartment. We peppered it with her personality and worked to give it a coziness that felt like her home. We shopped at IKEA and bought an area rug along with some other odds and ends. I also gave her the same Costco treatment that I had given Cara, and while the sun had been shining, it had not been as hot. There'd been a strong northerly wind sweeping over the plains (*brrr*).

Eliza and I had a fun few days together. We ate out, ordered pizza, slept in her king-sized bed, and toasted to her future. All night train horns blew announcing their presence at a crossroads of the tracks, the sound only slightly familiar to me from when I was a little girl and train tracks ran behind our home. This was not my home, though, not a past home, a current one, or one for the future. This was Eliza's fresh start, and there in Kansas City, just like in Tempe, I left another one of my baby girls. We shed tears when she dropped me off at the airport. The air in my lungs stifled a bit, my voice cracked inside. On the outside, though, I reassured her and affirmed her move because I knew she, like her siblings before her, was ready to fly, fly away.

I am a woman who connects. I am an introvert, but I am drawn to authentic relationships. To be able to have community with my children is more than I could ask for. Being with Eliza did my heart good. I enjoyed seeing her apartment, helping her where I could, and creating some special memories in her new stage of life.

BEACH, BEACH, BABY

Since the initial writing of this book, Eliza moved again—south to Florida to be near the ocean, my dream location when it comes to beaches. I always wanted to live on the ocean and be able to walk out my door and onto the sand. It is my holy space, my ultimate connection to God and the universe at large.

In retrospect, I don't think that I "knew" I could move out of town. It's not that I was told not to live away from my parents. It's just that I thought that's what I was supposed to do. I went away to school (finally) and lived in London for a semester, and I guess it seemed like that was it for me as far as living away goes.

At any rate, Eliza, her boyfriend, and their pups are as happy as I've ever seen them, and I get to visit them. However, what I've come to realize is that my dream of beach-living can still become a reality. It's never too late. Is it?

CHAPTER THIRTY-SIX

SHIFTING SAND

If you teach your kids to fly, then you've gotta let 'em fly high in confidence and with love. If you're an empty nester, how does it feel? Have you had challenges? Do you worry about your kids making it on their own? What about how this affects you? I'm talking about the "Who do you think you are?" you. Are your kids months away from moving out or years away? You may not want to consider it now, but I wish I had—not because I needed a plan to know what to do but because it's like I'm holding my breath until the last one leaves.

Where did I make room for me when I helped move my children out? Where was I in the process? Lost? Did I even know who I was? Maybe not in the moment, perhaps only in reflecting. My joy was connected to, even contingent upon, the happiness of my kids. I suppressed reality. I did not want to feel any sense of abandonment or touch the chords of sorrow that I felt deep down. All I wanted at the time was for each child to understand they were being launched with every bit of love and approval that I had within me. In the years following, I allowed what I had pushed down all that time to surface. Rather, maybe it's not that I allowed it to surface, but that I no longer had control of it, and the wholeness of the question: "Who do you think you are?" has come roaring to the forefront.

On his podcast, *Ten Percent Happier*, Dan Harris interviewed Dr. Gabor Maté, renowned doctor and best-selling author. During their discussion, Dan asked Dr. Maté about his journey to becoming a "real boy." In essence, the question centered around self-discovery and at what point you find yourself, or for the purposes of this book, when can you answer the question, "Who do you think you are?" Maté replied, " . . . this task of becoming a real boy is really a lifelong one."[9] He goes on to say that the process of becoming is emotional work, relational work, and spiritual work. In my process, what I surmise from his observations is similar to what I've discovered in my life's research from past to present. We are always becoming. There is no end to change. We can refuse to accept it, but it's there, nonetheless.

Life with kids living all across the country has moved the needle of expectations of both me and my adult kids. I'm straddling the line of some still having a dependence on me, but four of them fully independent. When life looks a whole lot different, how do you adjust and create your "new norm"? As Don and I raised the kids, the years seemed to crawl along, but in hindsight, those years slipped quickly through my fingers, like handfuls of sand that I couldn't hold onto.

The adjustment was hard. As I write today, I am fifty-four. We began moving our children from college campuses to career destinations in 2013. It's 2024, and we still have one to go.

CHAPTER THIRTY-SEVEN

YELLOW PETALS

In the late winter of 2021, our family suffered a devastating loss with the untimely death of Don's sister, Elaine. Elaine was a light and a joy. At times when I didn't know who I was, when I suffered from imposter syndrome, she was always there with the perfect card for my circumstances, an unexpected gift, a handwritten note left on my kitchen island when I wasn't home, and always, always, *always* a compliment that I felt undeserving of. Whether by a good word about my parenting or my personality, she brought a smile to my face.

Elaine wasn't just this way with me, though. She adored the kids and followed in the footsteps of her mother, Dee, with sentimentality, excursions, gifts, and love. We waited until early spring to memorialize her when the seven of us could all be together as a family. We joined together on a beach trip, specifically to remember Elaine.

Knowing of our loss, our Airbnb host left beautiful yellow flowers for us when we arrived. One day, I pulled a couple of the roses out of the vase, peeled off the sunshiney petals, and gathered them in a bag. Our whole crew went down to the ocean. Waves scurried to the shore in a bit of hurry, only to draw back as soon as they arrived. The sky was hazy, and the rays of the sun were diffused through the clouds giving off a soft light. That day on the Gulf, though, the wind was brisk. My hair whipped around and slapped me in the face until I got a hold of it and pinned it back.

Because of the northern breeze, the cloud cover, and the fact that it was barely 70 degrees, there was a noticeable chill in the salty air. As we adjusted to the temperature and spread out our blankets on a rather lonely beach, I took out the rose petals. I gave each person their own handful of petaled gold. One by one, we walked into the surf, spoke personal sentiments, and whispered goodbyes. Each in our distinct way tossed the rose petals toward the ocean. We watched as ribbons of yellow whipped and twirled in the wind. Little golden boats landed on the water, and rested on the waves—back and forth, the tide washed them forward and backward, to and fro until they could no longer sustain the grip of the water's current; and they were wooed out to sea toward the horizon.

I'm a person who enjoys rituals, personal ceremonies, and intimate conversation. Saying goodbye to Elaine on the petals of roses over the ocean was each of those to me, a new ritual of remembering, a personal ceremony between Elaine and me, and an intimate conversation with echoes of love whispered in the breeze. Part of who I am is a poet, and memories that mimic poetry are always sure to remain in my mind. This special time was no different.

Elaine, you remain forever in our hearts, forever in the sweet memories of the times we shared together.

CHAPTER THIRTY-EIGHT

WE'RE MOVING OUT

When we returned from our trip, the emptiness of the house, and my desire for change drove my thinking in the direction of a big move for us. Not only did it seem like the time to let go of our home of more than twenty years, but the real estate market was on fire.

When the pandemic was essentially over, our home began to quiet down again. Baker and Brennan were in Brooklyn. Cara was in Tempe, and Eliza was in Kansas City. Don, Jordany, and I were left in a big house with more room than we needed. Plus, our home needed major renovations and updates to properly house us. In all honesty, we were tired—tired of the upkeep, tired of appliances quitting one after the other, and tired of "keeping up with the Joneses."

It seemed as though everyone had the same idea about moving, only we weren't really prepared for the big surge of people across the country who wanted to move to our little town. Life had slowed down considerably over the past few years because of COVID, and the newfound freedom in the work-from-home-or-anywhere movement had lured thousands of people to hone in on quaint, boutique towns like ours was.

Franklin is thirty-five minutes south of Nashville. When Don and I had moved to Franklin in 1994, it was just beginning to sprout. Homes in Franklin were more affordable than in Nashville. The quality and pace of living was very conducive to families, and the public school system was ranked number one in the state. In the mid-1990s, there was a lot of allure for young couples to move from Nashville to Franklin to buy starter homes and raise families.

Honestly, I had never considered moving to Franklin until Don and I started to look for our first home. We kept driving south until we came to Franklin and found a cute, new construction home that we could afford. My parents gifted my car to us, and from the sale of it, we had enough money to make a down payment! We had fun picking out prefab selections, colors, and our facade. Once the home was finished, we packed up our townhouse in Nashville and moved south.

Our new neighborhood was in a large Planned Urban Development (PUD) that eventually topped out with around two thousand homes—from apartments to starter homes, mid-size and large, the neighborhood catered to middle- and higher-income families. We loved our first home, and one of the perks of where we had picked was that the market demand rapidly grew as did the equity in all of the homes.

Our first home was on sweet Summer Haven Circle, where after about a year we were pregnant with our first child, Baker. About two years later, we discovered that I was carrying our twins, Cara and Brennan, and another move ensued shortly after their birth. Eighteen months later, the proverbial baby bump erupted with Eliza, and we were on to our third home where we finally settled for the next twenty or so years.

In spite of the great recession in late 2007 to 2009, the homes in our neighborhood never lost their value, which was the case for most real estate in our county. When 2021 rolled around, and with the influx of West Coasters and big-city transfers, the housing market went through the roof—literally.

You may recall that decorating is a favorite pastime of mine. Put it up there with a love for architectural design, and you might not be surprised that another pastime of mine was ogling over new homes on the market. At one time my drive was "bigger is better." I welcomed the passing of that stage, though, because at my age now, I know that more is just more and is not always better—especially if you have to clean it!

My dad once told me, not too many years ago, that it took him decades to realize that with every purchase he made, came a new responsibility; and, unless you had loads of help (and money, and a place to keep all of it), carrying a never-ending load of accumulation is enough to break your back, your bank, and your desire for more.

There's a quote that runs through my mind on infinite repeat. It's one that I read and re-read from childhood. On my mom's bedside table, she had a framed, watercolor card that said, "Contentment is not the fulfillment of what you want, but the realization of how much you already have," (Author Unknown). That truth is seared in my mind. Do I adhere to it? Not as often as I wish, but I'm certain that the more that we put those words into practice, the better. Quoting it isn't enough, but it's a good place to start.

ROLL YOUR OWN WAY

At any rate, back to the housing market. Given my love for new houses and the allure of change combined with the astounding equity in the home where we lived at the time, it's no wonder that come spring of 2021, I had the moving bug. I didn't just have it; I had it bad!

Unfortunately, my unquenchable drive came on the heels of Elaine's death. Don had a lot to process, and it was too much for him to consider moving. He wasn't opposed to it, but he didn't have the capacity to do anything more than give a nod in agreement. When our real estate agent told us what he thought our house would sell for, it seemed almost a no-brainer to both of us. We didn't know that we would ever have this type of equitable opportunity again.

Was this the right thing to do now? In hindsight, maybe not the best idea at the time. Home prices continued to rise, but it was a seller's market. There were plenty of homes for buyers, but not without bidding wars and excruciating prices that escalated in a ridiculous manner. Again, though, we didn't have this information. No one did.

My wheels turned so fast at the prospect of paying off debt and buying a smaller home, that I pretty much rolled right over Don's feelings. Being a sensitive person, I knew, if only in the back of my mind, that I was pushing it. It's not that I didn't care about Don's feelings. I did, but I laser-focused on moving, and, in my "looking back" opinion, I selfishly took the opportunity and ran.

Consider this for a minute: Have you ever just gone on with something in a "damn-the-torpedoes" manner? Thinking about who I am, it was uncommon for me to roll this way. Remember, historically, I'm a pleaser. It's my nature to go with the flow and not upset the apple cart. However, there's also another way for me to reflect on this time in my life. It's rather historical—going "against" my nature, pushing for what I wanted. Inherently, there is nothing wrong with that. Look back at what I wrote previously. My sensitivity to Don is genuine, but did I shame myself as I explained my drive to move? I did. Was I really being selfish or were there needs of my own that were crying out to be taken care of?

Debt was a reality. Money from the sale of our home could relieve that stress. Home repairs were daunting. Moving gave us the opportunity to get out from under those looming financial obligations. Our home was large and only three of us lived there. Downsizing was a good idea, and being the primary housekeeper, I would have less to clean. A new home would be exciting, an adventure, and I was looking for a spark, a respite of sorts, a change of scenery. So, moving was self-care for me.

I've had to reconcile a lot of change—four adult kids gone, one tween home, new town, new schools, new way of life—so much unfamiliarity and a lot of adjustment. Life without hard things isn't really life, is it?

GET IT OR IT'S GONE

Don and I bid on more homes than I would care to go into. Bidding was draining, and losing was devastating, especially when I'd already imagined myself in the home and had mentally arranged the furniture. It was hard not to get attached. After all, we knew what we wanted in our next home, and when the dream was dashed, recovery was a challenge.

Recover we did, though. From losing a farmhouse built in the late 1800s (a blessing in disguise) to the possibility of building a dream home to the consideration of living in another tightly built neighborhood, our selections pretty much ran the gamut, but none of these homes were in our current hometown.

The more we looked, the faster the prices rose. The longer we took to "win" a home, the further away we were pushed from our desired location. Don and I were both set on finding a home with a little property, some privacy, a wooded lot, and no HOA. We couldn't find this dream home in our price range within a reasonable distance from where we wanted to be.

The anxiety and stress seemed to pile on. Looking for a home is fun, but it's also laden with important decision-making. The search started to take a toll on me, and I could feel anxiety, depression, and fear creeping in trying to make room in my being. Not only were these unwanted side effects of home shopping, but they were also markers that caused me to put my foot down harder on the gas pedal. Both Don and I felt the need to start compromising if we wanted our next home to meet the dream we had conjured.

PROMISES, PROMISES

Reluctantly, we widened our search circle and added a new zip code to include homes that better suited us both affordability-wise and aesthetically. Finally, after months of house hunting, we were introduced to a beautiful new construction home on a wooded lot with both privacy and neighbors, and no HOA! The only problem was that the house was located an hour from where we had been looking and fifty minutes away from my parents.

However, given the extraordinary circumstances of the market, its inability to provide us with closer options, and our desire to move from my parents' home where we had been for the last nine months, we decided that a compromise was going to have to be implemented. The new home was well-priced, or, at least, it was originally. We saw the house in February, and it wasn't completed until early April, but the agent/builder would not sell us the house prior to its completion. They, like so many others, wanted to put it on the "bidding block" and hopefully rope in a big, fat profit. One couldn't blame them, that's what all the sellers wanted, including us when we sold, but that had been almost a year ago.

The selling agent continued to encourage us to hang in there, lured us with (empty) promises on price, and we hung on because of the appeal of the home and the hope of an end to our fruitless search thus far. When it came time to bid on the house, the seller priced it at least fifty thousand dollars more than what we were originally told, and we walked right into another price war bidding against another alleged buyer.

THE CONCESSION STANCE

I'd like to say that this wrapped up in a lovely win-win situation, but I would be lying. Basically, we were "had." When you bid against another buyer, you have to decide if you're going to make concessions. One concession that was popular was to forgo the inspection. We were willing to do that on a new construction home. Thankfully, for the home built in the 1800s we did have an inspection, and that saved us from falling into a money pit!

Another concession that buyers often made at the time was opting out of the home appraisal. Doing this wasn't too much of a risk, if at all, because of the rapidly rising home prices. Your agent could run some comps of the area, and you could be pretty sure that the gamble of no appraisal would be worth it. That's what we decided to do. We needed to do something to make our offer look better than the other offer, and this did the trick. We won!

Well, kind of. Waiving the appraisal turned out to be a poor decision in this case. Unfortunately, the appraiser deemed our new construction home not worth the price we agreed to pay. The logic was that there were no "good" comps of other new construction homes. So, the appraiser shot low. Both our agent, and seemingly the selling agent, were flabbergasted. Don and I were devastated because we now had the hurdle of the bank approving us for a larger loan against a home worth less than what we needed to borrow.

When it was all said and done, we managed to get the money that we needed, but we failed to pay off all of the debt that we planned to eliminate, and we were stuck with a mortgage payment not too much lower than what we had with our previous home. Nonetheless, we were overjoyed to have a home, a new one at that, in a beautiful setting with no repairs needed.

CHAPTER THIRTY-NINE

WATERLOGGED

Finally, Don and I were able to take the next steps in our new chapter. The transition wasn't easy—not for us or for Jordany, who was pretty devastated about leaving the town he knew, the school he loved, and the friends he'd made. Jordany did, however, get to finish his sixth-grade year at his current school. During the week, he lived with my parents, and on the weekends, Don and I brought him to the new house. We did this for a month, and it worked out just fine.

Move-in day was super exciting. My creative energies were rolling and my appetite for change was being fulfilled. Our furniture had been in storage for nine months, and we were excited to see everything again—until, well, we weren't. As the movers unloaded boxes and hauled in our furniture, including antique family heirlooms, we began to notice a trend of wet boxes and damp dressers, hutches, clothes, and more. We unpacked boxes to the putrid smell of mold and mildew. Not all of our items were damaged but enough were that it was fairly devastating. Family pictures, framed art, photo albums, and other sentimental items including the girl's prom dresses, my mom's homecoming dress, and loads of knick-knacks and baskets from family trips.

I was disgusted. We were disgusted. Our storage agreement included insurance, dampness control, and a controlled temperature environment. We quickly learned that dampness and temperature were not a priority for this moving and storage company, at least not where our items were concerned.

The ruin of material things is insignificant in the long run. Obviously, memories and relationships are what we cherish most, but I'd be lying if I said my spirits weren't dampened (along with a lot of sentimentality). Eventually, we managed to work out a settlement with the moving company, but what we received paled in comparison to what we lost.

To this day, I find myself looking for an item that I cannot find anywhere, only to realize it was probably trashed or lost to negligence.

We rallied though. All was not lost, and we had a beautiful new home to put our personal touches on, and I fell right into my love for decorating and designing.

NATURE CALLS

We've experienced a lot of joy in this new home. I finished my book with my computer set up in my nook of an office, on my desk facing the woods outside. I've had the privilege of writing with an amazing background of nature: a beautiful, deep forest that is dense with green in the summer, filled with color in the fall, and tinted gray and white in the winter—sometimes with new fallen snow on branches and bushes. I watch the hummingbirds at my feeder filled with red deliciousness, where they vie and fight for a spot. One stands guard of the nectar; another dive bombs and knocks the keeper from his post. Back and forth they pounce on one another. It's a wonder anyone ever gets a sip.

There are not just hummingbirds to spy, but we also have all kinds of woodpeckers. Did you know there was more than one species? They're amazing. The jackhammer of their beaks echoes through the valley of trees, and their squawky calls linger in the air as they talk to one another. Birds, birds, and more birds are part of our life now as are the deer who birth fawn in the woods, the turkeys who strut their stuff down the driveway and, in the evening, leap into the trees, claiming a branch as a berth and pillow. Everywhere nature calls and gives its divine inspiration.

GETTING TO KNOW YOU

Over the last two-and-a-half years, our family has made new holiday memories. We've hosted friends for visits on our back porch, met new neighbors (some now like family), and we've worked to settle into this new start. Over the past forty-eight months or so, though, we've also been challenged in ways that we somewhat expected—making new friends, finding new favorite restaurants, and managing the sixty-minute drive to and from my parent's home.

What I didn't expect, though, is the depression that came with the move. Quite honestly, I thought I'd rally from feeling down and stressed over finding a house to buy. In a sense, I did, but a new home in a new town doesn't make up for what is lost to the old and familiar. Twelve months into our move, I hardly thought I could make it another year. I spent months glued to my chair in the living room, either on my computer or another device. I stuck my butt down hard on the lovely back porch bed swing and spent hours without moving. I wasn't moaning over the move all of this time because I was also enjoying the move at the same time. However, the din of down began to drown out the positives that I constantly worked on conjuring up in my mind.

At some point, I did make a concerted effort to get to know the town. I found some sweet, new spots to frequent for coffee and a couple of boutiques for browsing. I made friends with staff at my new favorite bakery, and I even managed to meet enough people that on occasion I would run into one or two at the grocery or hardware store. Getting to know my new hometown was a challenge, but I did make progress. What I didn't do, and am still working on, is find my place in this new world—my friends, my people, my heart.

Making friends is hard no matter your age, but in your fifties and in a new city, finding someone to gel with is impossible—well, not completely so, but tough, nonetheless. Even once you've found your people, friendships take time, energy, and commitment to blossom and grow.

I spent days crying until I could no longer cry, and once my tears were spent, I locked down the dam—I didn't allow even a trickle. I stopped moving my body. I stayed stuck. My hot flashes and menopause didn't help. I gained weight, like, every morning I woke up with something bigger—my thighs (God help me), my tummy (God help me), my boobs. Seriously, I would argue that I truly added a pound every day. My energy waned. My focus blurred, and my vision got weaker.

My fixer mode kicked in, and I buried myself in all the self-help that I could find. Books, courses, podcasts, inspirational sayings—anything, everything. I took a course on the vagus nerve and tried applying breathing tactics to help my stress riddled body. My weight gain caused me to hate my body, and hating my body caused me to move less and eat more. Even when I did start moving again, the pounds kept piling on.

I discovered a counseling site that offered help with eating disorders and a promise of insurance acceptance. I signed up for online treatment with a counselor until the company informed me that my insurance said they would not cover it. I did, however, have three sessions without charge.

Another better nutritionist came along, and after months of considering what she had to offer, I made the financial commitment and enrolled in her support group with four other women. I made inroads toward loving myself and gained a better understanding of my body and its needs. This was not a weight loss group. The focus was to learn how to eat to nourish our bodies, demystify food restriction and rules around what to eat and what not to eat. I had a lifetime of unlearning to do. The benefits I've gained from what my coach taught me are immeasurable and possibly lifesaving given my affection for disordered eating.

Despite all of the hard work of learning and unlearning, I still managed to feel completely alone—a loneliness I had never really known. In all honesty, I'm quite proud of myself for how much I put into relieving my symptoms of depression. It wasn't easy, but it also didn't warrant enough success to draw me out of despair. My psychiatrist was helpful, but more depression often meant more meds or new meds or both. Our insurance was horrible and continued to create more of a nightmare by denying coverage as I desperately tried to relieve my symptoms. I felt numb, indifferent, and stuck—very, very stuck.

IN THE WOODS

You know the saying, "You can't see the forest for the trees"? Well, that was me. All I could see were the trees in my way blocking my view of happiness ahead.

At some point the fun of the new house wore off, and I ached to find the joy that I had lost in our move. There is a path of thinking that tells us that what we really want when we are down is the feeling of the positive, exciting experiences we've had in the past. I get that.

I can conjure up what it feels like to be on a beautiful vacation, or with family at the holidays, or even the feeling that you get when you buy a new car. Those memories and what they felt like remain locked in our brains. We can turn our mind's record and our brain's memory into those feelings, and it helps. However, for me, I need—I want—my circumstances to change. The *feeling* of change is not enough for where I am.

Less than a month after we moved into our new home, Don lost his job, and over the course of the last two and a half years he has worked his ass off to bring in income. Don is a hard worker, an entrepreneur, smart, and successful, and despite those admirable qualities, launching a new business, building it from the ground up, and earning the support of new clients is not for the faint of heart, and it is not easy.

Over the years, we have been able to live on money that, quite honestly, I wish we didn't have to use. Our settlement with the movers provided a couple of months of income. My jobs brought in a minimal amount of support; we reluctantly pulled from our 401k, and, unfortunately, our savings had to do the rest until it was almost drained.

Our ability to get a loan was squashed. We couldn't move. Friends and family helped where they could.

Jobs came in, but they didn't stay long enough. We lived feast to famine. It felt and weird to live such a luxurious life with blessings a thousand-fold yet to be encumbered by the weight of financial responsibilities that could hardly be met and lack of income to boot. This combined with not loving where we lived wreaked havoc on my emotional state. Don would say as much himself.

Communication lines between Don and me have gone through strenuous and stressful times. There has been anger, compassion, annoyance, kindness, understanding, and confusion—all the feels across all of the spectrum. However, our love for each other remains.

I KNOW. I DON'T KNOW. I KNOW. NO, I DON'T.

Who am I at this stage of life? If nothing else, I am resourceful, but I'm also very tired. I know that my words don't fall on deaf ears. I know people who feel the same and live this same quality of life. Living this way is hard for the healthy person, but for the person who suffers from mental health issues, like I do, it's hard to see the light at the end of the tunnel.

Do I know that it will not be this way forever? I do. Things change. I have lived long enough and experienced enough to know that we will not stay in this same place. It's the dissatisfaction of knowing that pulls me down, sometimes. I can't see the forest for the trees. How does that work? Do you have to cut down the trees or do you get glasses? Maybe you do a little trimming and get your eyesight adjusted. I'm trying to figure it out.

What I'm grateful for is that Don and I are committed to one another. We are determined to get through this phase and onto the other side. I do want the greener grass—my grass, not anyone else's. I need a break. I'm ready for the season to change.

I would be dying to this never-ending season if it were not for my friends and family, my therapists, my medication, prayer and meditation, and the God of the universe who loves me unconditionally. If it were not for my job outside the house, I don't know where I'd be mentally, physically, and emotionally. I do know that I wouldn't be writing right now. I don't know if I'd even be able to get up. I do know that because of the intimate, sweet community I have in my new town at my new job, I'm able to get up each day and look forward to a few hours with friends. I don't know if they know just how much they mean to me. I do know, I will change that.

What I'm discovering about myself, in this stage of life, is that I'm not the same person that I was two years ago, much less two months ago. Thank God, I'm changing. I'm not melting away—yet. To get through what feels like the melee of life right now, I'll have to get through the trees. It's never easy "getting through." It's always hard, but I know that I have to do the hard things if I want to survive.

CHAPTER FORTY

DO THE HARD THINGS

Speaking of hard things, some of you may be familiar with the podcast *We Can Do Hard Things*, with hosts Glennon Doyle, Abby Wombach, and Sister (Amanda Doyle). I've listened to loads of episodes and have learned that I'm not alone in the hard things that I'm trying to do. There are so many women that I relate to and who relate to me. We are not doing life by ourselves even though it may seem that way sometimes.

As a culture and over the last few years, women have brilliantly emerged. We have recognized the blatant patriarchal society that was built, crafted, and created by men to reduce women in every way imaginable. While I know that this man-driven culture started forever ago, it boggles my mind that here we women are—still in our place. Things are changing, of course, but there is a lot of environmental learning that has yet to be undone. The notion of man as dominant has got to be hard to unlearn, but while unlearning it is critical to creating an equal society, we as women (especially those who grew up in hardened patriarchy) have behaviors that we need to change.

If this society (not exclusively Western society, mind you) has created cultural barriers that prevent women from being fully their own, then we have an obligation to do what we can, either in or out of our comfort zones, to break the cycle.

Stereotyping men or man-bashing is not my agenda; however, it's past time for men to recognize inappropriate cultural norms and where they stemmed from, and how they can change the course for future generations to treat women as equals. I, too, am learning to change my own behavior and recognize where I am succumbing to old patterns of submission to men. Slowly, but steadily, I am learning to speak up for myself. As an introvert drawn to codependency with a pleasing mentality, this is not an easy task, but it is empowering.

That very empowerment is one strength of character that Don and I longed to instill in our daughters. While we gave them encouragement to use their voices and stand up for themselves, as we reminded them that they can do anything they set their minds to, ultimately, this power was theirs alone to claim. They both did, and I am so proud.

I believe that as my daughters expressed their independence from patriarchy, I, too, gave myself permission to do the same. Both girls are examples to me in a role reversal—one I claim wholeheartedly.

This claim is meaty. Perhaps it is key to unlocking me. Maybe the very empowerment that I witness in my daughters is, even if indirectly or through osmosis, where I came to ask myself the question, "Who do I think I am?"

While I struggled to answer this question, and while I looked for direction, I happened upon episode 156 of *We Can Do Hard Things* entitled, "Jane F-ing Fonda." Great title, huh? Certainly grabbed my attention.

Actually, I hesitated to listen to this interview. Why? My first thought was that, despite the title being compelling, I didn't want to listen to someone amazing while I tried to figure me out. I wasn't feeling amazing at all and was down on myself and my writing.

Just as I decided not to listen, I just as quickly changed my mind and tuned in—mostly because I was driving and did not want to be distracted looking for something else. You know how it goes? Oftentimes, just what you think you don't want or need is exactly what you've been looking for. This was the case for me with Jane Fonda's story.

Jane's story is filled with pain, abuse, self-shame, and more. It is also filled with accomplishments, awards, accolades and strength for herself and for her causes. She's always been an activist. She is also human, and because she has been willing to be vulnerable, she has encountered transformation.

Part of this transformation for her came through her research on herself and her own journey. Jane says essentially that in order for her to find herself, she had to go back and see where she had been. This hit home for me and echoed possibilities for me in my own self-discovery.

Jane had a lot of her life physically documented—between being a famous actress today and having grown up as the daughter of Henry Fonda, her resources were thick with discovery.

However, what I took from these few words of Jane Fonda was that for me to understand myself, I too needed to go back and research where I had been. I needed to discover how my life circumstances had shaped me as a woman. In that self-reflection, I found the desire to extrapolate how my past circumstances gave way to the pleaser, the co-dependent, and how through the years, up until the present, I've been able to change the trajectory toward a woman who knows more about who she is.

I am valued and worthy. I have permission to speak up. I am strong. Being my own woman is definitely an all-encompassing definition of who I am and who I am striving to become.

CHAPTER FORTY-ONE

WRITE ON

I'm fairly certain that I was dealing with imposter syndrome long before there was a name for it. Who was I kidding? Sure, I'd written poetry pretty much since I had clear penmanship—hundreds, maybe thousands of poems. Sure, I'd submitted articles (with fewer posted than published). I'd helped edit others' books. I'd had blogs. Yada yada.

I'm not sure when I wrote my first poem, nor do I know where some of my earliest poems reside. For most of my life I wrote with pen and paper—sometimes it was a verse on the back of a church bulletin or maybe a poem inside my Bible. Certainly, many scraps of paper containing half-started ideas were tucked into the spines of books and journals.

My gift for writing came from my mom. She was always a writer and a wonderful poet. Her poetry inspired me to write my own. I started with basic rhyme schemes with one word in every line rhyming with another—sing-songy and simple.

As I grew and my life experiences became more intense, more meaningful, and more evident, my writing matured. Prior to that maturity, though, there were many emotional poems written over break-ups. Sad ones. Angry ones. Confused ones, and ones that were more prayer than poem, but they were prose, nonetheless.

Who do I think I am? I've come to know that I am a writer. I'm learning that I can do hard things. I'm emerging. I'm blossoming.

The Second Half of Life

When my voice cannot find the words
My writing often can
When I do not speak up for myself
My prose often does

My intention is to meld
My words with my voice
And to discover who I am
In the second half of life

CHAPTER FORTY-TWO

DROWNING IN DISORDER

Our world is filled with so much disorder.
Disordered thinking.
Disordered eating.
Disordered society.
Disordered expectations.

Our world is also filled with so much discontent.
I want to fight.
I want to move.
I want to start.
I want to go.
I want to stop.
I need to get back.
I can't go out.
I am stuck.

I believe Western culture has defined the concept of normal and abnormal behavior with unrealistic, insensitive limitations. We've become somewhat enslaved to ideas such as "more is better," "skinny is pretty," "fat is ugly," and so on. Striving for perfection has seeped into our subconscious and has created a perception that "perfect" exists within the parameters as defined by societal norms. Living a life constricted by these false claims that perfection is attainable in any form is unrealistic and chaos producing. Even so, we are trained to reach for the rungs of a ladder that goes nowhere yet has no end.

In my seventh-grade year, a new girl began attending our school. Through word-of-mouth, my mom connected with her mom, and Elizabeth became not just a carpooler with us, but also a friend. Elizabeth was a year younger than me. Her family had moved to Nashville from California to be closer to relatives.

With long, chestnut hair, smiling eyes, long legs, and a whole lot of enviable beauty, Elizabeth had a physical appearance that I longed for myself. At barely five-three, I obsessed over my short legs and wished they were slenderer and at least two inches longer. Up until this point, I hadn't thought much about exercise. I was an active child who played outside every day, ran through the woods, jumped on the trampoline (Thanks, Dad!), and joined many a kickball game in the field on our property.

In middle school, Elizabeth suggested that the two of us try out for track. I hadn't run track before, but I recalled that my mom had. At the time, I did enjoy running and being a part of a team appealed to me.

My motives for joining the track team were more complicated than just participating. Like I said, I was an active kid. I didn't overthink exercise. Moving was part of my daily routine. It was at this juncture, though, that I became more in tune with the mentality of exercising to lose weight or to keep weight off.

THIGH HIGH

Honestly, I don't know that the issue of weight gain in particular had been in my purview. However, the size of my legs had always been a source of contention in my formative years. Genetics were an unavoidable factor, and I was assured that "big thighs" were going to be part of my life forever. Despite this, my parents always complimented my beauty, my legs in particular, and in doing so they gave me a sense of contentment. However, buried behind that was a manipulative monster, a cruel inner voice waiting to pounce on my innocent heart. The haunting tape replayed over and again in my head, and I set myself on a course to prove it wrong.

Running made my legs stronger and prettier. Running did not, in my eyes, cause my thighs to shrink. Not too long after starting track, I discovered eating less and exercising more did give my legs a slimmer appearance because of muscle tone and weight loss.

Through middle school and high school, I had some sweet friends who suffered from eating disorders. In fact, looking back today with the knowledge that I have now, there weren't many of us who didn't suffer from some type of disordered eating or another. It wasn't uncommon for girls my age to over-exercise and eat very little to create a caloric deficit. Another similar approach was a diet restricted to favorite sweets and lots of exercise. I was vulnerable to disordered eating, and, while I did not want my friends damaging their beautiful bodies, I was unhealthily intrigued by their methods of achieving such beauty.

My mind churned as I tried to figure out how to produce similar effects to my own body. Throwing up wasn't an option for me. I tried gagging myself over the toilet, but I just couldn't do it. I intensified my exercise, running or walking more, and then I heard of a "trick" that the wrestling team put to use when they needed to make weight—you guessed it—laxatives.

Some of the wrestlers chose the wrong time to use their laxatives, though, and at least one surely regretted having taken one before running around the track. Regardless, with that, I had strategy for staying thin in mind.

While it never occurred to me at the time, what I know now is that I had fallen into the siren trap of the Western "perfect body" mentality. In fact, I was born into it. We all were. Disordered eating in America is hard to escape.

On and off through the years, I took Dulcolax to expel extra food. That I recall, I never revealed this about myself to anyone. Embarrassed and ashamed, this part of my life remained a secret up until this writing. The fat phobia mentality plagued my thoughts. I secretly compared myself with other girls my age. Sometimes the comparison helped me feel better about myself and other times, it made me feel worse and drove me deeper into a tangle of conflicting thoughts as to whether I was enough just as I was.

There were countless times when a comment about my size, my weight, my legs, or my thighs created negative tapes in my mind that stayed on replay throughout my life. One boy that I dated was warned by a male figure in his life to be careful about "girls like me." Why? Was I a bad influence? No, that wasn't the reason. This mentor to my boyfriend told him that shorter women were more likely to "get fat," and he insinuated that I would, too. Unfortunately, this guy thought it was appropriate to share this nonsensical information with me. The words were hurtful and shaming. Callous comments like these only strengthened the devil on my shoulder who told me that smaller was better. My resolve and determination to prove this theory wrong only led to me buckling down harder to fight the fat, the cellulite, and anything that might stand in the way of keeping my legs, at the very least, the size that they were.

In college, I exercised to eat. If I wanted dessert, then I needed to work it off. If I wanted that gourmet "forbidden" dinner, then I needed to refrain from eating for the whole day up until suppertime. If I wanted to drink alcohol, then I didn't eat at all—at least not until the munchies swept over me after midnight. Then it was no holds barred, and time and again I gorged, only to start the cycle all over again.

Recently, I talked to my psychiatrist about my eating behavior. In fact, I reached out to her because of this book. My writing opened Pandora's Box of disordered eating behavior, and it kind of freaked me out that I had tried so many schemes to stay my size or get smaller.

My psychiatrist asked me if I binged. Of course, I binged. But then she asked me if I purged. As I thought about her question for a moment, I answered, "No." I told her that besides taking laxatives decades ago, I didn't purge. Then she said, "Do you ever exercise more or harder after you've eaten what you consider too much?" I replied, "Of course, I have. I've even exercised more profusely *before and after* eating too much."

Her response stunned me. She said, "Well, then you've been purging." What? Her words really struck me. Whether I was oblivious to over-exercising as a form of purging or whether I had tamped that down to inexplicable depths, I don't know, but it was a revelation—an important one. We, especially those of us who identify as female, have ridiculous pressure on us because what the societal definition of "normal" is when it comes to eating and exercise. We exercise to eat. We vomit to eat. We stomach (or don't) diarrhea. We starve ourselves (and binge later).

Then the process repeats itself, over and over and over again.

Do you know what truth has been so clear in my mind lately? *We were born to eat!* Many nutritionists have said that if you are thirsty, you don't deny yourself something to drink—so if you are hungry, you shouldn't deny yourself food. At any rate, here I am, still learning after a lifetime of preoccupation with my body image, my self-image, and my food.

CHAPTER FORTY-THREE

DIET DRAMA

In high school and college, my self-imposed goal was to remain at one hundred pounds as best I could. I weighed often and exercised more. An extra five seemed to loom at every turn, and I was hell-bent on disproving the unsolicited fate of the freshman fifteen.

Do you remember the Fat Gram diet? If you eat fat you will get fat? Dang. It made so much sense to me.

The answer? *Duh.* Stop eating fat! I think this was when my serious, nutrition label reading began. Every single food that entered my mouth was vetted by its fat content. The closer to zero the better. All of that granola I was eating instead of eating lunch—well, it had to go, and suddenly I understood why I was having such a hard time losing five pounds. Seriously? How many times had I tried that one?

Later, as I matured into my thirties and forties, it dawned on me that any time you cut out a food group, you're likely to lose weight—if you don't replace it with something else.

This is called the "elimination diet," which is every diet. Anyway, it's all enlightening to me, and as I learn, I continue to become aware of where I eliminated, restricted, and purged.

After my study abroad program in London, I moved home to Nashville for the summer. I reengaged with hometown and college friends that I hadn't seen in a while. How I discovered this, I'm not quite sure, but one friend asked another friend of mine how I looked upon returning from overseas. Their response was that I looked good but had definitely gained weight.

With that, I took up another diet of sorts—seemingly healthy, but I'm pretty sure that the health benefits were only reaped if your food intake was more than one banana almond shake a day. Eating just that frozen treat combined with long runs up and down hills and valleys did the trick, and I got my weight back down in my comfort zone.

While my fear of getting fat remained, I did believe that I was pretty. My genes, despite the thunder thigh inevitably (insert eye roll), were really good. With blue eyes, lashes for days (thanks Dad!), and thick, blonde hair, I did turn heads now and again, but that was not a substitute for being at home in my own body. I also did not want to be liked or disliked based on how I looked—stereotypes easily come into play when we make judgements based on the cover and not the inside, but my thin mindset was constantly reinforced, unintentionally, by so many around me. Not only that thin equals beautiful, which is wrong on so many levels, but I was baptized in the cult of cultural thinness.

When I was diagnosed with major depressive disorder in my late twenties, I had Prozac to thank for a drop in weight. During that period, I vividly remember Don and I going to a party where we saw friends that we had not seen in a long while. I wore my white, bootcut Joe's Jeans and two-inch platforms—both excellent for creating a lean silhouette. Almost immediately, an old friend came up to me and said, "Laura Lyn, you look fantastic." *Boom!* I knew it was because I was several pounds lighter than the last time that he had seen me. Skinny mentality reinforced.

One Christmas, Don and I went to a party to celebrate the holidays. When we arrived, the hostess gave me a sweet hug and then said, "Laura Lyn, I didn't realize you were so small. Have you always had such a tiny waist?" *Boom!* Whether she meant it as a compliment or just a statement, I took it as fodder for my continued fight against fat.

Tiny. I liked being called tiny.

There were many instances over the next two decades when I was pumped up by being called "small." I gave myself three cheers when I was complemented for how good I looked, perhaps smaller than ever. "I've never seen someone so tiny," one person said (there were plenty of tinier people, but I thrived on this feedback). When asked about my children, people were always surprised to hear that at the time I had four kids. "How in the world do you maintain your size? I can't believe you have four kids, and twins? You're so little."

Yes, give me more!

The feeling of my flat stomach felt so good against any waistband. One year, while I was walking on the beach in Jamaica wearing a bikini and enjoying the ocean, a woman stopped me and said, "I've never seen someone with such a flat tummy. How in the world is it so flat?"

Ah, more skinny kudos for me.

The truth is my stomach was always flat. I did one hundred sit-ups and lots of pushups every night before bed starting somewhere in my early teens, and because I kept an eye on what I ate or exercised to negate the calories, it's no wonder my stomach was smooth and "fat free."

The first time that I ever experienced a plump tummy was with my first pregnancy, and with that pregnancy came loads and loads of permission to eat. I needed the extra food. The baby needed me to eat. All of a sudden, food was a free-for-all, and I had the perfect excuse to indulge everywhere that I wanted to, and in any sustenance that soothed my long-restricted body.

Other than premature contractions, I had a pretty healthy pregnancy up until I didn't. I gained seventy-two pounds and was swollen and sick with edema, toxemia, and preeclampsia. These issues primed me for the emergency C-section that I had at thirty-seven weeks. I recovered and somehow, lost all seventy-two pounds, and my stomach bounced back to its pre-pregnancy flatness.

The story was different when I was pregnant with our twins. The whole pregnancy was great. I gained about the same amount as the first, but, heck, I was carrying two! During those nine months, I eagerly returned to overindulgence but with a bit more restraint. I delivered healthy twins at thirty-six weeks.

This go around, however, my tummy did not spring back at all. My extra weight fell off fairly quickly, but because my stomach had been so thoroughly stretched over carrying two babies, its "fat" fate became an atrocity for me. With two hands, I could pull the mottled skin four inches away from my abdomen. There was so much loose skin that I had to tuck it into my pants. Honestly, I was mortified.

For a period of time, I tried to reconcile my unsolicited tuck-in teammate by reminding myself that this extension of my core represented a huge accomplishment—"battle scars," if you will, to reinforce the notion that I was tough, had the scars to prove it, and the twins to match.

THE INTERNAL SCALE

Over the next two and a half years, my depression and anxiety increased. The large flap of stomach skin continued to not just bother me, but self-inflicted disgrace ruminated in my head and, it became impossible to quiet the disordered voices that taunted. I felt fat. I could not see my beauty without defining it physically. I loathed tucking my tummy into my clothes and my OCD was over-the-top.

Less than a year after our fourth child, Eliza, was born, I was diagnosed with an abdominal hernia. It protruded through the ripped muscles of my stomach just above my belly button. The hernia was about the size of a small baking potato. It needed to be repaired.

I was thrilled. (I know, right?)

Because of my obsessive thinking, I had conjured up many thoughts about how to eliminate the sagging skin on my belly. A tummy tuck was the obvious answer, and in my mind, I had been angling for some way to get one. Suddenly, this hernia gave me the chance I wanted. As opposed to seeing a general surgeon about its repair, I went to a recommended plastic surgeon in Nashville. With an abdominoplasty, the doctor would be able to avoid a vertical scar up my middle and instead use my C-section scar as an entry to sew up my abdominal wall. With that, he could also pull all of the loose skin down and remove it.

I was thrilled (again).

Insurance covered only the hernia repair, but Don and I figured out a way to pay for the tummy tuck plus some liposuction on my thighs to get rid of my abhorrent cellulite.

The mindset that I operated from was akin to vanity, but it stemmed from an eating disorder and body dysmorphia—two serious issues that needed attention. Unfortunately, I didn't have enough information at the time to recognize my condition and society was quite affirming of my behavior. From the first time that I ever heard the term liposuction, I knew that I wanted to do that someday. I had been teed up for it. Oh, to be rid of the culturally unacceptable lumpy and dimply thighs that were my genetic fate.

There was nothing glamorous about my plastic surgery. The hernia repair and tummy tuck were painful. The recovery was worse than healing from a C-section. I could hardly look at the stitches that trailed like ants from the top of one hip bone, down the pelvic bone, across my pelvis, up the opposite pelvic bone, to the top of the other hip bone. There was a bag attached with surgical tape on the inside of my thigh that served as a collection point for fluid, blood, and puss that drained from the tube connected between the bag and my stomach incision. All of it was gross. I had a lot of pain. None of it was fun, but it's what I wanted, and the end results were worth it to me.

My stomach was restored to its pre-pregnancy flatness. The surgeon stitched me a new, odd belly button because the other one had disappeared when he pulled all of the skin down to remove. I walked away with a huge, U-shaped scar from hip to pelvis to opposite hip. My legs were slimmer than ever, and the cellulite less conspicuous. I was happy (for the moment), and I experienced a return to physical self-confidence that I had not had in a long while. The issue was that my concern for my body was because of a disorder, and when left untreated, unrecognized, or undiagnosed, disorders don't heal. They return.

Logically, it would seem this season of life would be wrapped up here, with my body issues resolved.

Flat tummy? *Check.*
No cellulite? *Check.*
Thinner thighs? *Check.*

As you can probably imagine, this was not the end of my fight against my body. Having the physical changes was one thing, but without a change in mentality or a repaired relationship with my body, my disordered eating and body dysmorphia continued and is still a challenge today (although I have gained tools to help myself through counseling).

Earlier I wrote that during my junior year in college, while I was abroad, I went vegetarian. As I said earlier, anytime you eliminate a food group, you can expect a change in weight. However, as you may recall, one thing that friends noticed when I returned from Europe is that I had gained some stones, not lost any. Well, the fact that some of the best vegetarian options overseas were butter and cheese sandwiches, one can only imagine why I didn't return home a Skinny Minnie.

Fad diets were a consistent part of my life. There was the fat-free diet, Weight Watchers, Nutrisystem, food combining, carbs only, no carbs, the Engine 2 Diet, liquid diets, fruit fasts, intermittent fasting, and on and on. Food restriction, rules around eating, and naming food "good" or "bad" was exhausting. Do you know how much of my life, my valuable time I spent not eating? A minute would have been too much.

Suffice it to say that I've experienced a lot of damage and deprivation around eating. I know that I am not alone. There has been a significant shift in society's acceptance of all body shapes, but it hasn't been enough. It won't be enough until the status quo of thinness is ostracized—no longer part of our learning curve, kicked out of the equation. It takes an exhausting toll on mental health with so much hyperawareness, and it's a lose-lose scenario.

Being painfully aware of my struggle, knowing that I need to love my body, stop shaming it, and treat it with the respect it needs is ever present in my mind; yet, it's difficult for me to answer the question of who do I think I am with respect to my self-worth and how I measure up because, for so long, the measuring stick was my own, internal scale (more or less).

The process of shifting my mindset is slow. The tools available are many but putting them to use is the challenge. I am working on it, and it's important work to me. I want to be free from the preoccupation with size and body image. I want to open my eyes more fully to the beauty around me and shift my focus from the size of my body to the beauty of who I am as a human being and what I have to offer. Easier said than done as age, change, and self-doubt creep in.

There are parts of aging that I have enjoyed. There are other parts that have kicked my ass because I wasn't prepared. How could I have been? The information I needed for the "transition" wasn't available. The research wasn't done. The generation before me had nothing to say on the topic because, well, it was taboo talk. What transition am I talking about? The one that told me, "You don't know who the fuck you are." The one that led me to say, "I'm going to find out."

CHAPTER FORTY-FOUR

(WO)MENOPAUSE

Wonder why it's called "*men*-opause"? Because men, yes, men, coined the term, did the research (not on women though), and closed the book. For centuries, medical and clinical trials only included men. Only in the last few decades were women included in the studies. Pretty crazy. Just think: Men always wanted to be in control of the woman's body, in everything from our right to choose to our right to female-based research studies. How else are we going to know how we, as women, are affected? Just like men shouldn't be treated based on a female control group, women should not be diagnosed based on how a male reacts. People of all races, color, and ethnicity need to be included in studies. Sadly, the White, male researchers did not see it that way at the time. Comparing apples to oranges will never produce adequate, much less accurate, results, and that has put us behind.

With that said, I recently learned that menopausal studies with women did not begin until the 1980s. Seriously. The 1980s! I've listened to many podcasts on the subject, including *The Mel Robbins Show*, episode 87, called *From PMS to Menopause*, where Mel interviews Dr. Amy Shah.[10] "Dr. Amy," as she's affectionately called on the show, is a leading expert in women's hormonal health. Not only is hormonal research on women fairly new, it's also a topic that has long been left off of the table, especially for menopause and the changes related to this monster nicknamed, "reverse puberty." As more people talk about, write about, and read about menopause, the door will continue to open and help take away and explain the scaries.

For me, perimenopause started early as did menopause. At age fifty four and having been postmenopausal for several years, I wish that I had had more information to prepare me for what my generation of women and doctors didn't know. Too often, the unknown becomes unspeakable, and morphs into a topic never highlighted or put on the table for discussion because it's "inappropriate." My hope is that this mentality is finally over and better understanding, acceptance (by all genders), and acknowledgment of its reality will rule the future. In some countries, menopause is celebrated. That's right. It's a milestone worth acknowledging–a job well-done. Guess what? These women experience more positive symptoms. It's worth looking into and reading about. Think about it. Mindset. How we view something can dramatically change how it's perceived, negatively or positively.

As I've aged, my weight has shifted. Blame whatever, but it's just a fact. Talk to my friends. They'll tell you the same about themselves. This is a wild phenomenon. In the U.S. and in Western Culture, we're a band of sisters experiencing a similar metamorphosis.

Clothes that I used to wear no longer fit. I wore these clothes for decades! I do not know who I am in my *new* body. It is a new body. I dare someone to say otherwise. The changes are real. I have more curves in different places. I have fuller hips. I have larger thighs, more cellulite, and a pudgy tummy. I even have boobs!

Can you believe that most of my life, aside from puberty and pregnancy, I've been a teacup? I had a friend who used to tell me, "A champagne glass full is enough." Think old-fashioned champagne glasses—the shape of a martini glass. Picture holding one up to your breast and tucking it inside. If it fits, it's enough. If it overflows, then you don't need this analogy. Ha.

Seriously, though. Rarely could I find a push-up bra that would actually give me cleavage. A lot of times I set them free and no one was the wiser. Now? My boobs have flourished into a lovely size that's about four times that of what they were. I don't know what to do with them. They get in my way when I sleep on my side. They cannot go uncontained during exercise, and they will not fit in a martini or a champagne glass. However, now I have cleavage!

I've written a whole chapter on my body, my food intake, my disordered eating all of which when summed up equal an eating disorder. So, all of these physical changes have been quite difficult to process. For help along the way, I have worked with an intuitive eating counselor to help me walk through the unfamiliar—someone who gives me "permission" to eat when I'm hungry rather than seeing skipping meals as good behavior. I have ditched food rules and restrictions to the best of my ability; however, those rules sometimes creep back in. Being aware of them helps. If you find yourself anywhere in my camp, or on the opposite spectrum focused on not accepting your larger body (people in all sizes can have disordered eating and eating disorders–look it up), seek help. I'm not an expert, but my newfound knowledge also comes from accredited professionals and *not* TikTok.

When I finished my sessions with the nutritionist, I began a virtual course called Embracing Food Freedom led by its creator, Kate Brock, CNS, LDN. Let me tell you, Kate is amazing. (Look her up on Instagram @KateBrockNutrition.) Her goal is to help women ditch the cycle of dieting, develop a healthy relationship with their bodies, and curate sustainable ways to eat so your body is getting its necessary nutrition. Our virtual group consisted of three clients. We met for sixteen weeks. I'm not "cured," but I walked away with a much better sense of the importance of eating, not assigning value on how my body looks (or doesn't), and honing in on the newfound freedom from constant dieting.

I'm a work-in-progress—a woman who is open to new ways of living and learning. I am striving to believe that I am enough. I'm trying to move in ways that feel good to my body and not because I want to negate the food that I've eaten. I'm listening to my hunger cues, taking care of my mindset, and failing—but getting back up to try again. I am worthy of the work, and so are you.

Whether you will or can relate to menopause or not, if you're a woman or identify as female, you deserve to know more. If you're testosterone clad and have a female in your life, this is for you too. Knowledge is power. It is also mercy and understanding—which can hopefully lead to sympathy and acceptance. It's past time to talk about it. It's time to celebrate our womanhood, kick the hot flashes, and dance.

CHAPTER FORTY-FIVE

AN UNENDING LOVE SONG

There are some of us who may think that loving others is the most important part about living and giving, but while I agree to some extent, selflessness is not the key to happiness. Too many of us have been beaten down with labels, underserved, unwarranted, and unkind. Many of us long to experience acceptance, grace, mercy, and unconditional love. In a world full of contingencies looking out for only themselves, their own interests, and their own agendas, it's easy to feel silenced—discarded even. Unlovable? That message spreads like wildfire.

There is a difference between self-love and selfishness, but I believe, that selfishness may be the gateway to self-love—selfishness that is not harmful to others, and I only bring this up because it's all too easy to dismiss ourselves and focus on someone else. The irony, though, is that it's very difficult, if not impossible, to love others well if we do not love ourselves.

For me, part of learning to love myself has been writing this memoir. Whether you relate to my story or not, we all have a story worthy of telling. No life is any less important than another. Struggles are unique and should not be measured on a scale of significance because every aspect *is* significant to varying degrees, of course, but how else should it be? You deserve to be heard. You are worthy of love, from yourself and from those around you.

Admittedly, learning self-love demands a lifetime of learning, and a life filled with growing. Thankfully, though, the opportunities for change and growth are not stagnant. Each follows our timeline. It's up to us what we do with what is before us. We are not the same people today as we were ten years ago—maybe not even ten days ago (thanks, overnight muffin top)—but we are all invaluable, priceless.

If my book only impacts one person in a positive way then it is successful, whether I ever know it or not. Should my self-exploration and musings give way to your own personal discoveries, then I have achieved my goal. If you walk away with only one message, "You are loved," and you learn to believe it, then, to me, that is the greatest gift of putting my own story out there.

In January of 2020, I wrote my husband a poetic love song. I titled it, "To be Revised: Unending Love Song." The phrase "to be revised" is important because love is a never-ending evolution taking on many shapes, sizes, and stages over the years. It's an unending love song because love, in its purest form, should never come to an end.

I leave you with my poetry, a part of me, of who I am, of how I long to love myself, my family, and my friends, and how I long for you to be loved!

To be Revised: Unending Love Song

To the love of my life.

If I were to write you a love song, my love, t'would be an anthem of lyrics from poets and prose, lovers, composers, and writers of old.

I would poignantly paint the richness of color in the myriad sunsets we've shared . . . a tribute to lovers, a reminder of days.

Your unabashed love would be the refrain, and the melody a dance tuned in the key of your hand wrapped in mine, your lips on my lips, our bodies entwined.

If ever an oracle were to be penned, it is the story of you and me . . . our soulmate love and ceaseless provision.

My chorus would ring with beauty and telling . . .

Laced with lines of your ocean eyes and defining dark lashes . . . blue infinity pools . . .
    heavenly formed orbs for falling in love . . .
    and staying in love . . . transcendent, translucent . . . yet opaque and intense . . .
    Luscious and lovely . . .

The orbiting aria, a balm for the weary . . . a redeeming immersion that cleanses the soul.

If I were to pen you a ballad, my love, its words would be full of strength, restoration . . . unceasing verses . . . one after the other. . .
    Pure expressions of love, beckoning, longing . . .
    An echo of love,
    an eternal song.
You are loved. May the banner over you always be laced in love.
Every day is another beginning.

ACKNOWLEDGMENTS

I am ever grateful to those of you who have come alongside me in the process of writing this book.

Thank you, Mom. You are my mentor, my best friend, and my inspiration. I want to be you when I grow up. Dad, thank you for your unconditional love and belief in me.

Thank you to my friends who are all part of my story and part of my growth. I love each of you.

Traci, you are my best girlfriend. We have shared decades of life together—a lot of it spent walking and talking and a lot of it spent holding one another up in the good times and the not so good times. Your constant support during this journey has been instrumental to me.

Thank you to my "twin-cousin," Mimi. You have been a source of encouragement throughout my life. Thank you for cheering me on along the way and for reminding me that sometimes we are in a specific place to accomplish a specific purpose.

David, thank you for taking it upon yourself to stay connected and for driving to Columbia to keep my spirits up when I needed a friend.

Fran, thank you for believing in my dream, for loving me in spite of myself, for your encouragement, and for being my first Substack follower!

Thank you, Celeste, for your continued encouragement. From the mountain top to the valley, your friendship has never wavered. I love you, MaaMaaa!

Thank you, JuLee. You are much more than a publisher to me. You are a friend, and I am ever grateful that we returned to each other's orbit. I could not have written this book without you. You have a gift for championing women, for coaching a stronger story out of us, and for giving us permission to be vulnerable. Thank you.

Thank you, Virginia. I had no idea what an immense impact an editor could have on a book. I'm grateful for you, your constructive advice, your line edits, your grammar knowledge, and for your ability to take a writer's words from good to great. JuLee, thank you for putting Virginia in my story, and Virginia, thank you for showing up in such an incredible capacity.

MY KICKSTARTER TEAM AND BACKERS

My book would not be a reality today if it were not for you. Thank you, Baker, for coming home to help me put the campaign together, for teaching me time savers on Canva, and for creating icons for the rewards. Your input and knowledge were essential to its success. Thank you, Don, for urging me on to practice recording videos, and thank you for setting up your fancy video equipment and lighting when I was finally ready to record.

Thank you to all of the tremendous Kickstarter backers. Not only did your contribution make my book possible; but the very act of supporting me financially gave me strength, courage, and fortitude to plow ahead. Each one of you is invaluable.

Thank you to all who selected the reward that included having your name listed in my book: **Rob and Jenny Baker, Christian and Kyle Baker, Carrie O. Banks, Eileen Beehan, Kate Brock, Jennifer Cooke, Chaz Corzine, Brennan Donahue, Cara Donahue, Baker Donahue, Eliza Donahue, Mike and Lynnda Donnelly, Mary Anne and Simon Griffin, Allan Heinberg, Jessi Hook, Dr. Teresa Titus-Howard and Donald Howard, Bob Hutchins, Fran and Wayne Kirkpatrick, Tiffany Larnicol, Brendan O'Malley, Traci Orton, Kevin and Simonne Poff, Sunny Qiu, Willa Wang, and Beth and Robert Weedman.**

ENDNOTES

1 Beattie, Melody. *Codependent No More: How to Stop Controlling Others and Start Caring for Yourself,* (Center City, MN: Hazelden, 1986).

2 Nouwen, Henri. *You Are the Beloved: Daily Meditations for Spiritual Living* (New York: Convergent, 2017).

3 Rohr, Richard. *Breathing Under Water: Spirituality and the Twelve Steps* (Cincinnati OH: Franciscan Media, 2011), 9.

4 Rohr, *Breathing,* 63.

5 Rohr, *Breathing,* 32.

6 Rohr, *Breathing,* 12.

7 Rohr, *Breathing,* 32.

8 Brown, Brené. "Brené with Father Richard Rohr on Spirituality, Certitude, and Infinite Love, Part 1 of 2 Father Richard Rohr: Part 1," April 10, 2022, *Unlocking Us (podcast).* https://brenebrown.com/podcast/breathing-under-water-falling-upward-and-unlearning-certainty-part-1-of-2/#listen.

9 Harris, Dan. "Modern Life Is Making You Sick, but It Doesn't Have To, with Dr. Gabor Maté," April 19, 2023. *10%Happier with Dan Harris (podcast).* https://open.spotify.com/episode/3KusGYw9LJ4tzfBf6yHsSu.

10 Robbins, Mel, with Dr. Amy Shah. "From PMS to Menopause: How to Hack Your Hormones and Use Science to Lose Weight, Sleep Better, and Get Your Mojo Back," *The Mel Robbins Podcast,* July 27, 2023. https://podcasts.apple.com/gd/podcast/from-pms-to-menopause-how-to-hack-your-hormones-and/id1646101002?i=1000622473367episode 87.

ABOUT THE AUTHOR

Laura Lyn Donahue believes wholeheartedly in the transformative power of community and kindness.

Growing up in a quintessential southern home in Nashville, Tennessee, she learned the art of hospitality from her mother and father, who frequently gathered friends, family, and strangers for community and conversation around the table and in front of the fireplace.

Laura Lyn is happiest when she combines others' gifts with her own, including writing, editing, casting vision, and creating space for others to thrive. Her clients and her family attest to her success in serving others.

For most of her adult life, Laura Lyn has worked behind the scenes, helping others bring their stories to life. She turned that passion toward herself with the release of her first book, *Who Do You Think You Are?*

She resides in Columbia, Tennessee, with her husband, Don. They have five children, four adult children living across the country, and one child still at home.

Laura Lyn is passionate about family, friends, and kindness. She is a freelance writer, editor, and poet. Her pastimes include sending snail mail, walking her dog, practicing yoga, and relaxing on her porch swing.

Who do you think you are?

"I am a beloved child of God, who is fully accepted as I am with all my strengths and faults. I am commanded by God to love first, not judge, forgive others and ask for forgiveness, too. I am a devoted wife, mother, daughter, friend, and colleague who has learned to set boundaries. I am a life-long learner who is committed to continuous self-examination and growth. I am someone who seeks simple pleasures and joy in life with little patience for negative energy or attitudes. I know who I am and know who and what I am not."

—Dr. Teresa Titus-Howard

www.ingramcontent.com/pod-product-compliance
Lightning Source LLC
Chambersburg PA
CBHW032147080426
42735CB00008B/620